"*From the Shadows* lays bare the soul of the West Point Class of 1968 through the compellingly told stories of our twenty classmates who fell in Vietnam . . . and provides insights into the honorable warrior ethos that has developed and guided generations of the Long Grey Line in leading soldiers of our nation's army."

—D. David "Dutch" Hostler, '68 West Point Class President

"I am not a member of the USMA Class of 1968. I graduated from the Virginia Military Institute in 1967. However, upon arriving in Vietnam in February of 1969, that distinction all but vanished as all of us were joined as brothers-in-arms dedicated to carrying out our common mission against our enemies on the battlefield. Our common experiences carried forward even as we completed our tour and returned to 'the world,' as . . . we used to describe home.

"Upon returning, we found that our world had changed. It was difficult to find love or respect for our service and sacrifices.

"John Hedley has showered his twenty USMA classmates who died in service to our country with the love most never found. I believe that, even now, these men can feel the love John has infused into this tribute. But beyond that, with this tribute, John has spread that love to all who died in this war. When one reads the stories of these twenty gallant soldiers, remember that there are over 58,000 similar stories associated with the other names on the Wall."

—John I. Orrison, Co. C, 554th ENGR BN, Cu Chi, Lai Khe, RVN 196

"John Hedley has done a superb job of capturing the true essence of the twenty members from the West Point Class of 1968 who gave their all in Vietnam. His book is a lasting tribute to these gallant warriors and spellbinding for any reader."

—Ray Rhodes, '68, Lt. Col. (R)

"The Vietnam Veterans Memorial ('the Wall') is one of America's most powerful and personal. *From the Shadows* tells the stories of twenty young soldiers from West Point's Class of 1968 whose names are among the more than 58,000 hand-cut into the Wall's black polished granite, giving readers a personal connection to those men who did their duty when asked and paid with their lives. No longer will that multitude—all of whom made the ultimate sacrifice—be an inanimate collection of faceless names to be honored. Readers will gain a connection to William, John, David, and the seventeen others, bringing into sharp focus the magnitude of their Sacrifices and the losses to their family, friends, West Point classmates, and our nation. It is truly powerful stuff and a rare opportunity to learn about these twenty men which should not be missed!"

—**Rich Hubbard, Parent of a 2009 West Point Graduate**

"In *From the Shadows*, John Hedley shares an important and poignant chapter in our nation's history through a unique and personal lens. Sincere, enlightening, and often heartbreaking, John masterfully tells the story of the West Point Class of 1968 and those who gave their lives for their country in Vietnam. Nine hundred were sworn in as West Point cadets on July 1, 1964. Over their five-year term of required service, twenty made the ultimate sacrifice for their nbation, earning eighteen awards for valor. This book is their story. John provides an exceptionally meaningful tribute to his classmates and so many others that raised their right hand for their nation and gave their last full measure of devotion."

—**Col Patrick Roddy Jr., Commander, 3rd US Infantry Regiment "The Old Guard"**

"John's first book, *Saddle Up: The Story of a Red Scarf* . . . was an excellent book that took me out of the security of my O-2 at 1,500 feet and immersed me directly into ground combat. I smelled the smells, heard the sounds, and felt the emotions of the infantry soldier. John's writing in *From the Shadows* goes to a new level. The dedication must be read and re-read again and again. God is writing the dedication through John's hand. The words aren't from the brain; they're from the heart. No, they're from the soul.

"Using the writing of those who knew some of the twenty better than he was genius on John's part. It ensured the legacies of those he did not know was at the same level as the ones of those he knew well. It ensured their stories were all told by someone who felt the loss as deeply as those closest to them. There is a temptation to consider the deaths of such men as tragic loss of what they could have achieved. But in His way, God tells us to be thankful for what they managed to give us in their short lives. As John could attest, getting into West Point is not easy. Getting through West Point is even harder. Both require the best that talented and accomplished people can produce. High achievers must achieve more than they thought they could. The contributions of these men are not measured by either quantity or duration of life, but by their lasting endurance. They gave more in a short life than many give in a longer time. God calls no one home before He has ensured their destiny is fulfilled."

—Clark B. Russell

"This is an outstanding story of the life of twenty young men and their influences and camaraderie they shared with their fellow West Point classmates. They are still remembered and mourned fifty years later for their lives taken too quickly. These young men knew what lay ahead of them and still put their lives on the line for their country."

—Mark Feldman LCDR, USCG, Academy Class of 1979

From the Shadows:
A Tribute to the 1968 West Point Graduates
Who Gave Their Lives in Vietnam

by Lt. Col. John C. Hedley (Ret.), USMA '68

© Copyright 2022 Lt. Col. John C. Hedley (Ret.), USMA '68

ISBN 978-1-64663-655-6

Published by

 **köehlerbooks**™

3705 Shore Drive
Virginia Beach, VA 23455
800-435-4811
www.koehlerbooks.com

This book is dedicated to the West Point Class of 1968, with special tribute to the Twenty we lost in Vietnam and their families. Through their selfless service in a war that the country had already determined not to win, the class epitomized devotion to the West Point motto of Duty, Honor, Country, and selfless service to something larger than themselves. While maybe not members of the Greatest Generation as defined by Tom Brokaw, they are certainly the greatest of THEIR generation.

FROM THE
SHADOWS

A Tribute to the 1968 West Point Graduates
Who Gave Their Lives In Vietnam

LT. COL. JOHN C. HEDLEY (RET.)
USMA '68

VIRGINIA BEACH
CAPE CHARLES

TABLE OF CONTENTS

THE CORPS

"The Corps" is a poetic hymn associated with the United States Military Academy. It is second in importance only to the Academy's "Alma Mater." Even though it may rank as number two, it is more emotionally stirring. The words were written by West Point Chaplain Bishop H.S. Shipman around 1902. The accompanying music was composed in 1910 especially for the ceremonial closing of the Old Cadet Chapel and opening of the new Cadet Chapel. "The Corps" was first sung on the steps of the Cadet Chapel on June 12, 1910 and became part of the graduation ceremony starting in 1911. Today, "The Corps" is typically sung by the Cadet Glee Club in companion to the Alma Mater at alumni gatherings, graduation, memorial ceremonies, and funerals.

The original words to "The Corps," as written in 1902 are:

THE CORPS! THE CORPS! THE CORPS!

The Corps, bareheaded, salute it, with eyes up, thanking our God.

That we of the Corps are treading, where they of the Corps have trod.

They are here in ghostly assemblage. The men of the Corps long dead.

And our hearts are standing attention, while we wait for their passing tread.

We Sons of today, we salute you. You Sons of an earlier day;

We follow, close order, behind you, where you have pointed the way;

The long gray line of us stretches, thro' the years of a century told

And the last man feels to his marrow, the grip of your far off hold.

Grip hands with us now though we see not, grip hands with us strengthen our hearts.

As the long line stiffens and straightens with the thrill that your presence imparts.

Grip hands tho' it be from the shadows. While we swear, as you did of yore.

Or living, or dying, to honor, the Corps, and the Corps, and the Corps.

INTRODUCTION

I thought about writing this book for many years. Part of me wanted to give it a try, but part of me didn't want to get back into another emotional journey through the past. Writing my first book, *Saddle Up*, was a long and sometimes painful journey, incorporating lots of late nights and early mornings and several bottles of a fine single malt scotch. I didn't know if I was ready to do that again. However, a couple of events set in motion by classmate Pat Jonas were instrumental in my decision to give this a try.

In June of 2018, our class gathered at West Point to celebrate a special fifty-year reunion, always an emotional experience, but particularly so after that much time. There was a huge turnout, some returning for the first time since graduation. Friendships were rekindled among the living while there were heartfelt memories of those no longer with us, particularly after the memorial service in the Cadet Chapel. Since we had all trained to be soldiers, and most of us had served in Vietnam, our losses in the war were particularly poignant. It was probably doubly so for me, as I had just published my first book, *Saddle Up! The Story of a Red Scarf* about my time and my guys in Vietnam, the phenomenal soldiers I had been blessed to lead. Vietnam was very much in my mind and heart.

Before one of our evening meals, all of our classmates who had performed with the West Point Glee Club or one of the chapel choirs, gathered to serenade us with a song composed by classmate Pat Jonas as a tribute to the class. I was struck by his admiration and dedication to the guys I had grown to love over the years. These feelings, and the warmth and camaraderie of the reunion, got me thinking again about trying something like this book. I even talked it over with our class president, but once again I balked. I was too apprehensive of the thoughts and feelings that I knew would be stirred up by the effort.

Two years ago, around Memorial Day, Pat released another verse to his song specifically dedicated to our "Twenty on the Wall," and that was the deciding event for me. If he felt that strongly about our Twenty, then I felt that the rest of the class did as well, and maybe my efforts could be of service to them and the families of our fallen. The words to Pat's song can be found after this introduction. Knowing all too well that the life of '68 would ebb over the coming years, I thought to provide a lasting legacy to our Twenty, so that when we've all ridden the last bird to Valhalla, they won't just melt into those polished granite slabs of The Wall but will live on in my words. You'll notice that I capitalize Twenty when *referring* to these young men of '68 who gave their lives in Vietnam. I do so in reverence to them. It's not just a number.

I've also tied this book to the words of West Point's hymn "The Corps" because that hymn is an emotional tribute to the fact that we of the living Corps are forever mindful that we are a part of those who have come before us, and those who have given their lives for our country. Our Twenty who are memorialized in this book are truly with us in *ghostly assemblage* any time we get together, and for many of us, every day that we are blessed with life. We do *grip hands tho' it be from the shadows* with every one of them, and honor them for their sacrifice. We do feel *the grip of [their] far off hold* as we go about our lives, never forgetting that we are living for them.

The last two years have been an incredible journey, filled with frustration at times and incredible emotions at others. When I started, I could break the Twenty into three groups: those who I knew well, those who I knew slightly or knew of, and those whose names I didn't even recognize. After this journey, I now feel like they're all truly my brothers, and this has certainly enriched my life.

I've also come to understand a couple of other emotions that I had not thought much about before this. I've come to understand the depths of the meaning of the word *tragedy*. While all deaths can be tragic in one sense or another, and that word is certainly overused these days, there is incredible, real tragedy surrounding our Twenty and the loved ones that they left behind. I tell my Vietnam recon platoon guys that combat infantrymen never cry, although sometimes our eyeballs sweat a little. And some days while putting this together, my eyeballs sweated a lot!

There is another word overused these days: *hero*; it seems like everyone gets labelled a hero, from those who stock our grocery shelves to those who deliver our mail. To my mind there's nothing particularly *heroic* about those functions. First responders, police, and firemen can be legitimately called heroes at times for what they do to protect the rest of us. But combat is different, it's more visceral. It's twenty-four hours a day full of apprehension. There is always the presence of fear, the constant danger, the ever-present possibility of death or maiming, the personal uncertainty, and if you're a leader, the incredibly heavy weight of being responsible for the lives of many mothers' sons. Combat can put unbelievable stress on your body, causing some functions to quit working, or maybe sometimes work more than they should. And in this environment, to then step up and risk your life for others is truly heroic. John Wayne may have said it best: "Courage is being scared to death but saddling up anyway." When you read the stories that follow, you'll see that our Twenty were legitimate heroes.

All of this can be summed up in an overarching spirit of *dedication and commitment*, the willingness to go in harm's way for a greater good. This spirit sums up all that is encapsulated in the West Point motto of *Duty, Honor, Country*, a solemn creed by which we've all lived our lives, particularly in the perils of combat. It makes West Pointers what we are, what we always have been—and what we always will be.

This quest to document the all-too short lives of our Fallen has been an unbelievable journey. It's not easy to do after more than fifty years, for in so many cases family members, classmates, and roommates are no longer with us, and trying to find firsthand information about how they lived and died has been extremely difficult at times. And, as to be expected, I didn't know all of our Twenty and so didn't have direct information or experiences that I could fall back on like I could with a few of them.

Two of the Twenty were classmates of mine at the Army's West Point Preparatory School, then located at Ft. Belvoir, Virginia. One was Don Workman, with whom I played lacrosse, and the other was Bill Ericson, who was in my platoon and therefore the same

barracks for a year. I knew Don Colglazier very well all four years
at West Point, from being in the same squad in Beast Barracks and
subsequently the same company until graduation. Not being what
was considered academically gifted myself, I shared a lot of classes
with Rick Hawley, who was last in our class in order of merit.

This final product does not look like what I had at first envisioned
and put together. Since I had little material to begin with, I solicited
the class on several occasions for input. I asked for stories, vignettes,
and pictures, anything people were willing to send. I thought that I
would be better off to have too much than not enough. Then I wrote
a separate chapter for each of our Fallen by putting the input I had
received together. When I finished my first effort, I had more than
700 pages filled with 220 thousand words and over 150 pictures!
Much too big. My second effort was still more than 600 pages and
180 thousand words. Although it took some extra urging from time
to time, the class really responded to my requests.

To make the situation even more difficult, I performed what could
have been a real tactical blunder and set out to change publishers in
mid-stream—good cavalrymen know how unwise that is! I went to
Google, searched for publishers of military books, and essentially made
some cold calls. I had no assurance that this book would be published,
or if it would, would it be on time? Fortunately, my guardian angel
is still on duty, and I found a terrific company who put me on to a
wonderful editor who has been instrumental in helping me reorganize
my thinking.

This has been a more emotionally draining effort than I had
anticipated. After two years I've come to know each of the Twenty
more intimately. In many cases I've talked with their widows, sisters,
brothers, children, and soldiers who were with them when they
were killed. In some cases, I've learned of, and have been incredibly
touched by, the dedication of some of our classmates to one member
of the Twenty with whom they were especially close. Sometimes a
classmate asked if they could write the contribution on one of those
killed in action, and of course I was happy to include those. There
is no one more qualified to reconstruct the life of one who was lost
than a classmate who was a close and dedicated friend. The quotes
and contributions from these friends, family, and brothers in arms

of our Twenty and the other sources I have included here have been lightly edited for clarity, style, and consistency. In the case of quotes from The Wall of Faces, a virtual site maintained by the Vietnam Veterans Memorial Fund, and those posted on Westpoint.org, they are reproduced here exactly as they appear on those sites. The words as written sometimes reveal incredible emotion and are a true reflection of the man who posted them, regardless of punctuation, grammar, or style, and I want to respect the gravity of the feelings they experienced when writing those tributes.

I hope that this effort will establish a lasting legacy for those members of the class lost in Vietnam and ensure that they will never be forgotten. Any opinions or thoughts expressed in this book are solely mine. Graduating with this class has been the seminal achievement of my life, and I'm incredibly proud to be able to stand in ranks with such tremendous guys. I pray that I've lived up to my dreams for, and expectations of, what I wanted to do with this effort. I sincerely hope that this result is a fitting legacy for Twenty outstanding young Americans who gave their all in the service of our country. And I hope that I've lived up to our class motto: No Task Too Great for '68!

"LIFT A GLASS TO '68"

by Pat Jonas, West Point class of 1968

July the first of sixty-four, they answered duty's call
Their heads were shorn, their marching honed,
their mothers were appalled
At Trophy Point, they took the oath, they all stood straight and tall
"No Task Too Great for '68," their motto says it all

From plebe to yearling, cow to firstie, '68 stood out
Home for Christmas, got some slack with Navy win fallout
Stole the goat, and stole the bowls for New York Times to see
No Task Too Great for '68, even civvies in '73

Chorus:

No Task Too Great for '68, they answered duty's call
Lift a glass to '68, their heart was shown to all
From West Point to the world and back they served as they were called
Let's drink a toast to '68 with Twenty on the Wall

On June the fifth of '68, they left their Highland Home
Once they all heard "Class Dismissed," their West Point days were gone
Their class rings still remind them, of oaths and friends they've made
No Task Too Great for '68, now life is their parade
No Task Too Great for '68, their motto holds them all
To lofty standards everywhere, to serve, to heed the call
To Vietnam, where conflict grew, they went, they led, they saw
And when it all was over, they had Twenty on the Wall

Fifty years since "Class Dismissed" and '68 has changed
Civilian life encircles them and aging is their game
"Duty, Honor, Country," lights up all their names
"Well Done," the class of '68, you've earned your lasting fame

Chorus:

No Task Too Great for '68, they answered duty's call
Lift a glass to '68, their heart was shown to all
From West Point to the world and back they served as they were called
Let's drink a toast to '68 with Twenty on the Wall

INVOCATION

T his prayer was offered by classmate Jerry Hansen at our fortieth graduation anniversary, which we commemorated by gathering at The Wall. I offer it here as a blessing for our twenty fallen classmates whose names are inscribed thereon.

Dear God, our Father, as we gather today as classmates and families to honor those who fell in battle and as we reflect on the forty years since graduation that you have graciously given those gathered here today, we remember fondly, but sadly, the friends who departed from us so suddenly—in the prime of their lives, with so much to offer. We know that you alone know why, Lord, and you alone can heal the empty spot in our hearts and in our lives. We thank you for the grace you have given to the families and loved ones of our departed classmates, as they have lived lives of honor and service in tribute to their dearly departed husbands, fathers, sons, and friends. Although our days in uniform are past, duty still calls to place service to you, our country, our families, our classmates, and other veterans in need ahead of our own selfish interests. As we reflect on how best to invest the time you have given us, Lord, we pray that you will show us the way. Help us to unite as a class, to be there for others in need, and for the families of those departed. May we leave a legacy of honor, service, love, and that "courage born of loyalty to all that is noble and worthy." We pray that you will continue to bless our nation and our Army—and be with those soldiers who have filled our places in the ranks, who are in harm's way, engaged in the endless conflict to protect and promote freedom and liberty. May they know you, may they serve honorably, and may they come home safely to a joyous reunion, knowing they have done their duty to you and to their country. All of this we ask in the name of the Great Friend and Master of Men. Amen.

WEST POINT

On the first of July 1964, approximately 990 young men of the 1000 who initially accepted appointments, including three turned back from the class of 1967 and two foreign cadets (one from Chile and one from the Philippines), reported into the United States Military Academy at West Point, New York to become the class of 1968. By the end of that day more than 900 paraded to Trophy Point to be sworn in as new cadets.

By taking that oath we were potentially exposing ourselves to four years at West Point and five years of service thereafter—nine years of our lives—a commitment that would be legally formalized at the beginning of our cow, or junior year. We had no idea of what the future held, and probably few of us had heard of a small country in Southeast Asia that would loom so large in most of our lives—Vietnam. We were tired, many of us in shock from the rigors of the first day, and I'm sure that some were wondering just what the hell we'd done. Had we done the right thing?

That first day had been one to remember, still seared into our minds even now, more than fifty years later. My family had driven me down from Rochester, New York, my mom, dad, and sister; somehow Dad was able to get us rooms in the Thayer Hotel on campus. Dad and I spent some time the evening before that first day sitting on that beautiful veranda overlooking the Hudson River, sipping a good scotch. I don't remember much of what we talked about, but knowing my dad, a retired infantry officer, I'm sure he was trying to buck me up for what was soon to begin. The next morning, we had breakfast and then went out to the front to await the arrival of the bus that would take me through the gates of hell.

Our initial processing was done in the gym. Our height and weight were checked, I think we had to do some pull-ups, and we accomplished other administrative chores, including a final medical and dental check. In my case, we then moved to the area of the cadet barracks, and I wound up in Central Area as a part of First New Cadet Company. I know that we went to a myriad of places to draw equipment and uniforms and to be measured for our dress and full-dress uniforms. We were also issued new shoes that we wore to break in before the march to Trophy Point for the swearing in later that day. Central Area was a loud and busy place, with upperclassmen yelling in the faces of the new cadets: *Drop that bag! Pick it up! Drop it!* Over and over again they shouted, and our soon-to-be classmates answered in equally loud voices as if to impress the upperclassmen of their sincerity. Guys in all sorts of dress, civilian and military, ran around from one place to another. *Bedlam* is a great word to describe what was happening. The effect of all of this well-organized chaos on the new cadets of the class of 1968 can probably be described as *shock*, as very few had ever been subjected to such mental and physical harassment.

I remember going in and out of my room in the First Division barracks in Central Area to drop off gear and then pinging back outside to get a haircut similar to the one I had received in basic training, or draw more gear, or practice rudimentary dismounted drill to get us ready for the upcoming formation that afternoon. Sometime that day we received the feared order to report to the *man in the red sash,* a senior cadet officer, where we learned the only three answers that we were authorized in response to a question: *Yes, sir; no, sir;* and *no excuse, sir!* In time we were allowed to add, *Sir, I do not know!* Maybe that is also where we learned to salute. The culmination of the day was the march to Trophy Point, accompanied by the West Point Band, where we took the oath as a new cadet. What a proud time. We were dressed in the summer Sierra uniform, with no hats, and carried gloves in our left hand. The Sierra uniform was a short-sleeved white shirt with removable gray epaulettes, and dress gray trousers that had a black stripe down the side. It was during the formation preparation that we learned how to do a *dress off,* which entailed gathering the side seams of a classmate's dress shirt and pulling the excess material to the back and holding it there neatly against his back while trousers and belt were closed. The result was a clean and sharp appearance, even from the rear, if done properly. We must have presented quite an image with our shorn heads visible to all. I remember the pride I felt that day, and while we were told not to gaze around, I did see my family standing on the curb. For the first time in my life, I saw my dad with tears running down his cheeks.

We had a rude awakening when we went to the mess hall, hungry and thirsty after a full day. Having to shout answers to questions from the couple of upperclassmen at the table resulted in very little food being consumed; this was our introduction to the Fourth Class System. Eventually, we were given time to get our rooms into some sort of rudimentary order and meet our roommates. Reveille came much too early the next morning.

West Point was a far different place in 1964 than it is now, in many ways it was the old traditional West Point of the previous one hundred years. The physical footprint has been changed with the tearing down of old iconic structures like Central Area, and the construction of new barracks, three new wings on the mess hall, several new academic buildings, a fine library, and a student center. But beyond its physical structure, the very core of the Academy's mission, and therefore her graduates' mission, has changed. No longer are graduates required to serve in the combat arms of the Army. The philosophy of cadet training and life, academic requirements and degrees offered, the essence of the revered Cadet Honor Code and System, as well as cadet discipline bear little resemblance to what we experienced.

Our Corps of Cadets was comprised only of men; no one could have even imagined the possibility of female cadets. There were only two regiments, the First and Second, and the historic Central Area Barracks (circa 1851) and Washington Hall (circa 1929), the cadet mess, had remained unchanged over the decades. We were the last class to learn the complicated and confusing old Cadet Drill, used in parades and other formations in which every member of a squad had different steps to follow in making directional turns for the unit depending on the position in the formation he occupied, and every cadet had to know the choreography for all positions.

We were the first large class, eventually leading to a doubling of size of the Corps from 2,200 to 4,400. We were in fact a bridge class, entering into the world of the old Corps, yet transitioning in part into the new Corps. We were the first class to go home for Christmas as plebes—a fact we have never been allowed to forget by those classes that came before us. At the beginning of our cow year, many of us were split from our original cadet companies to form two new regiments, the Third and Fourth. And maybe most importantly, little did we realize on our first day that the West Point class of 1968 was destined to become a war class. During our four years at West Point, the Vietnam War developed from non-existent (except for a relatively few advisors and trainers) to a full-fledged conflict involving over 550,000 of our countrymen, and so divisive in nature that it was beginning to tear our country apart by the time we graduated.

The day after that first day, New Cadet Barracks, affectionately known as *Beast Barracks*, and our introduction to the Fourth Class System started in earnest. What a summer this would be, as we underwent the rigors of Beast while our erstwhile high school classmates were enjoying a summer of chasing women and drinking beer before many of them went off to civilian colleges—two radically different worlds. Beast Barracks and the Fourth Class System that governed our lives during plebe year were instrumental in the formulation and production of West Point's graduates, who have served honorably in every war since the Academy's founding in 1802. The class of 1968 was no different, as the system we were introduced to had not fundamentally changed over the years.

Inherent in Beast was also a philosophical requirement to become familiar with what had set West Point apart from any other institution of higher learning in the country: the Academy's motto of *Duty, Honor, Country*, and what that would mean to each of us, and the strict Honor Code and System. According to *Bugle Notes*, the small plebe bible published by West Point and containing information about West Point and the Army, "The three attributes of a soldier which are of paramount importance are Duty, Honor, and Love of Country."

Duty may be defined as "the sense of obligation which motivates one to do, to the best of his ability, that which is expected of him in a certain position or station." This becomes of critical importance because the lives of soldiers may well depend on an officer's sense of duty. In a macro sense, the very survival of our country could also be determined by a strong and driving sense of duty throughout the armed forces.

The concept of honor was firmly imbedded in the Academy's Honor Code and its attendant Honor System, and strongly infused in every cadet from day one. Simply defined, the Honor Code is stated as: "A cadet does not lie, cheat, or steal, nor tolerate those who do." The Code requires complete integrity in both word and deed of all members of the Corps and permits no deviation from those standards. The maintenance of these high honor standards is the responsibility of each cadet, and each cadet is expected to report himself or any other cadet for violations of the Code. After World War I, the superintendent, General Douglas MacArthur, was instrumental in formalizing the Honor Code and System and making it an integral part of cadet life. It is perhaps the most cherished teaching of the West Point of our time, was zealously guarded, and applied to all parts of life by cadets and graduates.

Some of the general principles upon which the Honor Code is founded include, "A cadet who violates the Honor Code should resign at once, as there is no place in the Corps for anyone who cannot abide by the principles of the Honor Code and offenders are *never* (emphasis is mine) granted immunity."

A key concept of the Honor Code was that it was administered by the cadets themselves, not by the academy command group. Each year the third class, or yearlings, selected an individual from each company to serve on the Honor Committee. During the second-class year, these cadets assisted the first-class honor committee in the conduct of their work. This committee conducted investigations of violations, and if a cadet was found guilty, made a recommendation to the commandant for appropriate action. Very rarely, if ever, was a cadet found guilty of a violation and allowed to remain a member of the Corps. It was a black-and-white system; there were no gray areas in compliance, guilt, or enforcement, and no quibbling allowed. There was no sense of having to develop an understanding of the prohibition of lying and cheating, it was assumed that everyone entered with a basic knowledge of right and wrong, and the requirements of compliance with the Code were driven home from day one.

The Honor Code became an essential block in the character of every graduate. In the Army, it is imperative that you be able to rely on the word of those to your left and right, and that you can believe reports and evaluations of combat conditions. An officer's word is his bond, maybe a trite and overused phrase today, but it was something in which all graduates believed, and which we all strove to live by. This code also carried over to the civilian world, and this expectation of high personal integrity is a large part of what sets a West Point graduate apart from others in the conduct of personal life.

Love of country is something that needs little elaboration, one either has it or does not. I think it very likely that each individual of the class of 1968 shared a strong love of the country in which he lived and carried a natural desire to protect it and all that it stood for. We had been raised by fathers who were World War II or Korean War veterans, or sometimes both. We had been taken to Memorial Day and Fourth of July parades that featured veterans in uniform riding in honored places in cars or open trucks. The most emotional and meaningful tribute to our motto of Duty, Honor, Country can be found in the stirring words of General of the Army Douglas MacArthur's farewell address to the Corps of Cadets, delivered in Washington Hall on May 12, 1962, and which can be found immediately after this chapter. These words were spoken during the General's last visit to West Point, an institution that he loved and cherished his entire life, and one on which he had incalculable influence during his long and devoted career.

Another source of the importance of that motto is found in the words of the Cadet Prayer, which was recited every Sunday during mandatory services in the Cadet Chapel:

> Encourage us in our endeavor to live above the common level of life. Make us to choose the harder right instead of the easier wrong, and never to be content with a half-truth when the whole can be won. Endow us with courage that is born of loyalty to all that is noble and worthy, that scorns to compromise with vice and injustice, and knows no fear when truth and right are in jeopardy.

The motto of Duty, Honor, Country, and the Cadet Honor Code, provided the bedrock of what West Point—and West Pointers—stood for. And those, in turn, provided the basics of the belief system that her graduates took with them from those gray walls out into the Army, into combat for many of us, and eventually into the civilian world. They shaped us and provided the foundation for the decisions we made and for how we would live our lives.

Beast Barracks was probably the most intensive military training period during our time at West Point. Starting on the second of July and ending the last week of August, we underwent what was essentially Army Basic Training, although Beast was much more inclusive and demanding, a point to which I can personally attest. Not only did we have the military training, extensive drill and ceremonies, and a rigorous physical training schedule, but we were also introduced to the full gamut of the Plebe System. While *hazing* had allegedly been eliminated years earlier, there were still traditional *rites of passage* that had to be navigated and endured to be successful. We learned how to *brace*, meaning we squeezed our chin back into our neck as far as it would go. This would be the required posture whenever we left our rooms after Beast as well, for our entire plebe year. Don Colglazier, a member of my Beast squad and also featured in this book, developed a severe physical malady as a result of this practice called *brace palsy*, an affliction of the muscles of the neck and shoulders which excused him from bracing for a while. We were not allowed to talk with anyone while outside unless addressed by an upper classman and were required to walk in straight lines and make ninety degree turns if we wanted to change direction. Bracing was also the required position in the mess hall unless we were allowed to *fall out* by order of the table commandant, which meant we could relax, eat normally, and even talk with our classmates.

The dining table was another adventure all unto itself. Three plebes sat at the end, opposite the table commandant, and were responsible for announcing food as it was delivered by the waiter, serve hot and cold beverages after memorizing the requirements of each of the upper classmen for each of the beverages offered (one of us was the *hot beverage corporal*, the other the *cold beverage corporal*), and the plebe at the end of the table, the *gunner*, was responsible for holding up and announcing the dishes as they were delivered by a waiter, and for cutting deserts into the required number of equally sized pieces determined by who wanted a serving. To accomplish that, we plebes all carried a handmade template in our hats that marked equal shares for any occasion. The last thing the gunner wanted was for one piece of the desert to not be equal to the others for some reason. That could lead to being very hungry for a day or two.

We ate only small bites, raising our forks straight up to the level of our mouths and then making it do a ninety degree turn into our mouths. We then put the fork down, following the same path, chewed, and couldn't take another bite until the one in our mouth was swallowed. The bites were to be small enough to be swallowed after only two chews upon being asked a question or being required to recite some *plebe poop*. This was accomplished while sitting on the front three inches of our chair in the brace position. Of course, we could be interrupted at any time and told to recite any of the plebe poop found in *Bugle Notes*, or recite the movies of the week, or tell the first classmen how many days remained until their graduation, among a myriad of other requirements. As opposed to a *freshman fifteen* weight gain common to students entering civilian colleges, most plebes at West Point lost weight.

We also had clothing formations during Beast. We were called into a company formation in a certain uniform and were then told that we had a minimum amount of time to change into another uniform, maybe no more than five minutes. When we left our rooms after a hectic change, they had to be left in good order, as they were subject to close inspection by upper classmen wandering in the barracks. Of course, once we fell into formation, we were subjected to inspection by other upperclassmen, who moved down the ranks handing out punishment with an ill-concealed sense of glee. If a room did not meet standards, the occupants could return and find everyone's clothes and gear thrown into one large pile in the center, which had to be sorted through for the next requirement. If you were late getting into any of the formations, or had a problem with the uniform, you were subject to acute verbal harassment, maybe pushups, and maybe other requirements to *drive around* to an upper classman's room after dinner for even more verbal tongue lashings and physical exercise. Clothing formations normally required four or five changes of uniform. The obvious purpose of this seemingly ridiculous requirement was to induce a heavy load of stress on each new cadet and then see how he responded.

Another favorite rite of passage was shower formations. With the strenuous physical activity, and the heat and humidity of New York in the summer, showers were a daily requirement for the sake of everyone else. If you lived in any of the Central Area division barracks, the shower rooms and bathrooms were in the basement or *sinks*. A division was a separate entity consisting of four floors with four rooms each, two in the front and two in the back; this provided each room with large windows, which were necessary for light and ventilation. Each room also had a vestigial fireplace, no longer usable, and could accommodate two or three new cadets. Fortunately, each room also had a faucet and sink, so you could wash up, brush your teeth, and even shave in the safety of your own room without having to leave and go down to the sinks and risk a meeting with an upperclassman. Multiple divisions were connected by common walls that resulted in a large, three-sided barracks area, which was the perimeter of the rectangular Central Area. To go to the sinks for a shower, we could go only when authorized by an upperclassman, and were required to wear our light-weight summer bathrobe and carry a soap dish in our left hand extended in a ninety-degree angle from the elbow with a towel over the forearm. When we got down to the sinks, we lined up against a wall to await our turn in the shower room. While waiting we could be required to sound off with any number of responses, all while at the required brace, and respond until we had produced enough sweat that a penny could stick to the wall from behind our necks. Often, we were not allowed to actually enter the shower room for our very short shower until this had been accomplished.

At the end of August, when the three upper classes returned from their summer duties or leave, we were officially welcomed into the Corps with the Acceptance Parade and became actual Fourth Class Cadets (plebes) instead of just New Cadets. At that time, we were also assigned to a lettered company in one of the regiments. My assignment was to Company A, First Regiment (A-1), where I stayed for the entire four years. It was during this parade that we passed in review for the first time to the stirring chords of "The Official West Point March," known to cadets as "The Thumper" for the way it made your heart beat. I can still remember my sense of pride and wonderment that I was actually on the field and that this stirring march was now a part of me.

This started a whole new tough world for plebes. During Beast we had actually outnumbered the upper classmen, so with some thought and careful planning, we could avoid them at times. After the parade we were vastly outnumbered, so life took on a whole new format. We were required to memorize the names of all the upper classmen in our company by class. A favorite ploy of harassment was for an upperclassman to stop a plebe and demand "Who am I, smack?" (shorthand for *smackhead,* a special term of endearment) with his name tag covered by his hand. We would have to peek at the color of the brass shield on the upperclassman's uniform and then start down the memorized list for the appropriate class until we were stopped at the correct name. Woe unto us if we were stopped by the same upperclassman at a later time and didn't remember his name or face or recognize his voice.

Our days were filled with academics, physical training, intramural athletics, and periodic parades, both during the week and on Saturdays during football season. We assumed additional duties of closing windows, delivering laundry, newspapers or mail, and minute calling, among others. As a window closer, the plebe had to go to the rooms of the sleeping upper classmen just before reveille with a long pole and close the windows without waking anyone. As a minute caller, we had to stand in the hall and announce, in a loud voice, time to formation starting with a ten-minute warning and then from five minutes out at one-minute intervals. We also had to announce the uniform, determined by looking at flags flying from the Central Area Guardhouse if we lived in those barracks, and also announce the menu for that meal. After calling "One minute, sir!" the minute caller had to scurry outside to get into the formation on time. Needless to say, life for a plebe was hard and stressful, and some guys couldn't deal with it, so they quit.

As West Point and the national culture has changed, so too has the plebe or Fourth Class System. The rigorous requirements and constant *attention* were there by design; the purpose was to weed out those who couldn't stand the pressure, who couldn't operate effectively under the stress created by being a plebe. As we were training to become combat arms officers, there was a good chance that many of us would actually deploy to a war zone and command soldiers, and the philosophy was if we couldn't function under the pressures of life at West Point, then we probably wouldn't be able to function under the pressures of combat. That would be especially critical at that point because, as officers, we would be directly responsible for the lives of others as well. This was openly an attrition system—identify and dismiss those who didn't measure up. As opposed to attrition, the current system is developmental and it's almost impossible to be dismissed. No matter the failure, a cadet is to be counseled and worked with until the problem is corrected. Many times this also includes Honor violations. The old Honor Code and System, plus the Fourth Class System, were fundamental to life at West Point and instrumental in developing the character of its graduates. Neither exists today.

An appreciation of this world of West Point as it was in the late 1960s is necessary to understand the stories in the chapters that follow, the stories of our classmates who committed to service in the Army, even with a nasty and brutal war looming for all. Many volunteered to go to war, many actively sought those positions of greatest danger, and many risked their lives because of a commitment to Duty, Honor, Country. One needed commitment to those ideals to survive the demanding four years of life at West Point and then certainly the combat tour that followed shortly thereafter.

Academics plebe year were tough compared to a high school senior year. The only degree available to us was a bachelor of science with no major, so the curriculum was heavy in math and science. During our four years, we went to class on Saturday mornings, so for the first two years we had math class six days a week. If that was not your strong suit, then life could be pretty miserable. We were organized into academic sections, according to performance, in each subject for each grading period. First section was for the really smart guys who excelled or *hives*, last section was for those who didn't perform as well, called *goats*. Since for most of those first two years I held down a seat in one of the last few math sections, I developed a fond interest in anything edible, like the goat I was. I also became good friends with another of those featured in this book, Rick Hawley, who was the official goat of the class because of his standing at graduation as the last man on the order of merit list. Other goats featured in the following pages included Ken Cummings, Jim Gaiser, Harry Hayes, Jeff Riek, Dave Sackett, and Don Workman; guys who worked so hard to graduate only to see their lives cut so short. On the other end of the class spectrum, amongst the Star Men (top 5 percent of the class), was Don Colglazier. We could all check our grades weekly, as they were posted in the sally ports of Central Area. We were graded on a 3.0 system wherein 2.0 was passing and one needed 2.0 or above to be *pro*, or proficient. A cadet needed to be pro in order to participate in Corps Squad sports or to travel off post with any of the clubs. This became even more important for everyone during our last two years, when we were authorized to leave the reservation one weekend a semester. Many of us would fight for tenths of a point in order to stay 2.0 or above in all of our classes.

In addition to the tough academic schedule, every cadet was required to participate in an athletic program that included Corps Squad (varsity, junior varsity), clubs, or intramurals. Denny Johnson and Harry Hayes both played 150-pound football, Ken Cummings was the captain of the swim team, John Darling was a Corps Squad wrestler, Jim Gaiser was on the sport parachute team, Dave Maddux was a fencer, Doug Wheless was president of the Karate Club, and Bill Ericson was a brigade boxing champion.

We had to study hard at night, for we were required to recite in every class every day—there was no slack. We also had English classes, engineering classes, and tactics classes; three in the morning and two in the afternoon. After class we had intramural sports and then supper, study time, and lights out. All three meals every day but Saturday and Sunday were mandatory. Breakfast was mandatory on Saturdays because of class, but lunch and dinner were optional. On Sunday there was a voluntary brunch where we found a wide selection of offerings. The dinner formation on Sunday evening was again mandatory.

On Saturday mornings during football season, after classes ended, the plebes were required to chant "Odin" as loudly as possible on the way back to their barracks. Odin was the Norse god of rain, so we were calling on him to do his thing so we would not have a full dress parade. Getting into our parade uniform, full dress gray over white under arms, was a complex operation. We wore the full dress coat with tails and rows of brass buttons over highly starched white trousers or *trou*. These were so heavily starched that we had to *break starch* with our bayonets starting at the cuff so that they wouldn't get wrinkled. Many guys would stand on a chair to put on the white trou so there would be no chance of a wrinkle. Once we put them on, we couldn't sit down for the same reason. We then put on our highly spit-shined shoes, often tied by a roommate. After donning coat and trou, we put on our white cross belts, which had a black cartridge box at the ends. Over where they crossed on our chests, we affixed a highly shined brass breast plate. The last item was a white waist belt, threaded through our bayonet scabbard, also with a highly shined brass plate buckle. The belt had to be so tight that it didn't sag at the front and passed just above the cartridge box in the rear. We then put on our parade helmet, or *shako,* with black pom-pom, shined visor rim, and highly shined academy crest. Last but not least was our M14 rifle with a highly oiled stock and shiny brass keeps or *frogs* on the sling. As we exited our rooms, we wet our white gloves at the sink so as to be able to keep a tighter grip on our weapons. As can be imagined, this was a time-consuming process. Once we fell into ranks, plebes were subjected to a close inspection, looking for a smudge on any of the brass or scuff on our shoes; haircuts and shaves were also closely scrutinized. Classmate and company mate Don Colglazier had some trouble with these requirements, which will be described in his narrative.

Our first procedure after everyone was accounted for in the company formation was to fix bayonets. West Point and the 1st Battalion, 3rd US Infantry are the only units in the Army authorized to parade with fixed bayonets (the 3rd US Infantry is known as *The Old Guard* for being the oldest active regiment in the Army). We then went through a sizing movement where we were told, "If you're taller than the man in front of you, move up" and then were given a "Right face" and went through the same move up drill. The end product of that procedure was that the tallest guy was at the right end of the first rank, and all ranks and files appeared to be of uniform height. As that tallest guy was normally me, I also became the *Right Guide.* After the company executed its last turn to come on line on the parade field, it was my job to come to port arms and double time out to the front of everyone to find the A-1 marker in the grass. Once found, hopefully, I would then come to attention and face to the right and dress on the band until the company closed on me and I could do a left face and align with everyone else. As we marched on to the parade field, we corrected the alignment of the rifle ahead of us. At any time during the march on, or even after arrival on the field, plebes could be ordered to recite the marches for the day's parade, or recite the movies for the weekend, or the menu for the evening meal, or statistics on our football opponent. A favorite form of punishment was to have the plebe hold his rifle an inch off of the field whenever we were at attention. This could result in quivering arm muscles, which made it difficult to perform the manual of arms, which in turn could add more punishment. While A-1 was always the first company on the field and therefore had to stand at attention the longest, we were also the first company to pass in review and exit the field. On football Saturdays we then changed uniforms and went to the game and were free until the required chapel formation on Sunday morning. This was followed by more free time until dinner formation that night and required study time. The bottom three classes marched in formation up the hill to the chapel. The firsties were allowed to saunter in on their own. This was a schedule that was basically followed for all four years.

The highlight of '68's plebe year was the Army-Navy game weekend. We had a vociferous rally in the mess hall on Thursday night, and then the night before the game we attended a large pep-rally bonfire. Very early on Saturday morning we boarded trains and moved to Philadelphia, which was the traditional site of the game, got off and formed up in company formation after a little free time to stretch our legs, and then paraded onto the field. The *March On* by the Corps was always a spectacular sight and always more military and impressive than when the brigade of midshipmen from Annapolis kinda strolled in. After a series of traditional cheers, we moved to our seats to watch the game; although, as at any Army football game, the Corps never sat. After the game was over, we were free until formation at the trains for the return trip back to West Point, usually around midnight. That was the first time most plebes had been off post, and we took full advantage of the restaurants and bars of Philadelphia. The return formation was always a sight with "slightly" inebriated cadets trying to find their company, some out of uniform, or wearing Navy hats they had traded for. Our plebe year was really remarkable because we beat Navy, which was being led by their famous quarterback, Heisman Trophy winner Roger Staubach. A West Point tradition was that if we beat Navy, the plebes could *fall out* until Christmas, which meant no bracing and normal meals when we could even talk with our classmates and eat without restrictions. This was even better because we also went home for Christmas.

After Christmas leave, we returned to West Point for the second semester, which was basically a repeat of the intensity of the first—except for the weather. The winter at West Point was known as Gloom Period when everything was gray—the skies, the uniforms, the buildings, and even the ground when beautiful freshly fallen snow turned gray with age. The wind howled down the Hudson River Valley and was bitterly cold. If we had a date on the weekend, time could be spent in the small snack bar in Grant Hall or in the weapons room in the gym, which was a larger snack bar where we could get things like hamburgers and cherry cokes, and dance to music on the jukebox. There were always movies in South Auditorium of Thayer Hall or some relief in the restaurants of the Thayer Hotel. In good weather we could take our *drags* or dates for a stroll down Flirtation Walk, which was off limits to officers and all others. There was a famous Kissing Rock overhanging the path, and legend said that if your date refused a kiss the rock would fall on you both and the foundations of the Academy would crumble. It was not unusual to see a cadet with his date, and a small blue, rectangular suitcase walking toward the entrance on their way to Flirtation Walk for a picnic—maybe with something a little special to drink. Normally in the bag was a blanket or something similar, and I'm sure in some cases a bottle of alcoholic beverage, for a "picnic." As public displays of affection were never tolerated on the campus, there's no doubt that a lot of affection occurred on Flirty. It was a very special place in an all-male environment.

As cadets, we were not allowed to drink alcohol within fifteen miles of the Academy grounds and as plebes we weren't allowed off the base to begin with! Another significant difference from a civilian campus. There was a favorite and famous drinking establishment named Snuffy's that was precisely fifteen miles down Rte. 9W and a popular hangout for cadets who had the freedom and means to get there.

When spring finally rolled around, the upperclassmen took off for a week's spring leave break while the plebes had the run of the campus. There were a lot of parents and girlfriends who made the trip to spend time with us and to get a chance to really see West Point. The highlight of the week was a Band Box Review, during which we conducted and commanded a parade for our visitors in Central Area.

Band Box Review in Central Area

This was a great week to blow off Gloom Period and to get ready for the last few weeks of plebe year. We celebrated 100th Night a hundred days before graduation. This was one night when the plebes could harass the firsties, there was a great show performed by cadets, and a good time was had by all.

At the end of the second semester occurred the most important event of the whole year for plebes, the Recognition Parade. When the company returned to Central Area after the parade, and in a real barrage of harassment and physical hazing, the plebes were recognized as accepted members of the Corps. We lined up in a couple of ranks in Central Area and the upperclassmen walked down the ranks and shook the hands of each plebe, introducing themselves by their first name. Of course, there was time for one more round of hazing by having the upperclassmen stomp on our shoes or run wet fingers over our brass. My brass breastplate has a couple of dents in it made by the rifle butts of some upperclassmen. What an incredible day that was. We had made it! We had survived the rigors of our first year and would soon become yearlings. The relief was palpable, and we could finally enjoy ourselves at any time. No more plebe duties or spouting plebe poop, we could really enjoy the fine food of the Academy's mess hall, and now we could even have stereos in our rooms! There is no feeling quite like that which we experienced that day. All of a sudden, life was great!

While I suspect that we didn't realize it at the time, successful completion of plebe year created a more confident and mature young man. Trials and tribulations we had never before even conceived of had been met and conquered. We had become immersed in the concepts of Duty, Honor, Country and the Cadet Honor Code, values that would stay with us our entire lives. We had become soldiers with basic combat skills, we stood straighter, and were more polite in our dealings with people in general, offering "yes, sir" and "no, ma'am" when dealing with our seniors and folks at home, even if we hadn't been taught to do that before. We had been tested beyond what we ever thought possible, both physically and mentally, and had conquered every one of those tests. Many of our classmates had not been so successful and had dropped out or been forced out along the way by the rigorous demands of the Academy's academics or discipline. A value system and sense of duty had been instilled in us that would lead most of us to a combat tour in the steaming jungles of Vietnam a few years in the future. This year had resulted in an incredible transformation that we didn't yet recognize, we just reveled in the fact that the mess hall would now become a friendly place!

As a reward, June brought all of us a thirty-day leave—a whole month away from the Academy and time to do what we wanted. I suspect that most folks went home and reconnected with families and high school buddies and girlfriends who had completed their first year of college. Others set off on adventurous trips across the country and overseas. For those that went home, it became obvious that a gap had been created between us and our buddies. In addition to a tough academic schedule, our stringent military training had set us apart. The strict discipline and the rigors of the Fourth Class System had made us into guys who didn't resemble those of a year earlier.

At the end of that wonderful leave period, we returned to West Point to spend the summer at Camp Buckner on the shores of Lake Popolopen. If Beast was the most intensive training period we would experience as a cadet, the two months at Camp Buckner, although also intense, were the most enjoyable. While we underwent intensive tactical training in the five combat arms, our free time was spent in an incredible environment with recreation areas available for swimming, water skiing, basketball, and skeet shooting, among others. A large screened-in dance area in Bartlett Hall extending over the lake was the place of summer hops, often in our dress white uniforms. We were organized into new companies, so we had a chance to get to know our classmates from other companies. The meals at Buckner were every bit as good as those in Washington Hall, and we didn't have to brace or recite poop anymore!

The tactical training in the combat arms branches was enjoyable and educational. We learned to fire all of the standard infantry weapons, including mortars. The infantry section was capped by *Recondo*, an intense five days of patrolling, hand-to-hand combat training, mountaineering techniques, and confidence courses. In the armor phase, we learned to drive and fire the main gun of tanks and armored personnel carriers and participate in field problems. The climax was a combined arms attack of armor and infantry to demonstrate how the two branches worked together. During the artillery phase, we learned the basics of duties in the fire direction center, gun crew drills, how to adjust fire and then actually fire the 105mm howitzer. With the engineers we learned about all types of bridges, field fortifications and obstacles, demolitions, and land navigation. The Signal Corps section taught us about basic field radio and wire communications. Leadership and instruction was provided by first classmen and the officers and soldiers of a regular army unit. All in all, those two months at Camp Buckner were extremely enjoyable, both from a training and recreational standpoint. We were now really upperclassmen and were ready to go back to the main campus and experience a whole new West Point.

The first major event back on campus was another Acceptance Parade when we welcomed the plebes of the class of 1969 into our lettered companies. The year settled down into the normal routine of academics, intramural sports, football games in the fall, and weekly parades. Food in the mess hall continued to be outstanding. As I remember it, once a week we had steak or some other large cut of beef, and about once a month we actually had lobster. The food was almost as good as Mom's! Before we knew it, yearling year had been completed and the class of '68 became cows, or juniors.

Second Class summer was another adventure-filled experience. The first phase in June consisted of a general orientation of the roles and missions of the Navy and Air Force. This started with a three-day trip by USAF transports to Ogden Air Force Base in Florida for demonstrations and orientation in Air Force combat power. After returning to West Point for a short period, we set off for a three-day Navy orientation at the base in Newport, Rhode Island. The highlight of that trip was a short trip out to sea on a Navy warship. Classmate Ray Rhodes and I were on board a frigate on a day of relatively heavy seas— at least to us. While most of our classmates were leaving the contents of their stomachs in all kinds of inconvenient places that had to be cleaned by the crew, Ray and I were topside, above the bridge, enjoying the trip immensely. This event may have set the precedent in later years for cruises together with our wives to various parts of the world. We then returned to West Point for a seven-day Marine Corps orientation, which included weapons training, map reading, physical education, and the Army's methods of instruction (MOI). For the second phase of the summer starting in July, the class was divided in half. One half went on leave, the other half was divided again, with some providing squad-level leadership in Beast Barracks for the class of 1970 and the other half going off to play *third lieutenant* in regular army units in the US or Germany (AOT or Army Orientation Training). For the second phase the half of the class that had been on leave returned to pick up the Beast Barracks and AOT requirements while the first half went on leave. All in all, it was another great summer.

The school year of 1966–67 was a seminal year for the class of '68 and for the nation. Given the age of 1960s technology in which we lived— no cable TV, internet, email, twenty-four-hour news cycle, World Wide Web, etc.—we were generally unaware of what was happening outside of our cloistered world at West Point. Our main source of news was *The New York Times,* which could be delivered to our rooms by plebes. Even when we were home or other places outside the gates—when TV reception was sometimes tied to putting tin foil on the rabbit ears on top of the TV and then moving those around to get the best reception of the three channels offered—there was little awareness of what was happening across the country unless you lived in one of the areas affected.

Much like today as I write this, America was facing a time of racial upheaval, with African Americans protesting unfair treatment in many parts of life, including the justice system. In many areas the protests turned to riots. My hometown of Rochester, New York, New York City's Harlem, and Philadelphia, Pennsylvania all saw riots in 1964. The infamous turmoil in the Watts area of Los Angeles, California took place in '65. Omaha, Nebraska erupted in '66, followed by Newark and Plainfield New Jersey, and Detroit, Michigan in '67. Riots took place in Washington DC; Baltimore, Maryland; Little Rock, Arkansas; and Cleveland, Ohio in '68. And '69 saw the first gay rights protest in New York City. This period of social upheaval, protests for civil rights, and the incredible destruction of life and property in many of our major cities had a telling effect on a nation that was not accustomed to such unrest. And it also had a deep effect on the young men who would fill the ranks of the US Army in Vietnam, particularly the African Americans.

While this was occurring there was another protest movement that was gathering steam: the rising anti-Vietnam War sentiment that was beginning to appear in some of the major cities. Participants included a growing number of disaffected people, including young, draft-age men and even, in increasing numbers, returning veterans. In the initial phases of the war, national sentiment had been largely pro-war and patriotic. The year 1965 had seen the big battle in the Ia Drang Valley, the first full scale combat between the US and North Vietnamese Armies (NVA). Even though it was heralded as a defeat for the NVA, the US casualty list was long, and folks back home wondered why we had just given that blood-soaked terrain back to the enemy. There were increasing incidents of young men burning their draft cards and chanting "Hell no, we won't go!" Some protesters even began to run off to Canada.

While these movements were occurring, the West Point class of 1968 took another oath to complete our last two years, accept a commission in the Army, and then to serve for five years instead of the commitment of four years required of previous classes. By this time many of us had heard of Vietnam and began to realize that one of the motivations behind admitting larger classes was to provide more lieutenants to the meat-grinder war in the jungles of the Republic of Vietnam. There was a growing shift in awareness in the class, maybe some resigned because of this, while most of us probably became more serious in our studies, particularly those that had to do with the conduct of combat. Since the great majority of us would be required to accept a commission in the combat arms, and since there was a growing number of funerals in the West Point Cemetery for members of earlier classes that had gone to war, we began to take a more serious and sober look at what we had committed to do. At home, as live TV coverage of the war became standard fare on the six o'clock news, our families were also becoming more knowledgeable of what we were facing.

Cow year was the first time that we assumed any chain of command or leadership responsibility for the conduct of activities in the Corps. Many of us became squad leaders at one time or another during that year and proudly wore a single chevron on the lower part of our dress gray and full dress uniforms. We were responsible for our classmates and the members of the two lower classes assigned to our squad. While this didn't normally come with a lot of duties, it was still a start for assuming some responsibilities for others. The academic year of '66–'67 was like those preceding it, with a different course schedule. The only exception to this is that we were now allowed two elective courses, one each semester. Taking these two courses, and two more the next year, had no impact on our BS degree. The signature events of cadet life also passed as before, and before we knew it the year was over and the class of 1968 had become first classmen, or *firsties*, now seniors and a short time away from entering the Army.

The highlight of our last summer at USMA was the Firstie Trip, a visit to the combat arms branch homes, including Ft. Benning, Georgia (Infantry); Ft. Sill, Oklahoma (Field Artillery); Ft. Bliss, Texas (Air Defense Artillery); Ft. Knox, Kentucky (Armor); Ft. Monmouth, New Jersey (Signal); and Ft. Belvoir, Virginia (Engineer). At each stop we were wined and dined and treated to demonstrations of that particular branch's unique role in the Army. There was also a hop at each installation where eligible young ladies were assembled as prospective blind dates for the cadets. The trip was a real adventure and helped to solidify our thoughts about which branch we would like to serve. For the rest of the summer the firsties rotated through either Beast Barracks or Camp Buckner, AOT, and a thirty-day leave.

While the firstie academic year was like all the proceeding ones, there were several unique events that marked our progress toward graduation. The first was the receipt of our class rings, which we had selected the previous spring. This was a major fall event and marked by the Ring Hop, one of the grandest of our four years. West Point had been the first college-level institution to offer these symbols of attendance and graduation in 1835 as a yearly tradition, with rings that were designed by the class as a symbol of class unity and remembrance of time spent together.

In early winter of 1968, the class gathered in South Auditorium of Thayer Hall to select our service branches. Then, by order of merit, our names were called, and we each stood to announce our choice. There was a large chart on a screen with all five branches and the number of slots available for each. As each person announced his choice, it was noted on the chart by reducing the available number of openings in that branch by one. Historically and traditionally, the first branch to be filled was the Corps of Engineers, primarily by our class hives. Some of the smart guys selected other branches, but the majority wanted to be an engineer. As we moved down the order of merit, other branches began to fill as well, until toward the end only Infantry was left, which had the largest number of requirements anyway. While that would have been my selection no matter where I stood on the merit list, some of my contemporaries felt that they were ranked into Infantry, as there were no other choices available to them and it had the largest number of openings. Many had no desire to be a grunt. At this point one of our classmates stood and requested that the remaining members of the class be called on individually to declare their branch and ended with "I choose Infantry, sir!" The presiding officer complied with that request. To become a grunt was not particularly welcomed by some because of the short life expectancy of infantry lieutenants in Vietnam.

The other major choice to be made was unit of choice for our first assignments. To start with, we had two major options, to either volunteer to go to Vietnam on our first assignment, or to choose another option of maybe going to Germany or a stateside installation for a full two-year tour before going to Vietnam. I volunteered, as did many of my classmates, to go to Vietnam first. With that choice, after the branch schools, Airborne and Ranger schools, we were to spend six months in a stateside unit to get the hang of being a platoon leader, and then would deploy to the Republic of Vietnam. As before, we could volunteer for specific units in the war zone, again by order of merit. My desire was to go to the Fourth Infantry Division, as my dad had served there as well. I served my stateside time in the 197th Light Infantry Brigade at Ft. Benning before boarding a plane for the Far East. Those who elected to go elsewhere as a first assignment again went through an order of merit selection process to choose where they would like to serve.

Before we knew it, our firstie year drew to a close with June Week graduation festivities. There were parades, banquets, hops, and time to be spent with family and girlfriends. We enjoyed a beautiful week of weather to close out this incredible final week of our West Point experience. On the fifth of June, 1968, we marched into Michie Stadium—706 strong—to hear our guest speaker and to receive our diplomas. The guest speaker was Gen. Harold K. Johnson, chief of staff of the Army. General Johnson was a survivor of the Bataan Death March and had fought in Korea, and his presence with us was significant and an extra special honor, as he had a son in the class of '68 who did not graduate with us. After the ceremony, we were administered the Oath of Service as commissioned officers in the Army, individually or in small groups. My dad swore me in—a very proud moment in both of our lives. And then the line-up began at the Cadet Chapels, as many of our number started their military service with a new wife along. This was a significant end to our four years as cadets.

At the same time momentous events were occurring across the country and around the world. The racial unrest was continuing with major riots in several large cities. On January 30, the North Vietnamese Army and Viet Cong launched a nationwide offensive

LT. COL. JOHN C. HEDLEY (RET.), USMA '68

in the south, eventually numbering some 80,000 troops. This event has been recorded in history as the Tet Offensive of 1968. While they initially had some local successes that garnered the attention of the American press, it was later confirmed that militarily this was a resounding defeat for enemy forces when the general uprising that they had hoped for did not occur. The Viet Cong were decimated as an effective military force, necessitating more reliance on the North Vietnamese regular army for future enemy combat operations.

On March 16, troops from Company C, 1st Battalion, 20th Infantry of the 11th Infantry Brigade of the Americal Division, committed an atrocity in the Vietnamese village of My Lai. Five hundred unarmed villagers, including women, children, and old men, were murdered by troops gone wild. The news of this atrocity, conducted by US soldiers, stunned the country and the world. How could this have been perpetrated by good, clean-cut American boys? Lt. Calley, a platoon leader whose soldiers committed most of the barbarous acts, with him participating alongside them, was ultimately the only individual tried and convicted. Initially charged with the murder of 109 civilians, he was convicted of twenty-two of them and sentenced to life imprisonment. After three days, because of appeals, he was granted house arrest, and after three years his charges and sentence were reduced, and he was granted his freedom based on the time served in his home. In May of 1971, Major General Samuel W. Koster, then superintendent of West Point and who was, at the time of the incident, the division commander, was censured for the initial cover-up of the event, was relieved of his duties, reduced in rank to brigadier general, and retired.

These two events in the first three months of the year really stoked the fires of the American anti-war movement, leading to larger and more violent protests. Walter Cronkite's report in late February on the evening news, after returning from a trip to South Vietnam to look at the results of the Tet Offensive, in which he stated that the war was not winnable and would probably end in a stalemate, was one of the most important turning points in the American populace's support of the war. Cronkite was the most trusted newscaster in America, and his defeatist report that day scarred the minds of many in America who knew no better. Shortly after this broadcast, America learned of the crimes in My Lai. Anti-war feelings and demonstrations were ramping up just as many from the class of '68 were preparing to graduate and head to that very war.

On the domestic political front events were also stoking the fires of insurrection. On April 4, Martin Luther King was assassinated in Memphis Tennessee, and then on the very day we graduated, Robert F. Kennedy was assassinated in Los Angeles.

These horrible events, combined with the counterculture protest known as the hippie movement, all combined to produce a very troubled, and somewhat confused American public. Many of the building blocks of a fairly conservative country were being pulled down. The world in Southeast Asia was in turmoil, the world at home was being set on its ear, and normal conventions were flying out the window. Music had turned to acid rock, hippies were dressing strangely and smoking a lot of pot, the emerging feminist movement was burning bras and encouraging women to leave the traditional life of a housewife and mother and get into the business world. Civil rights and anti-war demonstrations were burning our cities and creating scenes of mayhem.

This was the country we re-entered on the fifth of June as we happily went on a traditional sixty-day graduation leave and then reported to our branch schools for initial training in the branches we had selected. Many of us were going to shoulder that awesome burden of responsibility for leading other young men in combat. And we were going to do this as young men ourselves of twenty-two to twenty-five years of age. We were a cohort of warriors, and many were filled with zeal to get to the war before it was over. Plenty of us considered the West Point of that day to be the Sparta of America. It may not have been popular, but in the minds of some of us it was the only war we had, and if we were going to be successful combat arms officers, we needed to get there to truly learn our trade.

The trials and tribulations of West Point, particularly those of Beast Barracks and plebe year, tested us and molded us into young officers who would go off to fight a war even though the national government had already decided not to pursue it to absolute victory. This was in direct contradiction of the words of Douglas MacArthur, who had declared that "there is no substitute for victory." I have spent a great deal of time recounting the experiences of our plebe year because I think that period was instrumental in identifying those cadets who did not have the character, desire, or intestinal fortitude to conquer what seemed at times unconquerable. In so doing, the system identified many who were probably not capable of leading soldiers in close, personal combat in what would prove to be a horrific and violent experience. There were, however, some who left us who obtained commissions through another source, Officers' Candidate School or Reserve Officers' Training Corps, who also went on to serve in Vietnam. For the rest of us, the West Point experience taught us to operate effectively under extreme pressure, it inculcated us with a sense of Duty and Honor, reinforced our love of Country, and inspired us to go to war in the image of all of those from the Long Gray Line who had preceded us.

Vietnam loomed on the horizon!

DOUGLAS MACARTHUR'S FAREWELL SPEECH TO THE CORPS OF CADETS, MAY 12, 1962

[The Thayer award is the Academy's most prestigious recognition of exemplary service to the nation. These remarks were from the heart; the general had no script or even notes].

General Douglas MacArthur

G eneral Westmoreland, General Groves, distinguished guests, and gentlemen of the Corps: As I was leaving the hotel this morning, a doorman asked me, "Where are you bound for, General?"

and when I replied, "West Point," he remarked, "Beautiful place, have you ever been there before?"

No human being could fail to be deeply moved by such a tribute as this. [Thayer Award] Coming from a profession I have served so long, and a people I have loved so well, it fills me with an emotion I cannot express. But this award is not intended primarily to honor a personality, but to symbolize a great moral code—the code of conduct and chivalry of those who guard this beloved land of culture and ancient descent. That is the meaning of this medallion. For all eyes and for all time, it is an expression of the ethics of the American soldier. That I should be integrated in this way with so noble an ideal arouses a sense of pride and yet of humility which will be with me always.

Duty—Honor—Country. Those three hallowed words reverently dictate what you ought to be, what you can be, what you will be. They are your rallying points: to build courage when courage seems to fail; to regain faith when there seems to be little cause for faith; to create hope when hope becomes forlorn. Unhappily, I possess neither that eloquence of diction, that poetry of imagination, nor that brilliance of metaphor to tell you all that they mean. The unbelievers will say they are but words, but a slogan, but a flamboyant phrase. Every pedant, every demagogue, every cynic, every hypocrite, every troublemaker, and, I am sorry to say, some others of an entirely different character, will try to downgrade them even to the extent of mockery and ridicule. But these are some of the things they do. They build your basic character, they mold you for your future roles as the custodians of the nation's defense, they make you strong enough to know when you are weak, and brave enough to face yourself when you are afraid. They teach you to be proud and unbending in honest failure, but humble and gentle in success; not to substitute words for actions, nor to seek the path of comfort, but to face the stress and spur of difficulty and challenge; to learn to stand up in the storm but to have compassion on those who fall; to master yourself before you seek to master others; to have a heart that is clean, a goal that is high; to learn to laugh yet never forget how to weep; to reach into the future yet never neglect the past; to be serious yet never to take yourself too seriously; to be modest so that you will remember the simplicity of true greatness, the open mind of true wisdom, the meekness of true strength. They give you a temper of the will, a quality of the imagination, a vigor of the emotions, a freshness of the deep springs of life, a temperamental predominance of courage over timidity, an appetite for adventure over love of ease. They create in your heart the sense of wonder, the unfailing hope of what next, and the joy and inspiration of life. They teach you in this way to be an officer and a gentleman.

And what sort of soldiers are those you are to lead? Are they reliable, are they brave, are they capable of victory? Their story is known to all of you; it is the story of the American man-at-arms. My estimate of him was formed on the battlefield many, many years ago, and has never changed. I regarded him then as I regard him now— as one of the world's noblest figures, not only as one of the finest military characters but also as one of the most stainless. His name and fame are the birthright of every American citizen. In his youth and strength, his love and loyalty he gave—all that mortality can give. He needs no eulogy from me or from any other man. He has written his own history and written it in red on his enemy's breast. But when I think of his patience under adversity, of his courage under fire, and of his modesty in victory, I am filled with an emotion of admiration I cannot put into words. He belongs to history as furnishing one of the greatest examples of successful patriotism; he belongs to posterity as the instructor of future generations in the principles of liberty and freedom; he belongs to the present, to us, by his virtues and by his achievements. In twenty campaigns, on a hundred battlefields, around a thousand campfires, I have witnessed that enduring fortitude, that patriotic self-abnegation, and that invincible determination which have carved his statue in the hearts of his people. From one end of the world to the other he has drained deep the chalice of courage.

As I listened to those songs of the glee club, in memory's eye I could see those staggering columns of the First World War, bending under soggy packs, on many a weary march from dripping dusk to drizzling dawn, slogging ankle-deep through the mire of shell-shocked roads, to form grimly for the attack, blue-lipped, covered with sludge and mud, chilled by the wind and rain; driving home to their objective, and, for many, to the judgment seat of God. I do not know the dignity of their birth, but I do know the glory of their death. They died unquestioning, uncomplaining, with faith in their hearts, and on their lips the hope that we would go on to victory. Always for them, Duty—Honor—Country; always their blood and sweat and tears as we sought the way and the light and the truth.

And twenty years after, on the other side of the globe, again the filth of murky foxholes, the stench of ghostly trenches, the slime of dripping dugouts; those boiling suns of relentless heat, those torrential rains of devastating storms; the loneliness and utter desolation of jungle trails, the bitterness of long separation from those they loved and cherished, the deadly pestilence of tropical disease, the horror of stricken areas of war; their resolute and determined defense, their swift and sure attack, their indomitable purpose, their complete and decisive victory—always victory. Always through the bloody haze of their last reverberating shot, the vision of gaunt, ghastly men reverently following your password of Duty—Honor—Country.

The code which those words perpetuate embraces the highest moral laws and will stand the test of any ethics or philosophies ever promulgated for the uplift of mankind. Its requirements are for the things that are right, and its restraints are from the things that are wrong. The soldier, above all other men, is required to practice the greatest act of religious training—sacrifice. In battle and in the face of danger and death, he discloses those divine attributes which his Maker gave when he created man in his own image. No physical courage and no brute instinct can take the place of the Divine help which alone can sustain him. However horrible the incidents of war may be, the soldier who is called upon to offer and to give his life for his country, is the noblest development of mankind.

You now face a new world—a world of change. The thrust into outer space of the satellite, spheres, and missiles marked the beginning of another epoch in the long story of mankind—the chapter of the space age. In the five or more billions of years the scientists tell us it has taken to form the earth, in the three or more billion years of development of the human race, there has never been a greater, a more abrupt or staggering evolution. We deal now not with things of this world alone, but with the illimitable distances and as yet unfathomed mysteries of the universe. We are reaching out for a new and boundless frontier. We speak in strange terms: of harnessing the cosmic energy; of making winds and tides work for us; of creating unheard synthetic materials to supplement or even replace our old standard basics; of purifying sea water for our drink; of mining ocean floors for new fields of wealth and food; of disease preventatives to expand life into the hundreds of years; of controlling the weather for a more equitable distribution of heat and cold, of rain and shine; of space ships to the moon; of the primary target in war, no longer limited to the armed forces of an enemy, but instead to include his civil populations; of ultimate conflict between a united human race and the sinister forces of some other planetary galaxy; of such dreams and fantasies as to make life the most exciting of all time.

And through all this welter of change and development, your mission remains fixed, determined, inviolable—it is to win our wars. Everything else in your professional career is but corollary to this vital dedication. All other public purposes, all other public projects, all other public needs, great or small, will find others for their accomplishment; but you are the ones who are trained to fight: yours is the profession of arms—the will to win, the sure knowledge that in war there is no substitute for victory; that if you lose, the nation will be destroyed; that the very obsession of your public service must be Duty—Honor—Country. Others will debate the controversial issues, national and international, which divide men's minds; but serene, calm, aloof, you stand as the nation's war guardian, as its lifeguard from the raging tides of international conflict, as its gladiator in the arena of battle. For a century and a half, you have defended, guarded, and protected its hallowed traditions of liberty and freedom, of right and justice. Let civilian voices argue the merits or demerits of our processes of government; whether our strength is being sapped by deficit financing, indulged in too long, by federal paternalism grown too mighty, by power groups grown too arrogant, by politics grown too corrupt, by crime grown too rampant, by morals grown too low, by taxes grown too high, by extremists grown too violent; whether our personal liberties are as thorough and complete as they should be. These great national problems are not for your professional participation or military solution. Your guidepost stands out like a ten-fold beacon in the night, Duty—Honor—Country.

You are the leaven which binds together the entire fabric of our national system of defense. From your ranks come-the great captains who hold the nation's destiny in their hands the moment the war tocsin sounds. The Long Gray Line has never failed us. Were you to do so, a million ghosts in olive drab, in brown khaki, in blue and gray, would rise from their white crosses thundering those magic words, Duty—Honor—Country. This does not mean that you are war mongers. On the contrary, the soldier, above all other people, prays for peace, for he must suffer and bear the deepest wounds and scars of war. But always in our ears ring the ominous words of Plato that wisest of all philosophers, "Only the dead have seen the end of war."

The shadows are lengthening for me. The twilight is here. My days of old have vanished tone and tint; they have gone glimmering through the dreams of things that were. Their memory is one of wondrous beauty, watered by tears, and coaxed and caressed by the smiles of yesterday. I listen vainly for the witching melody of faint bugles blowing reveille, of far drums beating the long roll. In my dreams I hear again the crash of guns, the rattle of musketry, the strange, mournful mutter of the battlefield.

But in the evening of my memory, always I come back to West Point. Always there echoes and re-echoes Duty—Honor—Country. Today marks my final roll call with you, but I want you to know that when I cross the river my last conscious thoughts will be of The Corps, and The Corps, and The Corps. I bid you farewell.

VIETNAM

As we departed West Point after graduation, our minds were still pretty far away from a future that would affect almost all of us: duty in a small country in Southeast Asia called The Republic of Vietnam, or South Vietnam, or just Vietnam, Nam, or The Nam. Vietnam was bordered on the north by the People's Republic of China, on the west by Laos and Cambodia, and the east by the Gulf of Tonkin and the South China Sea, areas that most of us were not familiar with, maybe couldn't even find on a map. We had sixty days of leave—freedom—ahead of us before we had to report to our first duty station, so probably few were thinking of that part of the world. It would soon, however, become all too familiar; duty there would be significant, as it would be combat duty for most of us.

Vietnam was a seminal experience that would fundamentally change each of us who experienced it, no matter which of the combat branches we served. It was an experience of man at the most basic and primitive of levels, trying to kill rather than be killed. A harsh description perhaps, but it's the experience of war boiled down to its basic reality. The war that we fought was a war of attrition—eliminate as many of the bad guys as we possibly could in the hope that it would discourage the government of The People's Republic of Vietnam, or North Vietnam, from sending any more of its young soldiers off to fight and die in South Vietnam. Unfortunately for us, and especially for the twenty classmates whose stories are told in the following pages, our enemy fought with the same strategy as ours; they would try to kill as many Americans as possible in order to turn our public and political opinion against the war.

Unlike previous wars, in Vietnam there were no front lines; we held no territory other than firebases and major logistical installations dotted across the landscape. After a successful fight, conquering and holding terrain was not the measure of success, as we often returned those bloody battlefield patches of jungle to the bad guys pretty quickly. Rather, success was measured in body count, how many of the bad guys did we kill, and how many blood trails were there indicating that the bad guys had dragged a body off of the field? That was success—the more bodies and blood trails, the bigger the victory. This concept was at the heart of our operations and led to our search and destroy missions.

What a diabolical system, yet it was the only war that we had, and if we were going to be successful combat arms officers then we had to go to war and operate in the most efficient way possible and kill as many NVA and VC soldiers as we could while losing or injuring as few of our own soldiers as possible. This was a tough task for the young lieutenants and captains of the class of '68.

Vietnam was a country with a long and turbulent history. Long occupied by Chinese warlords, Vietnam finally kicked out the last of them around the year AD 1000 and gained a form of local independence. From then until 1802 Vietnam was ruled primarily by local warlords. In 1802, the Nguyen Dynasty united all of Vietnam and served as a national figurehead government until 1945. To complicate things for the Vietnamese, in 1862 France occupied large parts of the area and colonized it until the 1950s, with a break for WWII. The French divided Vietnam into three areas: Tonkin or the very Northern provinces along the Chinese border; Annan, which was the biggest area stretching from Tonkin to the area of the Mekong Delta; and Cochin, which was the southernmost area. Many referred to the entire French protectorate as Cochin China. While in truth Vietnam was largely a French colony, the Nguyen Dynasty was kept as the face of the Vietnamese national government.

In 1940 the Japanese invaded Cochin China, wanting the raw materials and strategic location on the South China Sea, and occupied it until 1945, causing the French to abandon their colony. When this happened Ho Chi Minh formed the League for the Independence of Vietnam in Hanoi in 1941, whose military arm was the Viet Minh.

The Viet Minh, supported by the US and Nationalist China, fought the Japanese invaders until the Japanese defeat in 1945. With their surrender, Ho Chi Minh declared the formation of the Democratic Republic of Vietnam on September 2, 1945.

As the war ended, France wanted to reclaim her former colony. At the same time the Chinese Kuomintang Army, as opposed to the Chinese Communist People's Liberation Army, which didn't yet exist, arrived in the area to oversee the surrender and repatriation of Japanese forces. While this was happening, the Chinese were involved in a civil war between the communists and nationalists that continued from 1945 to 1949. Through negotiations, the three countries, Nationalist China, the Vietnamese, and the French, came to a basic understanding for governing Vietnam: the Chinese agreed to leave (wanting to fight Mao's communists and prevent them from taking over the country), the Viet Minh agreed to the return of the French in exchange for assurances of independence within the French Union, and the French agreed to give up certain rights in China.

With the departure of the Chinese, negotiations between the French and Vietnamese quickly broke down, resulting in the First Indochina War between the two countries, or the French War as it was called by the Vietnamese.

Initially the Viet Minh were poorly armed and greatly outnumbered by a militarily superior France. However, with the help of former Japanese officers and logistical support from China and Russia, the Vietnamese quickly gained training, experience, and strength. While the French Army and its colonial troops, as well as units from the French Foreign Legion, partially supported by the US and Great Britain, was initially successful in clearing the Viet Minh out of selected areas, they quickly became bogged down in the jungles and rice paddies. Time after time the French found that their superiority of numbers and weapons was eroded by the fighting spirit of the local Viet Minh cadres, the logistical support of Russia and China to the Viet Minh, and the support of the local populations for the Viet Minh and their knowledge of the countryside.

June 24–29, 1954, the French suffered a catastrophic final defeat along Hwy 19 linking An Khe and Pleiku through the famous Mang Yang Pass, an area that many of us would get to know very well. As the French began to consolidate forces into just a few major bases after their disastrous defeat at Dien Ben Phu, their troops in the An Khe area were ordered to move north and link up with other French forces in the Pleiku area. French Mobile Group 100, consisting of 3,500 of the best troops that the French had left in Vietnam, was ambushed shortly after leaving An Khe in the infamous Mang Yang Pass, and suffered enormous casualties. During those five horrendous days of constant combat, they suffered 500 killed, 600 wounded, and 800 captured as well as lost 85 percent of their vehicles, 100 percent of their artillery, 68 percent of their signal equipment, and 50 percent of their crew-served weapons. Many of the dead are buried on a hilltop along the pass, and it's said that they were buried standing up due to the scarcity of suitable terrain, facing towards France. Their grave sites were covered with quicklime to keep them from becoming overgrown and were still visible from the air during our time there, a truly eerie sight. This event occurred a year after the major French loss at Dien Bien Phu, which cost French forces 15,000 dead, missing, and captured. These two major defeats hastened the French withdrawal from the country and the end of the French War.

With the French gone, the United Nations divided Vietnam into two separate countries along the 16th parallel with the communists in the north with their capitol in Hanoi, and President Diem controlling the free south with a capitol in Saigon. It was agreed that elections would be held within two years to unify the country and to determine who would run it; but unfortunately, that never happened. Hundreds of refugees streamed south to escape communist rule, and the two sides quickly entered into a state of war.

The major emphasis of American foreign policy at this time was containing communism, both in Europe and the Far East. The term *Domino Theory* entered the American political lexicon, espousing the view that if one country fell to the communists, then others in the area were sure to follow, similar to a line of dominoes falling in turn after the first one is knocked over. Many in the American government began to fear that if South Vietnam fell to the North, then Laos, Cambodia, Thailand, and others were sure to follow. So, plans were made to strengthen South Vietnam's ability to resist the North to keep it from becoming the first domino. This, in turn, developed into material aid to equip the South Vietnamese forces and allow them to stand up to and defeat the forces of North Vietnam, the NVA, and the South Vietnamese Viet Cong, or VC, successor to the Viet Minh, who were being supported by North Vietnam, as well as the People's Republic of China and the Soviet Union with military material and advisors.

In the early 1960s President John Kennedy became much enamored of a new branch of the US Army, the Special Forces—the famous Green Berets. They were organized around teams, the basic unit being the A Team of twelve men, which gained fame in Vietnam for manning camps along the Vietnamese border with Cambodia. These teams were designed to be deployed deep into the countryside and to provide training and, in some cases, command and control of friendly irregular or guerrilla forces. They were to be a direct counterweight to the Soviet and Chinese advisors to the North Vietnamese.

Direct American military involvement in Vietnam began in 1957 when a Special Forces detachment ran a training program for South Vietnamese in Nha Trang. In 1962, President Kennedy established a formal program for helping South Vietnam in their conflict with local guerillas, centered on assistance provided by the US Special Forces. With the arrival of the first US conventional combat forces in 1965, there were already some 23,000 US advisors and Special Forces personnel in Vietnam.

In August of 1964, a US destroyer, the USS Maddux, was allegedly attacked by North Vietnamese gunboats in the Gulf of Tonkin. In response, the president was authorized by Congress to conduct a counterstrike and follow-on military operations against the North by passing the Gulf of Tonkin Resolution. In the first aerial attack on the North's gunboat bases, Lt. Everett Alvarez was shot down and became our first prisoner of war (POW). In conjunction with this resolution, President Johnson ordered the first deployment of American combat troops with an initial troop ceiling of 184,000. In March of 1964, US Marines splashed ashore in Da Nang. On the third of May, 1965, advanced elements of the Army's 173rd Airborne Brigade deployed to Bien Hoa Airbase outside of Saigon. The US ground war, the Second Indochina War, had begun.

By the time members of the class of 1968 began to arrive, American troop strength had increased to about 550,000. Several

Army and Marine divisions had deployed as the war ramped up, and rather than rotate additional units in and out of the continental US, Army replacements were assigned on an individual basis to units already in the field. This system led to many problems, and when coupled with the fact that our tours were for only twelve months, and not the duration, most units realized close to a 100 percent turnover of personnel in a year— certainly not the most efficient way to fight a war. Every soldier's date of estimated return from overseas (DEROS) became a date to live for, and in many cases caused a degradation in small-unit efficiency when several soldiers in the same unit expected to DEROS around the same time. For, as soldiers got close to their DEROS they became *short* (short time remaining) and therefore more cautious and probably less effective if actually out in the jungle. *Newbies* or *FNGs* (which stood for fucking new guys) were inexperienced and prone to making mistakes. In addition, the old guys frequently did not want to form close friendships with the FNGs, as they may have already lost some of their friends to combat or DEROS and didn't want to go through that emotional trip again.

By 1969, this rotation schedule was well established and we of '68 deployed to Vietnam as individual replacements. When we boarded our plane in the US to fly to Vietnam, we were alone, even though there may have been 200 other guys on board. Our trip from the US to Vietnam took about twenty-four hours—not much time to mentally prepare for what we were about to face. Our dads had gone to Europe and the Pacific with the units they had lived with and trained with for months or even years, in the States or in England. And they went by ship, so they usually had weeks en route for further training and time to go through the mental turmoil of preparing for combat. Most importantly, they had ample time to bond with their buddies. For most of them, their DEROS was the day the war ended—short of being wounded or racking up enough aerial missions, if they'd served in the Army Air Corps. The only individual replacements during World War II were the guys assigned to replace casualties. When our dads deployed, they pretty much knew that they'd serve with their assigned unit until the end of the war, and then they'd return with that unit as well. The return home was also by sea and took a few weeks, giving our dads time to decompress and mentally prepare for their arrival stateside and the rest of their lives. And they returned as heroes. If we survived to our DEROS, we returned home, again alone, with a bunch of other guys we didn't know, and arrived in the US about twenty-four hours after leaving Vietnam—no decompression time, no time to prepare.

And we returned as pariahs.

When we arrived in the war zone between 1969 and 1972, we were sent to combat-experienced units manned by combat veterans; we were given command of some of these combat hardened soldiers while still very much wet behind the ears. Our only advantage was that we didn't deploy as a much-maligned second lieutenant, who everyone else believed knew nothing and had no experience. We had all been to our branch basic officer courses, and most went to Ranger and Airborne Schools. Those of us who had volunteered for Vietnam as an initial assignment were also given six months in the US in a Regular Army unit to get our feet wet as lieutenants. The great majority of us arrived in Vietnam as first lieutenants or even captains for the later arrivals, and therefore packed a little credibility in that we'd survived our Army plebe year as *butter bars* (second lieutenants) whose rank insignia was a single brass bar.

Incoming soldiers, and classmates, were assigned to two major in-country commands, United States Army Vietnam (USARV), or Military Assistance Command Vietnam (MACV). If assigned to USARV the FNG would go to an American unit somewhere in-country. If assigned to MACV then the assignment was to an advisory team, collocated with a South Vietnamese unit as an advisor and source of logistical, tactical, and fire support. MACV normally operated in teams, the size of which was determined by the size and type of unit supported. In many cases the role of advisor was a little awkward, as the Vietnamese commander being advised might have been fighting his war for years. The MACV teams lived with their units and many times depended on them for food and all other necessities. The most sought-after advisory positions were with the Vietnamese Airborne and Ranger units, as they generally had the most accomplished leadership, the best troops, and the best support from both the Vietnamese and US governments.

Vietnam was a different type of war depending on your branch, and as an infantry officer serving primarily in the mountains and jungles of II Corps along the Cambodian border I can only speak from that perspective. It's interesting to note that with more than 500,000 troops in-country, on any given day only about 10 percent were actually in the field seeking combat with the bad guys. We had a one-to-nine combat-to-support ratio, so for every soldier in the field there were nine in support in some other function. The majority of those actively seeking combat by thrashing through rice paddies or climbing the mountains along the Cambodian border while hacking their way through triple-canopied, dense jungles were infantry units. There were also some armored cavalry squadrons and a few tank battalions in the field, as well as artillery officers assigned to these infantry and armor units to act as forward observers, and some combat engineers in direct support, but the majority outside *the wire,* were infantry.

The infantry soldier in Vietnam can be viewed as the last of the American jungle fighters. Life for these guys was very primitive, living off of only what he could carry on his back for the most part, and then living off of the land when that was gone, depending on the availability of resupply. For many grunts, that load could be 100 pounds or more. Most would hear the sound of incoming rounds of various calibers coming up range at them as they, in turn, sent rounds of various calibers down range toward the source of those rounds. This is a very simplistic explanation of infantry combat, which in reality was much more complex, and many times absolutely terrifying, for the dense jungle with limited visibility was a truly scary place and being shot at there an even more intensely scary experience.

Most infantry battalions operated out of a forward firebase, a cantonment area for 150–200 guys, defended by bunkers of various descriptions and triple fences of triple concertina wire. The firebases were home for the battalion headquarters and normally included at least one battery of 105mm howitzers that fired in direct support of the battalion's rifle companies in the field. These bases were defended by one of the rifle companies that rotated through for a period of rest and soldier and equipment maintenance, called a stand down, as well as admin and support personnel from the battalion headquarters company who supported supply, administrative, and medical requirements, and maybe at times the battalion reconnaissance platoon during their stand-down period. While pretty grim in atmosphere and services compared to a stateside post, the firebase was a place where guys could get a shower and a hot meal provided by the mess section. It was a place to heal jungle rot and sores, clean weapons, get a clean set of jungle fatigues, and sometimes just rest and recuperate. The primary duty requirement was guard duty and establishing a couple of ambushes at night, and sometimes running a patrol in the immediate area. Compared to living on the ground in the jungle, a firebase was a pretty luxurious place.

However, living conditions were not plush by any means. Most guys slept in sandbag bunkers that had little ventilation, so they became exceedingly hot and odiferous. In many cases, the bunkers were shared with huge rats who would come out at night to forage for food left out by the occupants. These rats grew to be as big as a cat and were the source of bites and vermin that carried a variety of diseases. There was nothing worse than to be awakened in the middle of the night by some strange weight on your chest, and to open your eyes and see two beady little orbs staring at you. This would elicit a scream or yell from the trooper, which would in turn wake everyone up, and result in a flurry of activity as everyone in the bunker attempted to track the furry monster and do him in. Enterprising soldiers in my unit developed what we called soap rounds for their .45 caliber pistols to be used on the creatures. The bullet would be removed from a round of ammo, and half of the powder dumped out. The shell would be then screwed into a bar of hard GI soap until the cartridge was full. Before guys would go to sleep for the night a designated rat patrol would take a flashlight, a .45 cal. pistol, and several soap rounds in a magazine, and enter to clear the bunker. If the hunter was lucky and managed to hit a target, one of the advantages of the special round was that it would kill the rat without making much of a mess.

Firebases were many times pretty quiet and relatively safe areas, but no place in Vietnam was totally safe, from the small battalion-sized firebases located around the countryside, to major installations that housed a division rear area or a major logistical base or airfield home to hundreds if not thousands. All US facilities in-country were subject to attack at any time by mortars, enemy artillery or rockets, and ground attacks frequently carried out by NVA special infiltration forces called sappers. That's why buildings and facilities were protected by fifty-five-gallon drums filled with sand and placed in a wall around the site. While these were no protection from a direct hit, they would stop most shrapnel or small arms fire. Most locations had bunkers scattered around for folks to get into in the case of an attack from direct or indirect fire. Although thought to be relatively secure, the major logistical and admin bases were subjected to attack by NVA 120mm rockets and mortars of varying size. Even the largest and most secure installations were surrounded by three triple concertina fences and bunkers manned on a twenty-four-hour basis. On bases that housed aircraft, ground attacks by NVA sapper units couldn't be discounted.

Sanitation was another of the somewhat improved facilities on a firebase. In the field one took care of body elimination functions wherever one could. In most cases, if the tactical situation allowed, soldiers would leave the close proximity of their buddies and find a secure place to take care of their needs. Each box of C ration meals included a small, tightly wrapped package of toilet paper. When this had been used, and if there had been no resupply, then field expedient measures came into play. On the firebase there were *crappers* which were normally two or three *holers* that at least had a more comfortable toilet seat and rolls of real toilet paper. Underneath each hole was half of a fifty-five-gallon drum to collect the waste. Each day these had to be pulled out, the contents mixed with fuel of some type, and then set alight and stirred to ensure that everything was consumed by the flames. A popular form of non-judicial punishment for minor transgressions was to sentence that unlucky soldier to be a *shit burner*, whose responsibility was to keep stirring the mess until all had been burned. If soldiers were fortunate enough to be assigned to one of the larger bases, then local Vietnamese were hired. In addition to the crappers, *piss tubes* were scattered around the firebase where empty shell containers were partially buried at an angle in a hole filled with gravel or some other such material. Since there were no women in the combat arms in those days there was no need for privacy.

The most popular location on most firebases was the shower tent, if you could call it that. It was even more popular than the mess tent, where we could usually get more palatable real food. Given the hot and humid atmosphere, showers were a necessity. In many cases, a cleaned-out Air Force wing fuel tank was put on a high scaffold and filled with water, which in turn was heated by the sun. Dangling from the bottom of the fuel tank would be two or three hoses with a shut off valve and shower head at the end. In most cases the showers were found in a shed or at least had a canvas wall. A soldier would enter, turn on the water to get wet, turn off the water while soaping up, and then turn on the water to rinse off. Most guys were pretty judicious in their use of water, as sometimes resupply and refilling was difficult, and there were always a lot of guys who needed the shower. It was sometimes really humorous to see a bunch of naked guys with towels and soap running for the showers right after a unit returned from the field.

Author at the grill—FSB St. George 1969

We also had grills on some of the firebases, fifty-five-gallon drums cut in half lengthwise to hold the coals, and grates made from wire fencing or some other similar type of material for the actual grill surface. With enough advance planning, or if one knew the right guy in the right place, steaks or chicken, and sometimes both, could be obtained and grilled for the troops, accompanied by cold beer or even a bottle or two of hard liquor. Having experienced two of those events, I can attest that they were a very special event for hardened jungle troops.

Conditions in the field, in comparison to stateside or even in-country firebases, could be hellacious. Normally, when leaving the firebase, troops in our area of operations carried a rucksack that weighed anywhere from eighty to one hundred ten pounds, filled with rations, ammo, claymore mines, extra radio batteries, ropes, sleeping gear, maybe a jungle sweater, poncho, poncho liner, entrenching tool, water, and other necessities. This basic load was intended to serve for five days before a resupply helicopter was needed. Most times we rode to our area of operations on a *slick* (troop transport helicopter), so called because they had no on-board weapons other than a machine gun in each door. When we landed, we found either a *hot* (we were being shot at) or *cold* (no one was shooting at us) landing zone (LZ). Once on the ground, we became ordinary infantry foot soldiers. We'd then move through rice paddies and triple canopy jungle to try to find our enemy. Both types of terrain could be tortuous in hot and humid conditions. If the paddies were full of water, their beds were mud so sticky it could pull your boots off. If in the jungle, conditions became even worse.

Most of the jungle in our area was triple canopy, which meant that there were three different heights to the top of the trees. These areas were always dark because it was difficult for sunlight to filter through and always damp, as moisture constantly trickled down through all three layers. The underbrush could be so thick that you couldn't see more than three or four feet during the day, and these areas had zero visibility at night. The jungles were filled with all types of dangers, apart from enemy soldiers, as they were home to many types of biting insects, such as red ants of a particularly ferocious breed, hornets and wasps the size of your little finger, huge mosquitos that sounded like a B-52 bomber when flying around your ears at night, many different species of venomous snakes (we killed a king cobra that measured well over twenty feet in length), and animals, including orangutans and tigers. We were once tracked by a suspected maneater for two days. One morning I woke up to find the tracks of huge paws just inches from my feet. The cat had entered and crossed our perimeter without being detected! I called for an extraction because of the danger; our battalion lost a soldier to tigers on two successive nights. Elephants and ferocious wild boar were other huge dangers. On a smaller scale, leeches would attach themselves to your legs or other parts of your body and suck blood until they filled up and dropped off. They injected a mild anesthetic so you couldn't feel them as they did their work. It just became standard operating procedure (SOP) to stop periodically to do a buddy check for leeches, especially after crossing a stream, if the tactical situation allowed it. Our jungles were often on mountains, which made the terrain even more difficult to traverse.

When we were on an operation, we seldom received clean clothes because back-haul of the dirty ones might be impossible. Therefore, many times we'd wear the same pair of jungle fatigues for weeks until they began to rot, especially during the monsoon or rainy season. Minor scratches or cuts experienced from the underbrush could fester, become infected and turn into jungle rot, which never healed, itching and oozing until we got back to a firebase and had a chance to dry out. We didn't wear any underwear because it would bunch up, become sodden from sweat, and cause the same problems. We ate parts of C rations that we carried with us, and sometimes could actually heat them and make them passable as food. While the Army issued heat tablets, these were smelly and slow to work. The approved field soldier method of heating food or water was with the explosive C4, which required only a little piece and burned hot and fast. We asked folks at home to send us garlic salt, hot sauce, and other favorite seasonings to make the canned field rations more palatable. Once we had consumed all of the water that we carried, we were dependent on streams, rivers, and sometimes even rice paddies for refills. The potability of these sources were always questionable, particularly the rice paddies as they also served as water buffalo latrines, so we carried Halazone tablets to kill bacteria and make the water drinkable. The only problem was that the water then had an absolutely terrible taste, so most grunts carried packages of Kool-Aid with them to cover the taste of the water and tablets.

Infantry units spent a lot of time looking for the enemy. Depending on where we were, we could encounter one of two primary types of enemy forces. One was the Viet Cong (VC) who were basically local guerilla fighters. Their strength could vary from one or two local farmers to main force VC units that were organized much like regulars but didn't have the level of training or firepower found with the NVA. VC units were masters of the ambush and would seldom stand and fight because of our superiority in fire power. They would snipe at us, or maybe even blow an ambush, both of which could cause casualties, and then they would disappear into the jungle. The NVA were a different experience altogether. They were regular soldiers and were usually well equipped, trained, and led. They would actually attack American units, if possible, and loved to get in close and engage in fierce combat. Their belief was that if they could get close enough, or *grab our belts* as they referred to it, then we couldn't use our artillery or air support. If a mission involved attacking NVA in fortified positions then the fight could be horrendous, like the infamous battle of Hamburger Hill (Hill 937) fought from May 10–20, 1969. The hill was heavily fortified as an NVA base, and was of little strategic value, but troops from the 101st Airborne Division (Airmobile) were ordered to take it. Doing so took many direct assaults up the hill's wooded slopes, and US forces were constantly thrown back. The summit was finally reached on the twentieth, the NVA melted away, and the cost to the 101st was seventy-two soldiers killed, and 372 wounded. American forces abandoned the hill a couple of days after their bloody capturing of the summit.

Aside from major fights like Hamburger Hill, the life of an infantryman has been described by many as hours of sheer boredom punctuated with moments of sheer terror. Units could patrol in the jungle for days and see nothing, and then all of a sudden be subjected to withering fire in a ferocious ambush. If the enemy was VC, they would disappear shortly after blowing the ambush; if NVA, the initial fire could be just the beginning fusillade of a protracted battle.

Many times, relief and support were provided by Army helicopters, many flown by classmates. Besides the slicks that were primarily taxis, there were also gunships and aerial rocket artillery (ARA) ships. The gunships could provide support with mini-guns and 2.75-inch unguided rockets, the aerial rocket artillery birds had extra rocket pods that enabled them to provide heavier supporting fire to a ground unit in contact. Wounded soldiers could be flown quickly to major medical facilities by medevac ships that weren't armed and included trained medics in their crews. Even the most grievously wounded soldier had a good chance of survival if a medevac could get him to a hospital quickly. Normally used for logistical purposes, big, twin-rotored CH 47 Chinooks could also transport a larger number of troops or a heavy load of supplies, to include 105mm howitzers and pallets of artillery ammunition sling-loaded underneath the bird. Vietnam is frequently referred to as the small unit war, and it was also the helicopter war, as they were the workhorses of the American infantry.

Vietnam had two primary seasons, dry and wet, or the monsoon season. During the dry season, temperatures could cross well over 100 degrees Fahrenheit, and humidity could hover in the 80-90 percent levels or above. Dirt roads would become inches deep in dust that could penetrate every pore in your body and make breathing difficult. At the same time, the high humidity made it feel as though you were walking through a sponge. During the monsoon season, it rained every day, sometimes all day, for a couple of months. If troops were out on an operation, it was impossible to get dry. In the mountains it could actually get cold at night, and if cold and wet it was almost impossible to sleep. One of the most sought-after items of issue was the camouflaged poncho liner made of nylon that was constructed so as to provide warmth to even the coldest wet body. Sometimes in the mountains we would tie ourselves to trees to keep from sliding down the wet slopes during the night. Clothes would rot, weapons rust, and skin would get sodden and appear prune-like. Feet were an area of special concern as a soldier with foot problems became combat ineffective and a burden if medevac was not quickly available. It was not unusual for soldiers to develop *trench foot* like in World War I. When that happened, severe cases made a soldier non-operational for the duration of his tour as he couldn't walk well or wear jungle boots.

Mail call was as important to us as to World War II and Korean War soldiers as there was no internet, email, or Facebook. We could send letters home postage free, a good thing since there were few post offices in the jungle, by writing the words *Free Postage* in the area where a stamp would go. We could write on anything available, to include carton flaps from C ration cases or boxes, and it would generally get home. It was a great morale booster to see a big orange mail bag on a resupply bird if you were out on a mission. In many cases, the mail would also include goodie boxes with homemade cookies or other treats. It was an unwritten rule that these would be shared with those not fortunate enough to get their own boxes.

Most units would spend a week to ten days on an operation before cycling back to the firebase for some rest and recuperation.

Once in a while, we might have a visit from a USO-sponsored band that would come out to play for an hour or so, but those were pretty rare on the battalion-sized firebases. There were some great shows, however, on the major headquarters and logistical bases. Bob Hope continued his string of visits to soldiers, sailors, marines, and airmen, as he did during WWII. US Army Vietnam did have a two-level formal rest and recuperation (R&R) system, which authorized one out-of-country trip and one in-country trip during a twelve-month tour. The out-of-country trips were for six days and five nights, and there were a variety of places to choose from, to include Hong Kong, Thailand, Australia, Japan, Hawaii, and others. Australia was probably the favorite of the unmarried guys, for the country was renowned for its beautiful and very friendly women. Hawaii was the favorite place for married guys to meet their wives for a welcome break. The primary in-country site was Vung Tau or the famous China Beach for a three-night stay. Here was a place to relax, get some good food, an endless supply of beer and sometimes even be able to visit with round eyed (a term used by soldiers to refer to Western women) American military nurses or Red Cross Donut Dollies.

Donut Dollies were young women who volunteered to work with the American Red Cross and whose mission was to bring some TLC and welcome feminine diversion from daily life to US soldiers. These were very brave ladies who would ride helicopters out to forward firebases to bring relief and enjoyment to the troops stationed there. Their mission was to bring a touch of home to soldiers who had just cut their way through the jungle, maybe walked point, or had seen their buddies badly wounded or killed. These young American women, mostly in their early twenties, in their powder blue dresses (often pretty short), with ribbons in their hair, make up and sometimes maybe a hint of perfume, were absolutely incredible. While they seldom actually brought donuts, they might have ice cream or games or candy of some sort, and just provided the opportunity to talk with, and maybe even hold hands with an attractive young American woman. A visit from them could boost morale and put a smile on soldiers' faces. Three of these young ladies gave their lives, one in a vehicle accident, one to disease, and one was murdered by a druggie soldier. A total of 627 of these incredible young women volunteered to serve and support American soldiers in Vietnam.

In addition to the Red Cross Donut Dollies, some 5000 service nurses, primarily Army, also served in medical facilities throughout the country. They were a welcome sight to wounded soldiers medevac'd for treatment. Given the things they saw and the horrors they experienced, many of these brave ladies suffered lifelong effects from their experiences, much like the young soldiers they attended. Eight of these ladies are remembered on The Vietnam Wall, having given their lives in support of military operations and while doing their best to support and heal young soldiers in absolute need of their caring.

There were also some enlisted Army women of the Women's Army Corps (WAC) who worked in the major administrative and logistical bases in-country. These ladies shared the exposure to and dangers of mortar and rocket attacks from time to time.

The field artillery guys from the class of '68 played a major role in this war, as did their counterparts from other commissioning sources. As mentioned before, every battalion firebase had at least one artillery battery collocated; sometimes they had multiple batteries, depending on location and mission. In some areas the artillery guys were famous for their mess services, which provided better food than the infantry mess facilities, or so most grunts believed. They shared the possibilities of frequent indirect fire attacks and ground assaults with their infantry brothers. Many times they'd be awakened in the middle of the night to fire illumination rounds or high explosive rounds to support an infantry unit in contact. The artillery forward observer teams, (FO), went to the boonies with the grunts. Normally a lieutenant with a sergeant radio telephone operator, these guys experienced all of the various joys, hardships, and terrors of being an infantryman in Vietnam. The direct support batteries moved with us every time the battalion headquarters changed location. There were also batteries of larger 155 mm, 175 mm or 8-inch guns assigned at division or corps level who frequently added their heavier firepower to an infantry unit in contact. As with the 105mm batteries, these heavier units fired night illumination and harassment and interdiction (H&I) missions. Many times, they also deployed on *hip shoots* to place a gun or two closer to the action so as to provide better support to infantry units and 105mm batteries on the firebases.

The majority of infantry commanders were very careful with the lives of men in their units. During our time in-country it was not unusual to use artillery against small enemy units or even snipers rather than put soldiers' lives in danger. The Paris Peace Talks were already underway with the North Vietnamese, and it was obvious that the US did not plan to win the war, but rather achieve *peace with honor*, whatever the hell that was. No one wanted to be the last American killed in Vietnam.

For bigger fights, ground commanders also had access to the Army's helicopter aerial rocket artillery (ARA) or gunships, and if the situation was really hairy, could call on the support of US Air Force, Marine, or Navy fighter bombers controlled in most cases by Air Force forward air controllers or FACs. These FACs were a breed apart, flying around in small, propeller-driven planes, sometimes equipped with a few white phosphorous rockets—WP or Willie Pete—which could be used to mark enemy positions. They had radios with which they monitored ground unit frequencies, and when they detected a unit in trouble, they would call for the *fast movers* and direct their attacks. Many times the FAC would fly low and slow to entice the bad guys to shoot at him so that he in turn could mark their locations as targets with his WP rockets for the jets. These guys were incredibly brave and often risked their lives to help units in contact below them. We have at least one '68 classmate who was a FAC. In one incident, my unit was undoubtedly saved by a FAC at a time when we were grossly outnumbered and had no communication with higher headquarters.

The fast movers could carry heavy loads of bombs of various sizes as well as napalm—jellied gasoline—which was very effective in making the bad guys back off. There is a common story among veterans that while we might kid, make fun of, or even fight with members of our sister services, when the chips were down, we'd die to help or save them. I am living proof, as I owe my life to the United States Marine Corps in one instance, and to the US Air Force in another. Although I never used it, I've heard stories of commanders near the coast being able to get Navy offshore gun support, even from the WWII battleships that had been recommissioned. Fire support, as long as the unit had communications and was in range, was seldom a problem due to the dedication and bravery of the field artillery units,

Army aviators and Navy, Air Force, and Marine Corps pilots.

Armor and cavalry classmates in-country had a whole different experience. Most of them rode around on M113 armored cavalry assault vehicles (ACAVs) or even tanks. The ACAVs, which we called tracks, were essentially M113 armored personnel carriers (APCs) with added turrets for their main .50 caliber armament, as well as two side mounted M60 machine guns with protective shields; this was a heck of a lot of firepower for a platoon of up to seven tracks. While the tracks provided some ballistic protection, they were of questionable effectiveness against road mines or rocket propelled grenades (RPGs). Soldiers assigned to a track often rode on top because of these threats. One major advantage other than enhanced mobility and firepower was that tracks could carry a lot of gear, to include coolers with ice cold Cokes, or even beer! No matter the mission or organization, cavalry troopers took great pride in their cavalry Stetson hats and spurs. Some of the armor guys in the class may have been assigned to tank battalions, as there were a few of them in-country. From my experience they were primarily used for point security, like bridges or other high value facilities. Due to the rugged terrain and wet, soggy conditions, tanks were not used much in combat operations in my area of operations. They could be used as convoy security or to ferry soldiers to a specific site and were often used in firebase security missions as well.

Classmates in the Engineers were involved in building facilities, destroying enemy fortifications, road construction, and mine clearing operations. Their duty was often hazardous and exposed them to snipers and ambushes. Signal Corps officers were essential in keeping the complex signal systems in the war zone operational at all times. Sometimes signal and engineer officers were used in the infantry battalions and pressed into being platoon leaders or company commanders because they were West Pointers and had been to Ranger School. I'm not sure how many had been assigned to MACV and used in advisory teams. It was close to impossible for combat arms officers in Vietnam to escape experiencing combat of some type. There were a few classmates who were not commissioned in the combat arms, and they fulfilled administrative and support functions on the major logistical installations.

Vietnam was a brutal war, and taking prisoners was not the normal procedure on the part of the VC and NVA. In most cases the enemy did not have the means to take care of a POW, either in the form of facilities or food. If a potential American POW was wounded, there was no capability on the other side to medically take care of him. Consequently, there were numerous accounts of VC or NVA clearing a battlefield by executing any wounded American soldiers they found. While explainable on one level, this atrocious conduct was inexcusable and a war crime. If an American prisoner was taken, he might be kept in an in-ground cage that didn't have enough room for him to stand or lie down. POWs were marched long distances in an effort to get them back to North Vietnam and Hanoi, often under terrible circumstances. Because of these stories, some American soldiers vowed to save one round for themselves rather than become a captive. Sometimes the US might need a prisoner for intelligence gathering purposes, but there were very few NVA in particular who were taken alive, primarily because they would fight to the end, much like the Japanese of World War II, or fade away into the jungle.

Combat could often be sudden, ferocious, and at close range, and often it was impossible to see who was shooting at you because of terrain or vegetation. The most feared sound after the shooting started was hearing someone calling for a medic, because that meant that one of your guys had been hit. One wounded soldier could cause a serious degradation of firepower in a small unit because one or two others might be needed to care for him. If it became necessary to medevac a wounded soldier, then the unit had to move to an open area that could be used as an LZ. Otherwise, one had to be created where the unit was by knocking down trees and clearing underbrush. If a medevac bird couldn't land, it had the capability to lower a basket or heavy jungle penetrator to which the wounded could be secured and then winched up. Doing this made the bird very vulnerable, as it had to hover in place until the operation was completed. Medevac pilots were some of the bravest men I ever knew, for many would risk their own lives and brave heavy enemy fire to get in and pick up a wounded GI. They were phenomenal men.

Most of us served one tour in Vietnam, a few did more than one. For those of us who survived, we were forever changed. Most of us who saw heavy combat have carried personal demons and dragons with us, even if we have been able to put them in the back of our minds. Unfortunately, for twenty of us the return trip was in a flag-covered metal coffin, frozen in time as forever young. The chapters that follow are their stories.

DUTY! HONOR! COUNTRY!

"STILL SERVING"

By Dutch Hostler, West Point class of 1968

When it comes to the final deployment,
all you've earned in this life is an urn
or a box in the ground,
o'er which TAPS' mournful sound
will be blurred by its echoed return.

And the riff and report of the rifles
render trifles of life's cares and woes
when they render to thee
the salute you can't see
as you rest in a final repose.

Death, my friend's not an end. You're still serving
the home of the free and the brave,
though too many may seem undeserving
of the unswerving service you gave.

But the service you rendered our Nation
will live on long as men can breathe free.
You're a part of our flag. You're a fiber

in the symbol of our liberty.
And whenever the honors are rendered,
s'lutes tendered the red, white, and blue,
we honor a free and just Nation
and those who preserved her—like you.

VIETNAM
1969-1972

VIETNAM:
JUNE AND JULY 1969

Donald Francis Van Cook Jr.   William Forssell Ericson III

The first of the class of '68 who had volunteered for Vietnam as an initial assignment began to arrive in-country in the spring of 1969, most arriving after completing Ranger and Airborne Schools and serving a six-month stint in a regular stateside unit to learn how to be a platoon leader. This was the culmination of those arduous four years at the academy, the rigors of our first training schools, and the learning process in our first exposure to leadership in the *real Army*. This was the ultimate test of man against man after all of that training, and we asked ourselves that recurring question all warriors who were about to experience combat for the first time have asked themselves through the ages—would we measure up? A pivotal year in the war, 1969 started with the Army in-country at its war-time high of more than 550,000 and ended with the first redeployments of units back to *the World*, as we referred to the continental United States. That year alone, 11,780 Americans died in Vietnam, second highest number to the 16,899 in 1968. The intensity of the combat that we experienced that year can be illustrated by the fact that the latter six months of 1969 were the costliest period of the war for our class, with as many classmates being lost (eight) as would be lost in the entire year of 1970.

Donald Van Cook was the first of us to arrive in Vietnam because his orders to Ranger School were cancelled for medical reasons and he was afforded an early departure date. The youngest in our class, Don was also the first of the West Point class of 1968 to lose his life in South Vietnam.

Donald F. Van Cook Jr. was born May 14, 1947, in Brooklyn, New York. His parents, Donald and Gloria, had been high school sweethearts. Donald Sr. was a WWII infantry veteran. Fifteen months later Donald was joined by a younger brother, William, and they were inseparable from that time on. At an early age, Don stepped forward and displayed innate bravery when a large and vicious dog belonging to a neighbor attacked his three-year-old brother. Four-year-old Don stepped between them and stared down the dog until an adult could step in. He was always there for his younger brother.

Don made academic success seem easy. After completing sixth grade, he attended Junior High School 135, where he skipped the eighth grade. Don was also developing as a multi-sport athlete. Although left-handed, he could bat from either side of the plate and played golf equally as well with right- or left-handed clubs. At Cardinal Spellman High School, Don was an effortless scholar, a class leader, and a multi-sport athlete. His handsome good looks and loyalty as a friend made him popular with both the girls and guys at school.

After a dispute between players and coaches on his senior year football team, Don played semi-pro football as an offensive and defensive back, and a punt and kickoff return man. Playing at this level later impacted his ability to participate in NCAA sports at West Point, despite being a superb athlete. Don fulfilled his need for physical action by participating in company-level boxing and wrestling intramurals and later, military triathlon. Through these efforts he built strong friendships during those four years.

During Beast Barracks, on the plebe hike, he quietly helped a struggling classmate as they climbed steep hills. What developed was a short but quiet friendship during that period. The man he had helped, Pete Bonasso, and others had their instruments for their rock band shipped out to the encampment. At one point during a concert Pete looked at the back of the audience and saw Don smiling at him and rocking to the music. After that hike Pete never saw Don again and was serving in Germany when he learned of Don's death.

Art Coogler remembered Don when he "joined Ross Nagy and me as a roommate in Central Area barracks during Beast. Of course, Ross would be steady as a rock in a hurricane, so Don and I both probably benefited from rooming with him. We seemed to make a good trio that worked well together, so we endured. Don would sometimes smoke two Lucky Strike cigarettes before reveille while we shined our shoes and brass. His fingers sometimes looked orange from the nicotine stains. He was a smoker athlete, and a good-natured fellow." Another classmate remembered him as being quiet, thoughtful, and kind. Beast was a struggle for Don; his independent spirit did not mesh well with an environment of strict discipline. Roommates Art Coogler and Ross Nagy can be given great credit for assisting him with seeing those first months through.

During yearling year, when a roommate was turned out in physics for failing the semester final, Larry Van Horn remembered that Don "made a tremendous difference in giving me motivation and helping me understand some of the concepts that were giving me problems. An image of Don is still fixed in my mind of Don lying on his bunk with a cigarette in his mouth, smiling and listening to the Doors. Jim Morrison and the Doors were his favorite and he played them frequently. I was also pretty quiet and kept to myself, but Don and I got along very well. He always got along well with everyone he came in contact with and he would go out of his way to help friends." Art Coogler remarked, "I always credited Don's family with helping me survive our first year, and interestingly, Don credited Ross and me for helping him survive. It was truly *cooperate and graduate.*"

Don and Larry tried to pull a practical joke on their third roommate, Dan Ryan, who was renowned for his ability to sleep deeply. They decided to stick his fingers with a needle one night when he was sleeping to see if that would wake him up. Even though they failed to rouse him, they got a big kick out of the attempt.

Many of our classmates remarked on Don's incredible ability to get along with anyone he met, and his willingness to go out of his way to help someone in need. When our classmate Dan Ingwerson was killed in a roll-over auto accident during our first class year coming back from Snuffy's, Don was first on the scene. Larry Van Horn remembered hearing him talk about it. "Ingwerson was driving a Triumph TR-3, I believe. When Don came upon the accident, he tried to roll the car off Ingwerson but it apparently rolled back on him and bent his ring in the process. I think he eventually did get it turned over enough to free Dan. I saw the out-of-shape ring."

Don's *Howitzer* entry reads as follows:

> Don came to the hotspot of the scenic Hudson Highlands with an appreciation of the finer things in life, and seventeen years, forty-eight days experience with them. At the end of four years, Don had acquired a lot of friends, and had also managed to amass a wide range of valuable experiences. He will be remembered in the years to come as the teeny-bopper with a knack of understanding people and a philosophy many preached but few could practice.

Donald volunteered for duty in Vietnam just prior to graduation because he felt it was his obligation as an officer of the Regular Army to do his part in this conflict. Perhaps an excerpt from the Cadet Prayer, which he tried to live by, was his motivation: "Endow us with courage that is born of loyalty to all that is noble and worthy, that scorns to compromise with vice and injustice, and knows no fear when truth and right are in jeopardy."

In August of 1968, while on graduation leave in Oklahoma, he had a major auto accident that totaled his car, followed by an almost career-ending, first-ever asthma attack; he fought and won a medical review of his status that almost ended his future before it could start. He was allowed to remain in the Army, however, his orders to Ranger School were canceled because of the asthma and he flew to Vietnam in January of 1969.

His first assignment was as a forward observer for an artillery unit. He was a passenger riding on top of an armored personnel carrier when it hit a mine, resulting in many casualties, including some who were killed. Don was seriously wounded and was sent to a hospital in Japan for almost two months to recover. Given an opportunity to return home, he refused and told his parents that he was where he needed to be. After recovery, he returned to duty to continue his efforts to help the people of South Vietnam defend their freedom.

Upon return to Vietnam from the hospital in Japan, his next assignment took him to Kontum Province as a fire direction officer for C Battery, 14th Artillery. In June of 1969, an enemy rocket ended his life when his battery came under hostile attack. It occurred exactly one year after he graduated from the United States Military Academy. Although Don was assigned to the 14th Field Artillery at Kontum, he was at Ben Het firebase when it was besieged by two regiments of NVA. During the indirect fire rocket and mortar attack, Don and his gun crew were inside a vehicle used for communication, which they exited in favor of three small bunkers; Don's took a direct hit. This dedicated young officer, easy going and able to get along with everyone, who fought an effort to medically discharge him at the beginning of his service and won, who had already been wounded and could have gone home but wanted to stay to help the South Vietnamese protect their independence, sadly lost his life alongside three others.

Classmate Dan Limbaugh later served for an artillery officer who was present when Don was killed. There are no finer tributes than those that come from fellow combat soldiers. "My battery commander at Bragg, Capt. Bill Cartwright, offered me an alternate perspective on the Army. He had already been to Vietnam, and I was just on my way. He was a draftee, OCS, easy going, and getting out after his commitment was up. I admired him a lot. When he heard that I was West Point '68 he asked if I had known Don Van Cook. I told him I knew him but not well. Don and Bill were on the same firebase in Kontum. I believe it was an 8-inch/175mm battery that provided general support for any friendly unit within thirty-two kilometers. They had sporadic mortar fire and rocket attacks, but according to Bill, nothing serious until Don was killed. One of the rocket attacks started and everyone took cover as usual, but one got through a slit in the concrete bunker Don had jumped into. Bill was devastated. He called Don the best man on the firebase, including the battery commander, and it had to be Don who was killed by an absolute fluke. In the telling, Bill just sadly shook his head."

Larry Van Horn recounted: "I remember my first visit to the Vietnam Wall in DC several years ago. My primary goal was to locate Don's name. I was surprised at how emotional it was for me to see his name among all those 50,000 or so names of guys we lost there. I felt a great deal of regret at not spending more time with him at school; he was a good friend, and I would have benefitted from more contact with him. I've never heard any of the circumstance surrounding his death, but knowing Don, I'm sure he was doing whatever he could to take care of his people and that they cared for him and strongly felt the loss of their leader."

According to our yearbook, the 1968 *Howitzer*, "Donald had a philosophy of life that many preached but few practiced." By his actions he proved the words written by his peers to be true.

Don was the youngest member of our class, the first to arrive in Vietnam, and the first to lose his life. It was only natural that he was also the first casualty of the class of '68 to be interred in the West Point Cemetery. He was buried where he is among men who lived as he did, to serve others. Unfortunately, the row in which he lies was filled rapidly with his own classmates who also served unselfishly in accordance with their belief in Duty, Honor, Country. When Art Coogler was told about Don's death and plans for burial at West Point, he had a tough time, "I was a poor lieutenant with a pregnant wife and not enough money to fly to West Point for the funeral. I was also reluctant to leave my wife at that time. I cried."

Clare Barkovic, Bill Ericson's widow, recounts a memory of the West Point Cemetery. Don Van Cook was the only interment for a while in that particular first row of '68 Vietnam casualties. Bill was then placed next to him. While Don and Bill were alone, the Van Cooks always sent the same wreath or floral arrangement to adorn Bill's grave that they sent for their son.

One of the girls who knew Don in high school, Rosanne Cutropia-Cummins, posted a very heartfelt tribute to him on The Wall of Faces at the Vietnam Memorial long after his death:

Donnie, you were my first love. I was sixteen and you were eighteen. We met on the high school's end-of-year cruise on the Hudson River in New York. You were my first real love; you gave me my first real grown-up kiss. You were so special, so handsome, my heart fluttered when I saw you. My mom and dad loved you. I was so proud of you when you went to West Point. I visited you there plebe year, driving up from the Bronx with your dad. We danced, and I watched you in formation with your white uniform, so proud, so military, so regal. We wrote to each other for years, with me trying to convince you to stay at West Point, because you wanted to leave. I was so proud of you when you graduated, a military officer. I heard you went to Vietnam and came home to my sister telling me that you perished on those remote fields in another land. My heart broke. I cried real tears for you. I couldn't stay at the funeral; your coffin was draped with the American flag, your picture on top of it, and everyone so sad. I left early, ran home, and cried. I prayed for you, and I will never, never forget you, dear Donnie. Someday I will see you again . . .

Love, your forever friend, your first love,
Rosanne

I suspect that these feelings pretty well sum up the impact that Don had on all of those around him in high school. He was obviously a very special young man, as were most of those selected to attend West Point.

After Don's death on the fourth of June, additional classmates were continuing to arrive in Vietnam. I arrived on the ninth of July, my twenty-fourth birthday . . . and no one had a cake for me!

Combat was frequent and violent as US forces were engaged by the North Vietnamese Army at an increasing rate. The local force guerrillas, the Viet Cong, had been decimated and virtually eliminated as an effective military force in '68 during and after the famous Tet Offensive in February. The NVA were regular soldiers and well-equipped and trained. As combat intensified, and more and more members of the class of '68 arrived, our casualties began to mount up. About six weeks after Don Van Horn's death, Bill Ericson was killed.

Bill Ericson was one of those members of the class who was almost larger than life. Bill was first, before everything else, every inch the soldier, a characteristic that I came to recognize well when I shared the second platoon bay with him at the United States Military Academy Preparatory School at Ft. Belvoir, Virginia from August 1963 until May 1964. In stature he was kind of a little guy; in presence and character he was a giant. Since he came to the prep school from the 82nd Airborne Division, he was already airborne qualified, which made him one of a select few in our class. Our prep school yearbook, the *Challenge,* states that Bill is "Airborne all the way. His war stories have us convinced that the 82nd is second to none." Bill walked with a slightly bow-legged jaunty swagger, not overdone but just enough to let you know for sure that he was an airborne infantryman.

Not only was Bill a soldier and scholar, but he was an accomplished athlete as well, as proven when he tried out for the prep school lacrosse team. Like most of us who played, Bill learned the sport as the season progressed. As noted in the *Challenge,* "most of us couldn't pronounce the name of the sport when we signed up for it, but we soon learned the pronunciation, plus a few other things. Learning to handle those monstrous, mutilated tennis rackets was especially painful." In addition, Bill played on the first ever prep school soccer team. Not to be satisfied with just these two sports, Bill also played on the golf and handball teams.

Bill loved to regale us with "war stories" in the evenings or on weekends. He would dress up in his uniform with all kinds of additional pieces of military decorations, prop a foot up on a footlocker, and hold us spellbound for hours. Most of the stories centered on his time in the 82nd Airborne, the thrills of jumping out of airplanes, which few of us had done at that point, and escapades in downtown Fayetteville, North Carolina on off-duty time. There were many stories about "interactions" between some of the local guys and the airborne troopers when young women were involved. And with all of this he never turned down a request for help, whether in academics or some other area. He was certainly one of the strongest personalities in our prep school platoon and would fill the same role at West Point.

In barracks life we were required to maintain our individual bunk area at a high level of appearance and orderliness. We all became very proficient in the use of a commercial floor buffer to spit-shine our floors, with each of us being responsible for the area around our bunks and then detailing someone to handle the center aisle, a favorite job of Bill's. Bill and I once had the task of cleaning the grout in the latrine floors with toothbrushes while on our hands and knees before a big inspection— and of course we passed!

Bill was born in Astoria, Queens, outside of New York City on February 23, 1944, the son of Mr. and Mrs. Richard F. Ericson. He was named for an uncle, a US Marine Corps pilot who was lost in World War II shortly before Bill was born. The first place he lived for a couple of years was the Army's Ft. Totten, New York, so it's really true that the Army was in his blood. Bill graduated from high school in 1961 and immediately enlisted in the Army instead of going to college. He did basic and advanced military training at Ft. Dix, New Jersey and then went to jump school at Ft. Bragg, North Carolina, a member of the last class conducted there. While there he applied for the prep school and was admitted in 1963, where, as I remember, he was the cadet candidate company commander. At the end of the year, Bill received a Regular Army appointment to West Point to enter with the class of 1968. He was off to a great start!

During Beast Barracks Bill was constantly in the running for the Best New Cadet honor for Second New Cadet Company. When Beast ended, Bill quickly made a name for himself due to his toughness and dedication to becoming the best that he could be. Mike Trollinger remembered, "Bill was older than a lot of the rest of us in the class because he had prior service in the Army before joining the Long Gray Line. Because he was more mature and had prior service, he was much more *strac* (a slang term that meant *squared away*) than a lot of us and had better military bearing than the vast majority of us rabble. He was extremely gung-ho and even went to Jungle

Warfare School in Panama during his leave time one summer. Bill was an accomplished boxer. I can remember him boxing in the Corps boxing tournaments just like it was yesterday. He was a tough guy who took as much punishment as he dished out; however, he could take it better than most and won a lot of his bouts. He was never intimidated by anyone bigger than he was. He was basically fearless."

Rick Fetterman had a remarkable experience with Bill during plebe year, both on the *fields of friendly strife* and also during an off-duty experience that illustrates the many facets of Bill's personality:

Bill and I had a short-term relationship that I have always cherished. As he rose to stardom in our class, I felt a connection to him based on a few months together that created a memory I will never forget. Here's Bill, this *man's man*, in the ultimate man's world, regular Army veteran, 82nd Airborne, twenty-two years old. And me, basically an eighteen-year-old snot nose. And he decides to be my friend. We met at plebe soccer practice in late August or early September and we both made the team. Those years, 1963 to 1966 or so are considered to be the *golden era* of Army soccer. Our plebe team, I'm fairly certain, was the first undefeated plebe team in the history of the school when we went 8-0. And make no mistake, it was a great team.

Our first game was an away game in early September against Adelphi College on Long Island. I remember our coach, during warm-ups, telling us not to look down to the other end of the field so as not to be intimidated by the obvious skill discrepancy. We won in a total rout, 7-0. But that's not the story.

The real memory for me was that we had until one o'clock in the morning to enjoy New York City before getting on the return bus to West Point. And Bill asked if I wanted to join him and roam around Times Square. Me? Bill wasn't the Bill he came to be in his cadet career, but he already had a developing reputation based on his prior service. Needless to say, I was thrilled with the invite.

So, we went into the city and that's what we did—we

roamed around, grabbed a bite to eat somewhere, and after dark, around nine o'clock or so, he suggested we go into the Club Metropole because he had heard that Gene Krupa was going to be performing on the drums. We went in, bellied right up to the front of the bar and we each bought one drink, scotch, as I recall. Sure enough, out comes Gene Krupa, mounts a small stage behind the bar, right in front of Bill and me. He played for quite a while, it was a great time, and we each nursed our one drink for the rest of the evening. That may seem like a simple story, but it's a memory that has stayed with me all these years.

During yearling year Bill became the chairman of our class Ring and Crest Committee, an appointment that would change his life in ways that he could never imagine. It was with that responsibility that he met and later fell in love with Clare Conlan, who was the representative from the Balfour Company that would make our ring. On October 24, 1965, Clare set up her display in a classroom in Thayer Hall. Clare remembered "I was starting to prepare for the return shipment and in walked a cadet, alone, who casually stopped to talk. He began a conversation that was abruptly stopped by the officer in charge (OIC) of the '68 Ring and Crest Committee. He took the cadet aside for a chat. During that chat the cadet turned toward me and noticeably eyed me up and down." The OIC made a formal introduction to Clare of Cadet Bill Ericson, the committee chair. The OIC departed and Bill asked Clare for a date the following weekend at West Point. In two days, Clare received a written invitation from Bill, and so started a love affair that would continue to grow. Clare remembered:

Bill was late for our first date. He left me sitting in the Thayer Hotel until I was the last date called for. He was smiling and cheerful when he walked through the revolving front door of the hotel. I was not. He apologized, offered a verifiable excuse, and we left to walk to Grant Hall. On the way, he said I could stop frowning anytime now. Two Cadets were passing by and Bill saluted. I liked his salute and told him so. He asked, "What do you mean?" And, unbeknownst to me,

I had a reply that he loved: "your salute is so much *sharper* than theirs." That weekend, we were relaxed with each other and enjoyed being together. The time to say goodbye came quite soon. No goodbye from my date. Instead, he said "I'm going to Vietnam. If you do not like that, don't come back." He was so passionate about the Army, about being a soldier and being the best in all things . . . how could I not come back?

I was amazed that this new friend of mine, Bill, had so many relatives not far from my home. Most surprisingly, he said he had lived in Roslyn, Long Island before high school. He had lived not far from me; I even knew his house. As a kid, with my dad and mom in the front seat of our car, driving me to the doctor for asthma treatment, I knew, if I could make it as far as the *Spanish tiled roof house* I could make it to the doctor's office. That was Bill's house.

While this romance was happening, Bill was continuing on his soldierly path. He enrolled in the Special Warfare School at Ft. Bragg, North Carolina to take the Special Forces Extension Course, which he finished in early '67, the first cadet to accomplish this feat. He was also instrumental in the creation of the Military Affairs Club and its publication *The Muster*. It's been reported that he even considered leaving West Point to volunteer for a Vietnam combat assignment but was talked out of that bad idea by a couple of senior noncommissioned officers whom he respected immensely. And of course, his relationship with Clare continued to deepen.

Clare remembered:

A few more dates would take place. Bill would either take the bus or train to my parents' home on Long Island, or I would return to West Point. He told me that he was born in Astoria, Queens, not twenty miles from my home. After meeting my mother, a woman very crippled with rheumatoid arthritis since I was born, widowed since my dad died in 1958, and strongly Irish, I became very skeptical of her approval. But Bill, relaxed, charmed her with stories of his background. In the spring of 1966, Bill surprised me with a West Point A Pin.

[The A pin is the capital letter A with the appropriate class crest super imposed. The A can be adorned with diamonds, pearls, or other precious jewels. The A is attached to a miniature academy crest by a gold chain. The pin is given to mothers, sisters, and OAOs (One and Only's). When presented to an OAO, it signifies a bond similar to going steady.] It was a significant step for us both. That summer he left for Jungle Warfare School. He was prolific in his letter writing. I received my first ever Western Union Telegram from him. He wrote: "You are more than ever in my thoughts at this time. Letters coming in fine. All My Love, Bill." That was the first time Bill ever used the *L* word.

In March 1967, Bill asked me to marry him. I was not worried about Vietnam anymore. He didn't give me time to worry. I said yes. I'll marry you. He poetically wrote:

Two years ago, we were so free. No one to care for you or me. We went our ways; we held our own. We laughed and played but all alone. One day in the fall of sixty-five, Bill met Clare and came alive. He thought his life had been so fine, till Clare stepped in and changed his mind.
    It is love—forever, for Bill and Clare.

While Bill was courting Clare, he was also continuing to make his mark on West Point and our class.

Clare also remembered: "In July 1967, Bill was appointed King of Beasts, cadet commander of the incoming class of 1971. He was immensely proud. I later learned from friends that following tradition, the King of Beasts was made first captain of the Corps of Cadets; the highest-ranking cadet in the corps. That summer of 1967, the tradition was broken. The commandant appointed another classmate of Bill's to that position. As in politics of old, I learned of this great disappointment to Bill through officer friends. He did not tell me of those results, nor more importantly to me, his disappointment."

He moved on to his next assignment, commander of the Fourth Regiment. Perhaps the commandant felt that Bill could better use his talents in the Fourth Regiment that needed *bucking up* than on leading the Corps. The first thing that he did in this new position was to give the regiment a new motto: *Strict, Tough, Military, Proud.* The Fourth did not have a great reputation, and Bill wanted to inspire them to be the best. The new motto continued for years. Just three years ago, when Navy lost their winning streak over Army, the year the Academy Catholic Chaplain was seen kneeling down and praying the Rosary for Army in the last few minutes of the game, when Army WON, four grads, sitting behind us in the stadium, shouted out: "STRICT, TOUGH, MILITARY, PROUD!" Of course, they were Fourth Regiment!

As the regimental commander, Bill worked hard to bring a sense of pride and military bearing to his command. Always the soldier, he had a tough time believing that others couldn't attain his soldierly standards. He also worked hard on his other responsibilities as editor of the class of '68 yearbook, *The Howitzer,* and continuing his pursuit of the brigade boxing championship.

Even with all of this responsibility, Bill had time to counsel and talk with classmates and other cadets of his regiment. Dan Nettesheim remembered a particularly significant discussion: "As a cadet I had interactions with several of our special Twenty that were meaningful to me. Bill Ericson and I shared several occasions where we discussed our future careers in the Army. About ten days before branch selection, Bill came to my room to make his final pitch. He knew that I was leaning toward the Corps of Engineers but that I was also considering and researching Infantry. Basically, he argued that if I were to select Infantry that I would be the first in our class to do so and he could not imagine a deeper honor. He talked about recognizing my leadership ability and how it could only be honed to its peak in the Infantry. I told him I would make a final decision in a few days and that I would let him know my decision. I selected the Corps of Engineers, but I told him that his comments meant a lot to me and made my final decision even tougher."

While Bill was always interested in his classmates and helping or counseling when needed, he also had time for others in need of counseling or a kick in the butt, sometimes in areas where least expected. Bill Barkovic '71 remembered:

In the fall of 1967, as a plebe from the class of 1971, I managed to run afoul of the disciplinary system in a big way not once but twice in the same month. The remaining how and why of getting so many punishment tours on the area and the accompanying special confinement is not the subject of this story, however. What I want to tell you about is what happened after I got in trouble.

The timing of these events was just before Christmas leave. Having been sentenced for our crimes, our fate was known, but serving the sentence would have to wait until after returning from leave. Upon my return to West Point, I immediately became the subject of an increased level of *character building* from the upper classes. After a couple of weeks of this I received a message in my room that I was to report to Bill Ericson's room after dinner. Even with a couple of years of enlisted service, including USMAPS, behind me, Bill Ericson gave the impression of being a stern and no-nonsense man to be reckoned with. And so, I approached Bill's room that night with a little fear and trepidation that I was in for a real ass chewing. Upon entering Mr. Ericson's room, rendering the smartest salute I could muster, and reporting as required, Mr. Ericson asked me to be seated. He noted that, like him, I was prior service, a prep school graduate, and chairman of my Class Ring and Crest Committee. He said that West Point expected more of me. He also told me that he heard from his classmates that I was about to resign. He said West Point had a lot to offer me, but that I had to perform up to expectations. At that point he allowed me to respond. I told him how it took me four years to get into West Point, and that I was not about to leave now. I admitted I screwed up and said that I would accept the punishment and then move on. I have to say that he impressed me with what he said and how he said it, showing true concern for a subordinate that was previously on the wrong path. Bill Ericson reached out to an underclassman and provided counsel and advice when I was in trouble.

Bill was an extremely talented and complex man, not just the consummate soldier but a bit of a poet, a stock trader, and a restorer of old cars. A tough guy but with a gentler side as well. A man who gave his all in everything that he did. One classmate, Alan Aker, remarked:

> I was privileged to serve as Bill's executive officer during the last detail of our senior year. Bill was regimental commander of the Fourth Regiment in North Area and the *lost 50s* [a secluded barracks area]. Bill probably seemed only straight and serious to most who knew him from a distance.
>
> I was both fascinated by Bill and sometimes entertained by things he did as we roomed together. On one occasion he had gotten a radio from an officer who had been living in the bachelor officer quarters over by Cullum Hall. One evening as we waded through our assignments, Bill noticed a platoon of cockroaches coming from the back over the top of the radio. He immediately got me involved in a staff meeting on how this invasion should be handled. I thought we should simply toss the radio out the window, but Bill had other ideas. He kept a container of lighter fluid around because he smoked a pipe. Bill was so funny. He used that yellow and blue can of lighter fluid to napalm the little buggers . . . but they kept coming over the top of this melting plastic case, wave after wave of them. Bill thought they were coming out one platoon at a time. We figured there were at least a few companies of New York's best cockroaches in that radio. Bill loved it but had grave concerns about the cleanliness of the BOQ. Those roaches were the only ones I had ever seen at West Point.
>
> The loss of a friend, a brother, filled with so much energy and drive at such a young age produces a sadness that words cannot adequately express and that time cannot fully remove. Ecclesiastes 9:10 tells us: "Whatever your hands find to do, do it with all of your might." That was surely Bill Ericson, a most remarkable member of the class of '68.

While rooming with Bill, Alan witnessed Bill's incredible skills with stock trading—and this was before computers and the World Wide Web. Bill got into trading commodities, in this case cotton and pork bellies. In three months, Bill took his $3,000 cadet loan from Marine Midland Bank and ran it up to $42,000 before June Week— three months of trading in the ancient times of 1968.

Like many of our classmates and their fiancés, Bill and Clare decided to get married at West Point and start their life together right after graduation. One chapter of life had ended, another was about to begin. Four days after graduation, Bill and Clare were married on the ninth of June. They then honeymooned in the Bahamas, where they fished, gambled, and even bought their china service, a necessary mission for the young Army wife of that period. When they returned to Bill's home in Connecticut, Bill restored a 1930 Model A Ford, learning to repair parts that were severely rusted.

After weeks of working on the car, they reported to Fort Benning, where Bill attended the Infantry Officer's Basic Course and Ranger School. During that time, Bill bought Clare a .38 revolver and taught her how to fire it. This was an obvious necessary skill for a good infantryman's wife. Schooling was completed and they returned to Long Island for Thanksgiving, where they also adopted a Siberian Husky puppy they named Velvet after Bobby Vinton's song "Blue Velvet." It was then on to Ft. Bragg for Bill's initial assignment, with a side trip back to Benning for Pathfinder School.

In early May, they flew to San Francisco to see the sights before Bill's departure for Vietnam. It was there that Bill gave Clare some clear instructions. "If the Army notifies you that I am missing and a prisoner of war, don't believe it. I will not be captured. If the Army notifies you that I was killed, ask them if they have proof and if they are sure. And if I'm dead, I want you to remarry. I do not want you to be alone. Wait two years. After that, get married again." On the fourteenth of May there was a quick kiss, hug, and a look, and then Bill disappeared into the airplane. On that day, Bill started the journey to Vietnam to show once and for all what kind of soldier and infantry leader he was. This was to be the ultimate test, to take command of combat-experienced soldiers as an inexperienced, wet-behind-the-ears lieutenant and go forth to *meet the elephant*, a popular grunt saying in those days meaning to experience combat.

Upon his arrival in Vietnam, he was offered a pathfinder slot with the 101st Airborne Division (Air Mobile). However, he turned down the slot with its extra jump pay because he wanted to command a rifle platoon. He was subsequently assigned as a platoon leader with A Company, 1st Battalion, 503rd Infantry (Airborne), 173rd Airborne Brigade. Unfortunately for Bill, the class, and the US Army, Bill's combat time lasted only two months. It's still hard for me to believe, after more than fifty years, that all of that training, all that he had accomplished, all of that spirit and drive, all of that bottomless potential could end so quickly. And at home, his young bride was anxiously awaiting his letters, which came almost every day. Bill was killed on the fifteenth of July, the date that he was originally scheduled to depart for Vietnam had he not volunteered to leave early. On that day, Bill's unit's night defensive position (NDP) was attacked by a large NVA force. Bill detected them first and gave the alarm. After the attack was repulsed, Bill led a patrol through the wire to track the retreating enemy. He was killed in a sudden burst of small-arms fire.

The day before his death Bill wrote: "Our old AO [area of operations] is pacified. As I left the valley, it was memorable to look across those beautiful rice paddies with their quaint unique farmers and characteristic water buffalo and note the development of the area in the few short months that we were operating in it. There is little or no fear that the VC will steal the rice and use the farmers for forced labor or recruitment into their unit. The Vietnamese Army is now in force and can provide the security we won for them. Now it's combat assault time. The entire company is back at LZ Uplift preparing for an aerial combat assault into an area known as Crescent Valley."

Clare remembers that Bill's prep school and academy classmate, Bob Stroud, was her official escort at his funeral. "Bill's casket was met at the Catholic chapel doors by none other than the 82nd Airborne, coincidentally at West Point for summer training of cadets. They were the bearers of Bill's casket to the altar. Between family, friends, and our West Point community, Bill was met with honor. On the way to the cemetery, our dog Velvet, ran along Washington Road with a nephew hanging on to her leash. We were met at the cemetery by

Fourth Regiment cadets who were serving at Beast Barracks. The announcement of Bill's death was made to all cadets in the mess hall and the Catholic chapel. This was quite a shock to the class of 1971 cadets that Bill had led upon their entry to West Point."

Bill was laid to rest next to his classmate, Don Van Cook, the first 1968 classmate killed in Vietnam. There would be eighteen more 1968 classmates killed in Vietnam before the war ended.

Clare did remarry, to another grad, this time from the class of '71; that lucky guy is Bill Barkovic. Bill did end up graduating from West Point and served a career in the Army, during which time they had four children. Bill Barkovic is an amazing man; he recognized that he was marrying not just Clare, but the memory of Bill Ericson as well. He has worked hard with Clare to keep Bill Ericson's memory alive.

Bill's legacy and memory live on in many ways, not the least of which is at the United States Military Academy Preparatory School from which he graduated in May of '64. With the USMAPS class of 2014, who were to become members of our fifty-year affiliation class of 2018, a new element was added to culminate their cadet candidate basic training. This crucible was named the *Ericson Challenge* that was mentally and physically tough and designed to test the cadet candidate's skills and progress.

In the spring of 2016, I had the honor of being with Clare at Bill's graveside for the *Inspire to Serve* exercise in the West Point Cemetery for our Fifty-Year Affiliation Class. Several of our fallen classmates were featured in this program, and it was an honor to talk with the yearlings when they came to our site. I tried to impress on those young cadets the price that might have to be paid for their commitment to Duty, Honor, Country. It was kind of sobering to stand along that line of headstones for '68 and to reflect on all of those classmates having given their all for their country. In a way it seems almost a waste, but in reality, so many of us benefited in a big way from our short time with Bill Ericson and the others, and I concluded that their deaths were a sacrifice, extremely meaningful, as they had paid the ultimate price in selfless service to their country.

June and July were tough months for the class with the loss of Don and Bill, but unbeknownst to us, things were about to get worse, as more classmates made it to Vietnam. September and October would prove to be even more costly.

Don on a trip home to
Greenville, NC—1965

Don and Art Coogler at Hotel Thayer—1965

Bill as "King of Beast" —1967

Bill and Clare's Wedding,
West Point—1968

Bill (R) with the 173rd Airborne
Brigade, Vietnam—1969

VIETNAM: SEPTEMBER AND OCTOBER 1969

Denny Layton Johnson   Kenneth Thomas Cummings   David Lee Sackett

June and July had seen the first losses for the class of 1968, and in August we had a bit of a break, as no one was killed. But, things were about to become much worse for the rest of the year. September and October saw the loss of three more from the class: Denny Johnson, Ken Cummings, and David Sackett. More classmates in-country and more intense combat had some grim results. The first to be lost during this time was Denny Johnson and I thank classmate Ralph Tuccillo for his efforts in researching Denny's life.

Denny Layton Johnson was born on January 6, 1947, in Alexandria, Louisiana to Dallas and Mavis Johnson. Their first son was born in 1941 but passed away from unknown causes about eight months later. In 1944, Danny was born, followed in a couple of years by Denny. The Johnsons lived in Alexandria for most of the '40s, and finally settled in Bunkie, Louisiana in the early '50s. Dallas worked at the Columbia Carbon Plant for thirty years and eventually became the union president for all plant employees. Denny's mother, a very religious woman, worked for Vanguard Insurance as a secretary and administrator. They were a solid, hardworking, middle-class American family.

In the early '50s, all three males of the family became infected with the mumps. While their dad and Danny recovered quickly, Denny did not. He was subsequently diagnosed with mumps meningoencephalitis, which he suffered from for the next couple of years. While rare and often fatal, Denny successfully fought the disease. It affected his physical and mental development, but he eventually fully recovered.

The family enjoyed fishing and camping as the boys grew up. Danny talked about the wonderful family summer vacations where they would go about sixty-five miles to Trout Creek, where they might camp out for two weeks. In the early days, they would string a large tarp among several trees and sleep on the ground. During the day, they would fish with simple rods, like a tree branch or pole with string and a hook with a worm. Even with this simple rig they caught a lot of fish, which were cleaned and cooked for dinner. They had fun playing in the creek on hot days and exploring the surrounding woods.

Denny enjoyed playing Superman, jumping off of higher and higher objects until he finally broke his arm. Not to be deterred, even though he wore a cast for several weeks, Denny continued his quest to defy gravity. He also loved to play with his toy soldiers, which he set up on the ground on a dirt battlefield and would use firecrackers to simulate explosions.

Denny and his friends were active in Cub Scouts and his mom was the den leader. She kept the kids busy with scout projects and also provided outstanding snacks for all. After the meeting they would all go to a friend's house that had a mulberry tree to see how many berries they could eat before being called home. He and his brother would go home with stained uniforms, hands, and faces, and his friend Jimmy Earles remembered "then we would get an old fashion butt whipping that would last about six days, and on the seventh you knew where we would be."

Denny continued to grow and mature. One of his friends related a story about Denny as they were both trying out for a lineman position on the Bunkie High School football team. In one drill they lined up for one-on-one drills against other linemen. Denny found himself facing a 250-pound first team defensive tackle; Denny weighed about 150 pounds soaking wet. The coach told Denny to stand back, he was too small for this guy. The other players, knowing Denny's toughness, started chanting his name, so the coach let him go. He took the big lineman down three times and made the team. Although small in stature, he had a heart and mental attitude second to none. There was an ugly incident one day in the football locker room. Denny stepped into the chaos, separated the players and then began to chastise them. His words had a strong effect, and it soon turned into a room of teammates instead of arguing football players. The coaches watched what was happening without getting involved and knew that they had a real team leader.

Denny was very active in high school, was elected as the president of the student council his senior year and was selected to represent his school in Pelican Boys State—a premier leadership development program for young men sponsored by the American Legion. He also had a strong interest in science and joined the science club, where he built a rocket. He used a mixture of fuel and oxygen as a propellant, and in its first test the rocket launched and gained an altitude of several hundred feet. He was also selected for *Who's Who*, a publication that identified students who excelled in all facets of their lives.

Denny also exhibited a strong love for his family, and frequently spoke of his mother, dad, and brothers, especially the one that was lost as an infant. He also loved his church and felt close to God. The Johnsons were an extremely close and warm family.

Denny Johnson worked hard to realize his dream of going to West Point and received an appointment from his local congressman to the class of '68. He arrived on June 30, 1964 and booked a room in the Thayer Hotel on the Academy grounds that he shared with two other guys. They all wound up playing 150-pound football together and later served as infantrymen in Vietnam. The other two new cadets were Harry Hays, who is also featured in this book, and Dave Ohle, who was to demonstrate incredible heroism while rescuing another classmate from a downed helicopter in Vietnam. Fate brought these three young men together on the eve of entering West Point; two were killed in action, while Dave had an eminently successful Army career and retired as a lieutenant general. Dave has never forgotten the tragic loss of his two friends. Denny may not have been big in stature, but he proved to be strong in character, body, and mind all through West Point and service in Vietnam.

Denny was assigned to the Second New Cadet Company for Beast Barracks and did well in this rigorous environment until the final training exercise. This was a twelve-mile forced march through the mountains to a bivouac site, carrying full combat gear, a forty-pound rucksack, and an M14 rifle. After three days in the field conducting rigorous exercises, they marched back along the same route to the main campus. Denny struggled with the mountainous terrain and a load that was more than a third of his weight. Two guys recruited to play Army football helped him finish that grueling march and started a lasting friendship. Those guys were Nick Kurilko and Hank Toczylowski, who both went on to be superb members of the Army football team.

At the conclusion of Beast, Denny was assigned to company L-2, later becoming E-4. There he quickly established himself and made some great friends. Don Davis remembered that Denny was an outstanding person who loved to joke around "but was also one of the kindest, most gentle spirits in the company. He was a true Southern gentleman." Don also remembered that Denny was a whiz at calculus and advanced sciences like electrical engineering and nuclear physics but struggled with writing term papers. He was challenged with spelling and spent as much time looking up words in the dictionary as he did researching his paper." Don added, "We joked about this all the time, but Denny always put his best effort into everything he did and never let any shortcoming hold him back."

Don Davis and Denny became close friends and during cow year were assigned together as squad leaders for Beast Barracks. Don's parents came by to visit and after that experience adopted Denny as their fourth son. During spring break, they decided to tour Washington, DC, as they both liked history and Washington was filled with a lot of attractive and single women; they had a ball. A few days after graduation, Denny was one of Don's groomsmen, the last time they would spend any time together. Don went on to the Berlin Brigade while Denny went to Vietnam. When Don learned of Denny's death, he called his folks, who grieved like Denny was one of their family. They were all devastated.

Playing 150-pound football became central to Denny's life at West Point. The team was composed of tremendous athletes who just weren't big enough to play on the college varsity level. Many of the team's members had been stars on their high school teams and all just loved to play the game. Many struggled to lose pounds to make weight at 154 pounds two days before the game; Denny never had that problem. He played right offensive guard, the same as in high school, and wore number sixty-two on his jersey. His teammates had great memories of Denny. Dennis Burrell said, "When others were down, Denny was always cheering them on," and Jack Reid remembered him as being "the consummate teammate, always willing to give all of his effort to win and support the team in winning. I remember him to be charismatic and a confident football player. He was a happy man that people wanted to be around."

Denny and Lyle Pirnie went to Ft. Polk the summer of firstie year to act as "third lieutenants" and train with soldiers in the active Army. Although they didn't know each other at the academy, being in different regiments, they became close friends. Because they were only about fifty miles from Denny's home in Bunkie, they stayed with his family on weekends when they had time off. Lyle quickly became part of the family and thoroughly enjoyed his time with them. During June Week, just before graduation, Lyle had the opportunity to see the Johnsons again and to express his gratitude for their kindness.

They both selected Armor and saw each other in Ranger School and the Armor Officer's Basic Course at Ft. Knox. Denny remarked that he felt it was his duty to volunteer for Vietnam; with that, Lyle also volunteered to go as an initial assignment. They were in Vietnam about the same time, but Lyle didn't learn of Denny's death until his return from that combat tour. "I will never forget the physical sickness I felt when I learned of Denny's death . . . the shock of losing a good friend and kind soul can be overwhelming. I will never forget him and his family. Denny, his mom, dad, brother, and sister-in-law were some of the nicest people I've ever met."

After graduation Denny went to Airborne School after attending several classmate weddings. He then reported to Ranger School, the Army's premier course for small unit leadership training. His Ranger buddy, classmate John Johnson, was responsible for getting Denny through the course successfully, just as Denny was responsible for John's success. They had not known each other at West Point but became close because of the rigors of the course. They were a *Mutt and Jeff* team, with John standing six foot four, while Denny could stretch himself to five foot six. This difference caused some interesting times during hand-to-hand combat training; Denny's small size sometimes gave him a distinct advantage, which Denny claimed one day with a big grin on his face while handling John, bringing smiles to all around them—a rare incident for Ranger students.

John also recalled Denny severely spraining his ankle on a forced march during the Benning phase. Denny went down and the ankle quickly swelled to twice its normal size. Going to a medic might have caused him to have to leave the course and be recycled at a later time to start all over again. With great determination, he muttered something about *not* being recycled and finished the march, although in considerable pain. He was a tough guy. That was proven again on a river crossing when Denny, who had removed his boots, tied them together, and put them around his neck to swim across, lost those boots when he went underwater in the deep river. Denny just put on extra socks and continued with the mission—truly a tough guy.

After successfully graduating from Ranger School and earning the coveted Ranger Tab on October 29, 1968, they both went to Ft. Knox for the basic course, and then on to Ft. Hood, Texas to serve with troops for six months before deploying to Vietnam. It was there that he met Lt. Tom Niebling, an ROTC graduate from Niagara University. In the short six months they had together, they became close friends, spending a lot of time in the officers' club or driving around the local area. They talked a lot about Vietnam and Denny explained why he had volunteered and asked Tom to come with him. Tom called his assignments officer, had orders cut, and left for Vietnam about six weeks after Denny left at the end of July.

Upon arrival, Denny was assigned as a platoon leader in C Company, 2nd Battalion, 8th Cavalry, 1st Cavalry Division (Air

Mobile). On the seventh of August, his parents received a letter saying "My dream of Infantry blue came true! I am a grunt platoon leader in C Company" [each branch of the Army has its distinctive color; Infantry is light blue].

At that time, the division was operating about seventy miles northwest of Saigon, the nation's capital, interdicting NVA forces coming off of the Ho Chi Minh Trail, which came south from North Vietnam through Laos and Cambodia. Denny's mission was to find and destroy enemy forces infiltrating into South Vietnam off of the trail. In this area, the NVA also constructed extensive bunker complexes and supply caches containing food, weapons, and ammunition. The region was primarily jungle terrain with triple canopy, which made navigation a real challenge. The general term used for Denny's type of mission was aptly called search and destroy.

Enemy activity was on the rise during the summer, and it was suspected that there were tens of thousands of NVA troops in Cambodia and Denny's area of operation (AO) in that region of South Vietnam known as III Corps. The enemy in this area were battle-hardened soldiers and tough infantry fighters. For Denny it was not unusual to have some kind of enemy contact almost every day; he was wounded on the seventeenth of August, less than two months after his arrival and received his first Purple Heart. Details are not known, but since he stayed in the field, the wound was apparently not too serious.

On September 1, Denny's platoon, call sign *Log Chain,* was backup for 3rd Platoon, call sign *Lonely,* led by Staff Sergeant George W. Mays, its platoon sergeant. SSgt. Mayes recalled that the men were nervous, as they knew there were NVA in the area and their visibility was only ten to twelve feet because of the dense jungle. All was eerily quiet, until all of a sudden, all hell broke loose; Mays' platoon had walked into a classic horseshoe-shaped ambush and were taking intense fire from three directions and suffering heavy casualties. Mays reported the situation to Denny, who maneuvered his platoon to the enemy's flank, causing them to withdraw back into the jungle. Denny's platoon quickly secured the area and tended to SSgt. May's wounded, estimated at two thirds of his total strength. Fortunately, no one had been killed.

Denny called for *dust off* or medevac helicopters to take out the wounded. Because of the triple canopy jungle, the dust off bird had to use a jungle penetrator hoist designed to lift wounded soldiers straight up through the tree canopy to the bird when it couldn't land. His quick action and leadership got many of the more seriously wounded out before nightfall, preventing any deaths. SSgt. Mays was med-evac'd the next day due to the wounds he had received. According to George Mays, Denny was up all night, checking to ensure that the wounded were as comfortable as possible and also checking on his own men securing the perimeter. He talked with the wounded all night, assuring them that everything would be okay.

The next morning, Denny's mission was to move out and find the enemy. His platoon was in the lead and Denny positioned himself and his radio/telephone operator (RTO) right behind his point element, leading from the front. They came across a well-worn trail showing recent heavy use. As his platoon moved toward the trail, they came under intense automatic and small arms fire.

From his Silver Star citation:

> First Lieutenant Johnson, with complete disregard for his own personal safety, immediately engaged the enemy with fragmentation grenades and rifle fire. Unable to silence the enemy from his position, First Lieutenant Johnson attempted to flank the enemy and allow the rest of his point squad to move in on the enemy. The enemy countered with an intense burst of small arms fire, wounding First Lieutenant Johnson. Although he was seriously wounded, he continued to fire on the enemy position, killing one soldier and driving the rest from their position. As the remainder of the point element reached First Lieutenant Johnson, they found him fatally wounded.

A potentially rewarding career was cut short after only about one month in-country. Denny hardly had a chance to demonstrate all that he was capable of, but the soldiers around him saw some of it.

George Mays was devastated when he learned of Denny's death. Denny had stayed up all night caring for the wounded and assuring the security of the perimeter, and George believed that if Denny had been able to get some sleep that he would have been more alert. His exhaustion may have contributed to his walking into the ambush that took his life. George Mays felt somewhat responsible because Denny had to look out for his troops as well as his own and carries this guilt even today.

SSgt. Mays had the utmost respect for Denny because of his professional and leadership qualities and had been reassured when he expressed doubts of his own leadership ability in combat to Denny. Denny had told him to just relax, and when the bullets started flying to rely on his God-given common sense. Some thirty years after Vietnam SSgt. Mays found Denny's brother Danny and was able to share with him what happened during Denny's last fight.

Captain Robert Turrell, Denny's company commander, also shared his respect for Denny and described him as one of his "best lieutenants, a consummate leader, very bright and likable, great attitude who had quickly gained the respect of his soldiers." This was reflected in his letter to Denny's parents where he wrote:

> *News of your son's death came as a shock to all who knew him, and his loss will be felt keenly in this organization. I sincerely hope the knowledge that Denny was an exemplary soldier and died while serving his country will comfort you in this hour of great sorrow. Denny's enthusiasm and devotion to duty, no matter how difficult the mission, identified his outstanding abilities as a soldier. He displayed the finest example of soldierly bearing, discipline, and conduct. I am proud to have served with him.*

Denny had written a farewell letter to his family in case he didn't return. He left it in his belongings at home, in a sealed envelope addressed to his mother.

> *Dear Family,*
>
> *I know that this is a difficult time for all of you and that it will be some time before you will be able to adjust to the fact that I am never coming home again. Though the burden is great, I*

hope that you will never forget that there is One who is always
here to comfort us. When you turn to Him, He will not turn
you away. I am with Him now and at peace forever . . .

And so, my last gift, I give you again the words of our Father
and Master from His book, the Holy Bible.

Matthew 11: 28-30

Psalm 23

John 3:16

I must go now. I am thankful for the days I have shared
with you.

May God bless you all forever,

Love Denny

P.S. I am not dead. I am at rest in Jesus. I live with you. Your
life is my life: your joy, my joy, your sorrow, my sorrow—
always remember that.

Lieutenant Tom Niebling, Denny's friend from Ft. Hood, didn't
learn of Denny's death until after he arrived in Vietnam in September
1969. He had managed to get assigned to the 1st Cavalry division so
that they could be together. He was devastated. In July of 1977, he
wrote Denny's parents after the birth of his son, whom they named
Denny: *"I just hope he grows up to be half the man that your son*
Denny was. I still miss him." Tom also commented, *"I have grieved all*
these years that Denny did not live, and I survived. He was a special
friend. I have kept his picture in my wallet to this day."

Denny's parents expressed their appreciation and gratitude in
reply:

Dear Thomas,

We thank you, so much for taking the time and caring enough
to write us. Joy filled our hearts as we read the news of your
son and that you would call him Denny. What a wonderful
friendship you and Denny must have had that you would

honor his memory by calling your son Denny . . .

Our loss was great. We could not have been able to bear the loss of Denny, had it not been for God and friends. Bunkie really mourned his loss as well as the surrounding area and the many states with friends who knew him . . .

Part of our comfort was in a letter he left to us . . . He included several Scripture Passages from the Holy Bible . . . He also tried to comfort us with the words, "I am not dead. I will live in you and with you and others. I have Eternal Life with my Father in Heaven." We never knew just how many lives he touched and what he meant to them until his death. Everyone has been so kind . . . May God Bless you as a family and keep you safe in His care. May God grant unto you a great peace in your heart, that Denny knows and is greatly honored by your thoughtfulness and memory of him, and that you shared it with us.

Sincerely,
Dallas and Mavis Johnson

The Reverend Carl A. Hudson, a longtime friend of Denny's and his family, wrote a memorial article shortly after the funeral:

Lieutenant Johnson lived a full life revealed by the mature marks of a true Christian soldier . . . The phrase "All American Boy," was used more than a few times to describe this determined, courageous, and happy young man. This spirit was geared into his life and with deep consideration for others—others in his family, others in school, others on the team, others in the community, others in his country. After being in Vietnam less than six weeks, this unselfish virtue marked his gallant acts while engaged in combat which led to the mortal wound . . . When the contemporaries of Denny Johnson, as well as his many adult friends, spoke of him, such words as faithful, polite, Christian, thoughtful, determined, disciplined, cooperative, happy, and numerous other gracious words always entered the conversation. Denny *didn't* die. He will long live in the hearts and lives of his classmates of Bunkie High School, of the United States Military Academy, and the scores of friends who had the happy privilege of knowing this real soldier. And most of all, his assurance of eternal life with the God he worshipped and served.

Classmate Don Davis went on a search for Denny's grave in 2014. He had read in a newspaper article a couple of years earlier that it was standing room only in Bunkie's First Baptist church with many more gathered outside for Denny's funeral. Denny had been well known and well loved. In 2014 Pastor Hudson and many others had passed away but Don did find a bank vice president who had primary responsibility for the cemeteries in Bunkie. In a phone call, the VP told Don that he could "walk him to Denny's grave blindfolded." He had known Denny well and talked about the impact of his death on the community. That was years after Denny's death and Don stated "We are talking forty-five years. I think that testifies to the caliber of the person, the man, and soldier that Denny had become."

In the words of classmate Ralph Tuccillo, the following is a fitting eulogy: "Denny was on a quest to serve his country, to defend our constitution, to preserve our freedom, and to help other people in other lands have the same freedoms for which we are blessed. He worked hard to develop his mind and body to qualify for West Point and volunteered to seek combat in fulfillment of his quest. He fought on the battlefield of Vietnam to help the Vietnamese people achieve freedom, a noble quest caught in the quagmire of political chaos. He lost his life serving his country and the people of South Vietnam. He was a hero who led from the front and won many battles and at the same time saved many lives. Denny L. Johnson fulfilled his quest and is resting in peace with the Lord."

In fact, during our cow year Denny had written a poem entitled "The Quest," found by his brother Danny in his mother's belongings. A friend noted it eloquently captured Denny's ideals and philosophy of life.

"The Quest"

Beyond the far horizon
Where the weary sun must rest,
Upon the mountain high
And just beyond the crest,
There is a silent mystery
That draws me forth in quest.

There are better things
Those of which I dream,
Yet, across the great expanse
How far away they seem.

I've traveled far
And I've farther still to go,
Along the twisted trail
Where the thorns of life all grow.

Still moving, though more slowly now
Than 'ere I did before,
I push on to seek the endless dream
Restless all the more.

Will I ever reach that land
My home across the sea,
The land of peace and hope
Of all great things to be?
I feel I never shall
Though I try my very best,
For life is an endless trail
That winds on in noble quest.

Denny is interred in the Pythian Cemetery in Bunkie, Louisiana.

❖ ❖ ❖

Two days after Denny was killed, on September 4, a US Army helicopter UH-1H from the 177th Assault Helicopter Company crashed in Bien Hoa Province, RVN, after losing a blade from its tail rotor. Five crewmen and two passengers were killed in the incident. One of those killed was First Lieutenant Kenneth T. Cummings, our fourth classmate to die. This aircraft was the command-and-control helicopter operating with three slicks and two helicopter gunships with the 151st Long Range Reconnaissance Patrol (LRRP) teams. While flying at approximately 200 to 300 feet of altitude, a tail rotor blade separated from the tail rotor hub. About the third 360-degree turn, the mast snapped, and the main rotor blades fell backwards, severing the tail boom. The aircraft stopped spinning and fell straight to the ground in an upright position. Upon contact with the ground the aircraft burst into flames, destroying itself by fire and killing all aboard.

Kenneth Thomas Cummings was born in Brooklyn, New York to John F. Cummings and Marie Layden Cummings on August 20, 1946. John fought in North Africa during World War II and upon his return from the war became a New York City policeman, Marie was a homemaker. In 1950, the Cummings and many of their friends bought homes in the new Cambria Heights community in Queens, built for veterans returning from their service.

The young Cummings family and Cambria Heights neighbors attended Mass at the newly built Sacred Heart Parish, where Ken was confirmed. A first communion black-and-white photo shows a freckled eight-year-old with a wide, toothy smile, sporting a suit and neatly combed hair. A color photo would have shown that hair to be bright red.

Still a young family, John and Marie purchased a small summer cottage on Lake Panomoka, "mid island" as they called it. June to Labor Day the kids could leave the house in the morning, swim in the lake all day, walk to the potato farms, and play softball games and hide-and-seek after supper. Ken was a strong and accomplished swimmer, winning many local swim challenges. Laughter filled the night air as the parents gathered on lawn chairs for cocktails, nursing martinis and manhattans.

Ken's early swimming ability did not go unnoticed. He was admitted to St. Francis Prep, an all-boys Catholic high school in an urban Brooklyn granite building. St. Francis had a swimming pool and a strong swim team, and Ken was captain during his senior year. They won the city championship in 1963, another addition to the school's well-stocked trophy case.

During his senior year, he was offered a full scholarship to St. John's University in Queens, and an appointment to West Point. On the first of July 1964, Ken entered West Point with the class of 1968; the choice had not been difficult. He quickly established himself and began to form some close friendships. Renata Price (Renata transitioned in the mid 1970s) who roomed with Ken and Tony Medici, remarked, "There is not enough you can say about Kenny. He was just a really good, nice man. He and Tony Medici were like brothers to me."

Renata remembered that "in either the summer of '66 or '67 I trooped up to Rhode Island to visit Tony, hit the beaches, and attend the Newport Jazz Festival. If my memory is not failing me, Ken was the third member of that party. We had a great time trying to fit in with all the other college students and people who attend such affairs and had some good beach time and clam cakes and chowder."

Renata's clearest memories are of rooming with Ken during cow year, 1966–1967. "We were not being moved around to other duties outside the company, so roommates were not changing as much. It seems that by that time we were all pretty comfortable that we were going to make it through this thing we had gotten ourselves into. With that came some relief and I remember that we were constantly clowning around in the barracks, usually after taps. Ken was, of course, a Corps Squad (varsity) swimmer and was often freed from some of the more mundane and annoying aspects of cadet life. He was nevertheless serious about studies and leadership and making sure that we set the right example and tone for those that followed behind us."

Renata continued, "The memories get a bit sad for me here. I deployed to Vietnam on July 30, 1969. I was assigned to the 25th Infantry Division, 3rd Squadron, 4th Cavalry. I quickly heard that Ken was with the division and looked forward to seeing him. Unfortunately, before we could meet up, I learned of his death in a helicopter crash." Ken's death before they were able to meet in-country was difficult for her to handle and she mourned his loss.

Ken was an incredibly gifted swimmer but seldom won his events, most often coming in second or third. But he was elected captain of the team because of his attitude, his personality, and his leadership. He was an amazing young man. The most common comments about him from his teammates were about his personality, primarily his nice, friendly spirit. Many of his teammates didn't get to know him well, and when he was killed many lamented that fact, wishing that they had gotten to know him better, feeling they would have been blessed if they had.

Not only was Ken an accomplished swimmer, but also a great all-around athlete. During plebe year we had to run the hated indoor obstacle course for the first time. Ken's time was the second or third fastest in the entire class.

After graduation Ken went to Ft. Benning with many of his classmates for the Infantry Officer's Basic Course, and Ranger and Airborne School. There is a well-known story of Ken in Ranger School. His course was dubbed a *winter Ranger* course because even the water in canteens froze that winter in Florida. Ken's platoon was supposed to swim a rope across a fast-moving river at night so that the unit could cross. As the former captain of the Army swim team, Ken was elected to swim across while the rest of the platoon followed behind. Ken smiled, stripped naked, and plunged into the cold water, the heavy rope tied around his waist as he swam. Once on the other side, Ken didn't stop to put his fatigues and boots back on, but rather returned to the shore to help all of his comrades get out of the water safely. His entire body was as red as his famous red hair, true dedication to helping others and mission accomplishment.

Having successfully completed all of the schools, he reported to Ft. Carson, Colorado for some troop time before leaving for Vietnam. It was here that his life changed dramatically when he met Franki Bennett in the parking lot of their apartment complex. She had found a newly completed complex named the Oxford Club, which, quite by chance, Ken had also discovered. She and Ken passed each other several times as they drove in and out of the complex, where she shared an apartment with two employees of the El Paso County Welfare Department. Franki knew there was something different about the guy, maybe his smile, maybe his red hair?

And in January of '69 there occurred the perfect scenario for a meeting. As she returned one Saturday from running errands, she noticed his red Firebird with the hood open and him leaning into the engine compartment. Knowing something about cars, she parked alongside of him, got out, and asked if he needed any help. His answer was "Finally! I've been waiting to meet you." Working on the car was just a ruse he established hoping for a meeting. And so began a romance that would only grow stronger. They talked for a long while that day. "I leaned against my car, an eastward view of the plains and horizon, my lingering suntanned knees were visible between my plaid woolen Bermuda shorts and navy knee socks. He kicked imaginary stones and I folded my arms over my navy sweater, giggling too much. His Brooklyn accent sounded like the Mafia guys on TV. He was Catholic, I was Methodist. His dad a NYPD cop, my dad a plumbing contractor. He told me that his mom was a housewife, I told him that my mom was a nurse; he had one sister and I had three brothers. He graduated from West Point, I graduated from Colorado State University." So began an incredible romance.

They began to date, going to movies, taking walks and car rides, playing golf and going to dinners with her parents. With all of this exploring they fell in love with Colorado and with each other. Knowing that he would soon receive orders for Vietnam, he proposed on St. Patrick's Day, and they began to plan for a future of military married life. They talked about potential places for assignments around the world, talked about dinner parties and entertaining friends in their quarters, and chose their china pattern; they were excited about the future and Vietnam would be just a temporary interruption.

They made a trip back east, where she met his family. They visited West Point, walked around the campus, and visited places familiar to him that he wanted to introduce to her. He specifically pointed out housing above the Catholic Chapel, which he referred to as Catholic Hill because it was composed of large quarters—and they wanted to have many children. And, of course, he introduced Franki to Jack and Marilyn Ryan; Jack had been his swim coach. And then one day the orders they had anticipated arrived; Ken was to report on June 20, 1969 to Company D (Ranger), 2nd Battalion, 27th Infantry Regiment in the 25th Infantry Division. It didn't seem so bad, though, as they could meet at the halfway point of his tour in Hawaii for his R&R leave. He proposed that they get married before he left so that she could take advantage of the Army's R&R policy for wives, which provided a free space available flight to Honolulu.

Ken sprang into wedding-planning action. "I talked with Chaplain Hester. He agreed to officiate. I called the Air force Academy Officers' Club; we can have a reception there. And I've talked with your mom and dad, they have given their blessings," Franki remembered him telling her. Both sets of parents met and understood the urgency, as their lives had been touched by World War II. The honeymoon ended the day Ken had to report to the Denver airport. In Franki's words, "From the airport windows I watched him climb the portable stairs. Blinded by the Colorado sun, he turned, waved, and blew a kiss in the direction of where I was standing. Ken disappeared into the big bird, bound first for a layover in California, and then the final destination—Vietnam."

Soon letters began to arrive. Ken described the jungle and nighttime patrols, talked about the guys in his unit and his growing love for the Vietnamese people and their culture. Everything was new to him—a foreign land, culture, and language—and he loved and embraced it.

He was transferred from the 27th Infantry to D Company, 151st Ranger Battalion, 25th Infantry Division, where he served for a commanding officer who did not like West Pointers. He mentioned that he had been engaged in a heavy firefight on the twelfth of August, and that he had been nominated for an award of the Silver Star, the third highest award for bravery. "I checked out what a Silver Star meant as I sat with a dictionary on the library table before me. I was in awe of his obvious courage and leadership," Franki said. When she replied to Ken with the information that she was pregnant, "his written response was delight, glee and self-congratulations. I imagined the smiling redhead glowed with pride and joy."

From Ken's Silver Star citation:

For gallantry in action while engaged in military operations involving conflict with an armed hostile force on August

12, 1969 while serving as a platoon leader with Company
D (Ranger), 2nd Battalion, 151st Infantry Regiment, 25th
Infantry Division, in the Republic of Vietnam. On this date
shortly after being airlifted into an open rice paddy area, two
companies of the battalion encountered a large enemy force
situated in well-concealed fighting positions in a nearby
hedgerow. In the initial contact, the two companies became
pinned down by intense hostile fire and sustained several
casualties. While directing his platoon's advance, Lieutenant
Cummings repeatedly exposed himself to the enemy fusillade
to point out targets and place accurate fire on the hostile
troops. Under the cover of his element's counterattack, the
friendly casualties were safely evacuated. At one point during
the fighting, he spotted a wounded comrade, moved to his
aid, and carried him two hundred meters through enemy
fire to safety and medical assistance. After returning to the
center of the contact area, Lieutenant Cummings began
directing supporting fire upon the hostile positions. As the
friendly force began its final assault, it came under intense
machine gun fire from an enemy emplacement in front of
his platoon. Disregarding his own safety, he rushed forward
through the hostile fire and silenced the position with several
hand grenades and a burst from his rifle.

The officer's knock on the door, the notification, came two
days after the helicopter crash, on September 4, 1969. All seven
men perished in the explosion. Days later, Franki was still receiving
letters from Ken. And then the mail she received changed; brief and
brusque official yellow half-paper Western Union Telegrams from
Army Headquarters took the place of his beautiful and lovingly
written correspondence. A life had ended all too early, a little more
than two months after arriving in-country. Plans and dreams were
shattered after only two months of marriage, and a young widow was
left behind with an unborn child; I think there is no better definition
for the word *tragedy*. As one classmate so aptly put it, "That's the kind
of man and friend Kenny was. I am proud to have known Kenny; I
have missed him many, many times over the years."

Months after his death, Franki was contacted by the office of Major General Bernard Rogers, former commandant of cadets during our time at West Point, and then commanding the 5th Infantry Division at Ft. Carson, Colorado. General Rogers had known Ken at West Point and knew that he had been stationed at Ft. Carson before his departure for Southeast Asia. The general wanted to preside over the presentation of Ken's awards to his widow. The two families, Ken's and Franki's, gathered together again for this occasion as they had a few months earlier for the wedding. This time there was one notable person missing, Kenny, but there was one notable addition, Kenny's newborn daughter, Kimberly.

Some fifty-two years later, Franki was contacted by a platoon sergeant from Company D, which holds biannual reunions. One of the soldiers had captured Ken in footage that wound up in the Ken Burns' documentary *Vietnam*. It showed an excited Ken Cummings holding up a letter received during mail call. He was remembered by several soldiers with comments like "He never got us lost" (a major and necessary accomplishment in the triple canopied jungles) and "Lt. Cummings was the best platoon leader we had in Nam." Soldiers under Ken's leadership remembered, "Lt. Cummings did not demand respect, he commanded respect," and "He always had time to listen." There is no finer tribute than accolades like this for a lost leader.

One of the honors bestowed on Ken was his election as the captain of the swim team in his senior year at West Point. It was his positive attitude and leadership qualities that stood out so easily for his fellow swimmers to recognize. Ken, prior to attending West Point, was also elected captain for the St. Francis Prep swim team in New York. As further recognition of his leadership abilities, members from the swim teams of both schools formed Team Ken Cummings in 2008 and designed an award to be given annually to the captain of the West Point triathlon team.

THE KEN CUMMINGS AWARD
Class of 1968

From the very beginning, Ken Cummings displayed outstanding leadership abilities when he was elected in 1963 as captain of his St. Francis Preparatory High School swim team. He continued to lead at West Point, where he was elected captain of the 1967–68 Army Swim Team. It was not solely Ken's athletic ability that made him fit to be captain, though he was a great swimmer. What distinguished Ken as the leader was that he was always ready to lend a hand without regard to personal gain or glory. Ken led by example during every practice and competition with his commitment to be the very best. His loyalty to his teammates and honest respect for his opponents elevated him to be the true leader. His positive attitude and sincere determination to win were also valued leadership skills that he displayed.

Ken Cummings was killed in Vietnam on September 4, 1969, and this award is presented in his memory to forever capture his bubbling enthusiasm, his effervescent personality, and determination to be the very best.

From Ken's fellow simmers from St. Francis Prep and West Point, the Ken Cummings Award is presented to this year's member of the Army Triathlon Team who most exemplifies these same leadership qualities.

Ken Cummings was a truly phenomenal young man whose tragic end came much too soon. "Trustworthy, caring, kind, and driven by a higher purpose, this was Ken Cummings," Franki said of him. He had barely begun to live life, had barely experienced the joys of marriage with Franki, and never met the young daughter that was conceived on his honeymoon. So many plans for the future, so many dreams about life after Vietnam with the love of his life, and none of them to be realized. How does one rationalize such a story—and such a tragedy?

Ken is interred in the Ft. Logan National Cemetery in Denver, Colorado.

A short two months later, and only a little over four months since the first loss, the Class of '68 was to suffer the loss of another from its ranks. David Lee Sackett was killed on the twenty-fourth of October, 1969, less than sixteen months after our graduation; he also left a young widow, Pam Stokes Sackett, behind. Within five months of June 1969, with David's loss, five members of the class had given their lives in the service of their country. Who could have foreseen such a toll? Randy Pais '67, Jesse Gatlin '68, and Jim Swinney '68 worked together to present David's story.

David grew up in the coalfields of West Virginia with a good friend who preceded him by a year at West Point, Randy Pais, class of '67. The Pais family and the Sacketts were neighbors and good friends for years. Dave and his brother Frederick did not want to be limited to life in the economy of West Virginia. They both wanted to grow up and escape those confines. David accomplished that by being admitted to West Point with the class of 1968. There he succeeded while marching to the beat of his own drum, suffering his share of misadventures and brushes with the tactical and academic departments. During the course of these adventures, he formed a lasting and deep friendship with Jesse Gatlin, who was often his roommate. As a matter of fact, it was at Jesse's wedding in June of '68 that David met Pam. They were later married in April of 1969. Much like Ken and Franki Cummings, Pam and David were together for only a brief time before he left for Vietnam in late July of 1969 after a short assignment at Ft. Hood Texas. Just about three months later David was killed in an ambush by NVA troops.

Randy and David were special, lifelong friends, going to the same elementary and junior high schools and playing many of the same sports. Both boys were raised shortly after World War II, which had a profound effect on their love of country and sense of patriotism. Almost every day they went into the woods and refought the war against Germany. They played sports together on various teams and were active in the Boy Scouts. They could also watch a movie for twenty cents and buy candy and popcorn for five cents in the only theater in town. They attended Keystone Elementary School and then went on to Keystone Junior High, where they played basketball and football on the same team.

Keystone Junior High School fed its students into Northfork Elkhorn High School, a basketball powerhouse, holding a record for winning eight consecutive state basketball championships. The major *other than legal* activity in the county was the brewing of moonshine whiskey, which is still a local cottage industry. This area of southern West Virginia was also well known for being home to the infamous feud between the Hatfields and McCoys, which started after the Civil War and lasted until the 1950s.

In 1958, McDowell County celebrated its 100th anniversary. There were many ceremonies and special events during the year, which was capped off with a special pageant called *Our Changing Hills*, which was written by the same gentleman who wrote and produced the famous Cherokee county North Carolina production of *Unto These Hills*. Randy and Dave's Boy Scout troop participated as Native American dancers. David played a special part as the messenger whose role was to warn the Native Americans that their land was about to be overrun by new settlers from the east. The boys were so proud to be able to participate in this melodrama about the history of their county.

After completing junior high school, Randy went off to Staunton Military Academy, where he became interested in West Point. Randy was a year ahead of David, and in his senior year told David that he'd attend West Point if possible. This inspired David to do the same, and he set off to gain admittance. Randy entered with the class of '67, and a year later David and another Welch High School classmate, Don Roberts, entered with the class of '68.

Randy graduated in 1967, and in July of '68 went to Vietnam as an artillery officer in the 1st Infantry Division and then later as a forward observer with the 36th ARVN Ranger Battalion. Upon completion of that assignment, Randy and his new wife Jackie returned to Keystone West Virginia and attended a party for David and Pam, who had been recently married. David was preparing to leave for Vietnam and the 25th Infantry Division.

The next word Randy received about David was that he'd been killed in action, devastating news. He quickly made arrangements to fly to Washington so that he could be a pall bearer for David's funeral in Arlington National Cemetery on November 6, 1969. That Christmas night in 1969, the entire town of Welch lit luminaries—paper bags filled with sand and containing a lit candle—in David's memory. Welch was believed to be one of the first towns in the US to honor its war dead in this way. With twenty-nine killed in Vietnam, Randy's class of 1967 is one of two classes that lost more than '68, the class of 1966 being the other. Though these men of '67 were close friends and classmates of Randy, none of his class's losses had a deeper impact on Randy than the loss of David.

Jesse Gatlin had a close and special relationship with David beginning spring break of plebe year with a chance encounter in the sinks. There was an instant connection and they talked until about two o'clock in the morning. They decided to be roommates starting the following year and thus began an incredible relationship. Jesse and their other roommate, Mike Selvitelle, changed *David* to *Dave*, and nicknamed him "Snake" because of his wiry physique. "We kidded him that he would have to run around in a shower to get wet."

During the academic year Dave played brinkmanship with the academic departments, never trying to get more than a 2.0 out of a possible 3.0 (2.0 was just passing), thinking that anything more would be a waste of effort because it wasn't needed. Most often Dave won this contest, but sometimes he didn't and was turned out because he failed a final exam. He always passed the turn-out exam and stayed with the class. At one point he wanted to compete with Rick Hawley, also remembered in this book, for the last man in the class in order of merit prize, because he heard that that man would receive a dollar from every other classmate. When he found he couldn't beat Rick, he vowed to graduate in the 600s, which he accomplished, graduating number 699 out of 706.

In Jesse's words, "As a new first lieutenant, he departed for Vietnam in late July 1969 and was assigned to the 25th Infantry Division. I received a letter from Dave dated October 7, 1969, written a day before his twenty-third birthday, briefly describing the challenges of leading an infantry platoon in combat and wishing me well when I got assigned to Vietnam. In late October, I learned of David's death on the twenty-fourth while attacking a VC bunker complex. I was overwhelmed at the loss of my best friend. We buried Dave on a blustery cold November 6, 1969, near the west side of Arlington National Cemetery's Tomb of the Unknown Soldier. I stood at the foot of my best friend's casket, with tears in my eyes, rendered this outstanding soldier and true friend a final salute, and with heavy heart, trudged back to the Fort Meyer chapel. I have always wished I could see Dave's smiling face again. I miss him."

After the Infantry Officer's Basic Course and Airborne and Ranger Schools, Dave arrived in Vietnam in early August of 1969 and was assigned as the platoon leader of 2nd Platoon, A Company, 2-12th Infantry, 25th Infantry Division in III Corps, South Vietnam. The area where the 2-12th Infantry operated was close to the southern terminus of the Ho Chi Minh Trail, which started in North Vietnam, traversed Laos and Cambodia, and ended about fifty miles from Saigon. The trail was the major resupply route for the NVA and had numerous offshoots entering South Vietnam from the Demilitarized Zone (DMZ) to Saigon. This area is famous even today for the Tunnels of Cu Chi, a complex so huge that it surprised everyone with its breadth extenting to Cambodia after the war.

The platoon leaders of A Company were a tight group, living together in a small bunker at Firebase Pershing, with close friendships forged through almost daily contact with either the VC or NVA. One of the lieutenants remembered one of Dave's primary instructions to him when he first arrived was to "never ask your guys to do something that you had not done yourself." Following this axiom led to Dave being mentioned in the division newspaper, *The Tropic Lightning News*. One unfortunate incident occurred when he decided to lead by example and check out a tunnel before asking any of his soldiers to enter it. As he lowered himself feet first into what he thought was an abandoned tunnel, he was grabbed around the ankle by an NVA soldier who attempted to drag Dave deeper into the hole. The quick reaction by a couple of his soldiers resulted in a classic tug of war that freed Dave from the enemy below. One wounded and shaken NVA soldier was pulled from the hole after a couple of grenades were thrown in.

A soldier from Dave's platoon offered the highest possible accolade, "Dave was an excellent officer, and everybody loved him, and I felt very close to him." He frequently spent time with Dave because, at twenty-three, they were two of the oldest in their group. He recounted that when Dave arrived, the lieutenant recognized that the group had more experience in the field than he did, so he would always listen to their suggestions about situations. However, in the end Dave would make the final decision for any action. They all respected him because he listened to them first.

This same soldier thought that Dave was just days away from ending his time in the field. According to him, rifle platoon leaders in 2-12th Infantry normally spent three months in the jungle before being moved to a safer rear job. This policy may have been the result of the stress of constant combat in their area of operations. Vietnam has often been referred to as *the platoon leader's war* because most enemy contact was made by small US units.

Another soldier had similar thoughts about Dave. He remembered Lt. Sackett quite well. He recounted that right before Dave's arrival they were told that he was a West Point graduate. "We thought that the lieutenant was going to be a real gung-ho dick because he was West Point. Lt. Sackett turned out to be one of the better officers I have ever had the privilege to serve under. We realized quickly that being a West Point grad meant his love of country, his love for the Army, and his dedication to his men was of the highest standard. He was truly a man that you would follow into battle. And we did. And time and time again he proved his worth."

David Sackett was truly a soldier's soldier. In the space of five days in September he was awarded both a Bronze Star with V and a Silver Star. The citation for the Bronze Star, awarded for action on the twenty-first reads in part, "a gunship spotted an enemy soldier near a village. Arriving on the scene, Lt. Sackett spotted the muzzle of a rifle protruding from a hidden spider hole. Unhesitatingly, Lt. Sackett, with complete disregard for his own safety, rushed the emplacement and threw a hand grenade into the entrance, killing three enemy occupants."

From Dave Sackett's Silver Star citation, awarded for action on September 26: "While on a reconnaissance mission, Company A encountered a large enemy force. During the initial contact, the lead element became pinned down by the intense hostile fire. With complete disregard for his own safety, Lieutenant Sackett led four of his men forward through the enemy kill zone and swiftly destroyed the main enemy emplacements. Noticing that one of his men had been wounded, Lieutenant Sackett moved to his side and administered lifesaving first aid." In both cases he led his men from the front during an enemy contact and rendered first aid on the twenty-sixth to one of his wounded soldiers while under fire."

Just about ten days later he was awarded an Army Commendation Medal with V for courageously exposing himself to enemy fire while checking on his men during a heavy contact with the enemy. In all cases Dave was honored for his valor and selfless concern for his men during combat actions.

Not all of the time in Vietnam was spent in combat; there were lighter moments as well. During one period at FSB Pershing, David's 1st Platoon played touch football with the 2nd. There was also an incident with a rat one night crossing the mosquito netting over Dave's bunk. One of his fellow lieutenants thought it would be a good idea to wake Dave up, and when he opened his eyes, the rat was just above his face. Dave let out a scream and swatted the rat onto the netting of a nearby bunk whose resident never woke up. When the perpetrator thought it would be great fun to tease Dave about his scream, he was told that it just might not be a good idea and was sworn to secrecy. This is the first mention of the story since its occurrence! This same fellow platoon leader described Vietnam as "a bunch of young guys screwing around, followed by daily events of terror of the worst kind."

October 24, 1969 was one of those days of terror for A Company. It was warm and sunny when Dave's platoon walked into the perimeter of classmate Jim Swinney's cavalry platoon on the eastern edge of the Boi Loi Woods. Jim Swinney, who was present on that day, recounted the events. It was their first meeting since graduation almost a year and a half earlier. Jim offered Dave a cold Coke, one of the benefits of being mechanized with a lot of room in a track, and they talked for about an hour about West Point and the events from then to that day. Then a call came over the radio and Dave's platoon was to be airlifted about ten clicks (kilometers) into the jungle. This area intelligence had just identified a potential NVA assembly area on the western edge of the Ho Bo woods, just ten clicks east of their current position. Jim and Dave said their farewells and Dave climbed aboard a bird with his soldiers and lifted off for the LZ, up to that point, enemy contact had been sporadic. Then Dave's second platoon landed in what was later described as a supply and assembly point for the NVA 268th Regiment. According to reports of the action, Dave was the first man hit right after the helicopters lifted off; his platoon had landed in a well-prepared ambush by concealed enemy soldiers. As the platoon tried to continue their advance, others fell dead or wounded, and the platoon was stopped. For his conduct in that short period of time Dave was awarded his second Bronze Star with V device.

To reinforce the heavily engaged Second Platoon, the company commander, with his headquarters, and Third Platoon landed and entered the battle. In the words of one of the soldiers, "All hell broke out!" In this heavy fire, the Third Platoon Leader was also killed while leading his men. The company commander could not determine what was happening because the enemy appeared to be all around them and close.

During a lull in the fighting, the battalion commander directed his C&C bird to land. One soldier dragged Dave to temporary cover, not knowing if he was alive or dead, and then helped to load him on the battalion commander's bird and it headed to the 12th Evac Hospital at Cu Chi, the 25th Division's Base Camp. Unfortunately it's believed that Dave died en route to the hospital. Notes from that day say that A Company suffered about ten killed in action and fourteen wounded. Second and third platoons were reduced to nine and eleven men respectively. First Platoon was at the battalion firebase, as they had been on an ambush patrol the night before. They waited on the helicopter pad to be airlifted in to help, listening to the fight develop on the radio. The platoon leader remarked that he cried openly as he heard that Dave didn't make it to the hospital. There is nothing more frustrating in combat than listening to your buddies die in a heavy contact and not be able to help. This can lead to a common emotional state known as survivor's guilt.

The battalion commander requested help from the Brigade S-3 (operations officer) who was circling overhead, classmate Jim Swinney's 2nd Platoon, C Troop, 3/4 Cav was directed to move to the battle area and relieve the remnants of A Company. Jim's actions that day, as he went to the rescue of his classmate, neutralizing many of the NVA positions, were incredibly heroic, for which he received the Silver Star, and is remembered to this day by the survivors of A Company as a result of his effort to tell the story of that fateful day. Those who survived had a very difficult time, and morale was understandably low. The twenty-fourth of October had truly been a day of terror for them. Jim Swinney has remained in contact with the men of his cav platoon and has been invited to attend an A Company reunion this year because of his efforts with this book.

The best legacy possible for David Lee Sackett can be found in Jim's words:

> What was Dave's legacy and how are we to remember him? Dave Sackett's intrepidity in the face of the enemy in Vietnam is without question. He aggressively led his platoon from the front, and they unhesitatingly followed him into the breach every day. He was awarded the Silver Star for Gallantry in Action, two Bronze Stars and Army Commendation Medals for heroism in combat and the Purple Heart after only three months. His men respected him as their combat leader because he earned their admiration and love by his words and actions. His death was a tragedy that the men of A Company, 2-12th Infantry remember to this day.

One account of the battle of October 24 on the 2-12th Infantry web site from an aviator overhead summarized the bravery of all who fought and died that day. The website was put together by Sergeant Bruce Holzhauer, who had been wounded on October 21, and so was not involved in the fight on October 24. Bruce explained that the reason he set up the web site was "to find out what really happened on the twenty-fourth of October to A Company." Bruce gathered official reports, unit logs, individual diaries, notes, and memories that narrated the 2-12th Infantry's history over several years in Vietnam. One reflection on Holzhauer's website came from a 116th Aviation Cobra Pilot, Craig V. Fielding (call sign: Stinger 99): "I must admit that I had forgotten the date [October 24, 1969], but I will never forget the day. This was not the first nor last, nor was it the largest firefight I was involved with during my tour. It is, however, the day I am reminded of when I hear someone question the resolve or ability of the American infantryman. I will forever carry with me the individual and collective acts of heroism witnessed from 200 feet above in our gunship. I send a salutation to the men of A 2-12 Infantry and C Troop 3/4 Cavalry."

Before she died at the age of ninety, Dave's mother, Dora Lee Sackett, decided to give her collection of Dave's West Point diploma and uniforms plus a display case of his medals to Tony Whitlow, president of the Those Who Served War Museum in Princeton, West Virginia. Eight months prior, Whitlow had assured her that the museum would be pleased to accept Dave's uniform and would take good care of it. Priscilla Cecil, a Bluewell, West Virginia resident, was an LPN who cared for elderly people in the area, fulfilled Dora Lee's last request. Over their twenty-one-year relationship, Cecil had helped with light housework beginning in 1986 and became Dora Lee's best friend. After the deaths of Fred Sr. in 1989 and Frederick in 1991, she became executor of her friend's estate. Mrs. Sackett was meticulous about everything she did, especially taking care of Dave's shako parade hat in a glass case in her double-wide trailer home. The story came to light in the *Bluefield Daily Telegraph* when reporter Bill Archer learned that Priscilla had fulfilled Dora Lee's last wish to deliver Dave's uniform to Whitlow. "I've visited the Those Who Served War Museum, as has Jim Swinney, and have met Tony Whitlow, and was gratified to see the care and reverence with which Dave's memorabilia are displayed."

The Vietnam Veterans Memorial Wall USA website shows that West Virginia had the highest casualty rate in the nation, according to the US Department of Defense with 711 casualties, which is the equivalent of 39.9 deaths per 100,000 in the population. Oklahoma had the second highest rate.

Dave Sackett's West Point obituary in the May 1992 *Assembly* magazine may have summed up his character best and gives us his true legacy: "Leading was what Dave did best. His ability to understand, to cajole, and to bring humor to the most dismal of situations served as an inspiration to all. We did things for Dave because we knew that he would do them, ungrudgingly and with a smile on his face, for us." Although it was cut short, what better legacy for Dave's life than to be loved by so many.

Dave is interred in Arlington National Cemetery.

Denny High School Football

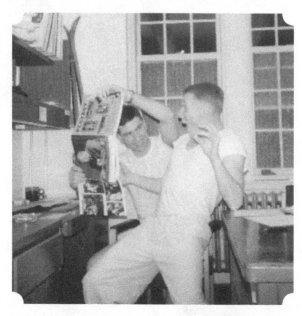

Ken discovering *Playboy* Magazine with roommate Tony Medici

SSG Mays of 3rd Platoon—
Credits Denny with saving
the lives of his soldiers

Platoon Leader, D company,
151st LRRPs

Dave (R) with his company
commander (name unknown)

Dave flavoring his "C" Rations

Dave and Pam, Cadet chapel, 19 April 1969

VIETNAM: NOVEMBER 1969

Peter Michael Connor   James Alfred Gaiser   William Francis Little III

From June through October the class of '68 lost five classmates, a terrible toll. We had just begun to join the fight and had already paid a high price for our commitment. The month of November 1969 would be the single most costly month for us and includes the worst week of the war for the class; three more were killed from November 4–11.

This week is particularly significant for me, as I should have been the fourth name on The Wall for this time period. Many of us who escaped death when we should not have by any amount of reason, celebrate an *Alive Day*, and I had two in the span of this single week. One of those nights I knew I was going to die. The second, a couple of days later, I had a premonition and had accepted that I would. No one knows why some of us survive while others don't; maybe it's luck or maybe a guardian angel. Living sometimes brings on survivor's guilt and causes one to question a lot. All I know is that every time

I visit The Wall to remember others, I think "there but for the grace of God, go I."

Pete Connor died on the fourth of November, doing what infantry officers did, leading from the front while protecting his men in a heavy contact. Pete, as is the case with the nineteen other incredible young men, was an inspiration to many who knew him. Although not prior service, Pete was an Army brat, so probably knew more about the Army than most of his classmates. And maybe because of that background, he knew how to work the system; as an example, he managed to keep the same roommates for almost the entire four years. This was probably a singular achievement for the class, almost impossible to accomplish, and as a result Dick McClelland, Bruce Korda,, and Pete became inseparable.

Pete was the oldest of five Connor kids. His father had received his commission through the Citizens' Military Training Camps in 1939 as a lieutenant of infantry. At the end of the second World War, he was commanding the 2nd Battalion, 2nd Infantry Regiment, 5th Infantry Division in the European Theater of Operations (ETO). By personal request from the division commander, Pete's dad served as the commanding officer of the 1st Battle Group, 87th Infantry, 2nd Division at Ft. Benning after the war. Pete attended Pacelli High School in Columbus, Georgia along with a couple of guys who later became West Point classmates. During their plebe year, the family was stationed at Ft. Leavenworth, Kansas, where his dad was chief of staff for the Combined Arms Group. On New Year's Day, the family was scheduled to attend the commanding general's New Year's Day reception, a time-honored Army tradition. All of the infantry officers gathered at the Connor's house to go as a group at the appointed time. Pete was to go along wearing his dress gray uniform. In preparation, he manned the front door of the Connor's quarters to welcome all of the visitors. His mom got a real laugh when the British liaison officer's wife complimented her on their splendid butler!

Not only were the British confused, Pete's brother Robert related another humorous story about Pete being home for Christmas that first year, this one involving another grad:

During Pete's plebe year we were at Ft Leavenworth; my dad was chief of staff for the Combined Arms Group there. Attending the Command and General Staff College (C&GSC) that year was a major who shall remain nameless. He was the son of the much-loved former commander of my dad's regiment prior to the war and a grad himself. As I recall, yours was the first West Point class allowed Christmas leave. Major X came over to our house regularly but when he came to drop off a Christmas gift, Pete opened the door in civilian clothes; Major X was in uniform. It was amazing how fast things went south. "What are you doing *here*, mister!" he yelled. Pete actually braced (I was standing in the hall). "Sir, I'm home on leave," Pete told him. The poor man was absolutely scandalized. "On *what*?" he shouted. By that time my dad made it to the front door and assured the major that Pete was not AWOL, that he had not been dismissed, and was, in fact, on Christmas leave. Major X, still plainly scandalized, put his hand to his forehead, slowly shook his head and actually said, "The Corps has," and meant it. [The phrase "The Corps has" is used by old grads to reflect on changes that have occurred at West Point since their tenure. These changes normally reflect a lessening in standards or requirements and basically is an abbreviated form of "The Corps has gone to hell."]

Classmate Robert Keller remembered an adventure-filled trip home to Cincinnati for Christmas leave yearling year:

Pete Connor and I were both from Cincinnati, Ohio and we ended up assigned to D-2/A-2 company. Although not acquaintances before entering the Academy, we became good friends while at school. Our yearling year we both decided to travel together to defray expenses as much as possible in going home for Christmas. We managed to catch a hop from Stewart AFB to Charleston AFB in South Carolina. Unfortunately, it did not leave until late in the day, but the flight met our minimum expense goal. We arrived in Charleston late in the evening and found no remaining flights in the general direction of Cincinnati, so we managed to catch a military bus ride to the other side of the runways where the civilian airport operated. There were no flights to Cincinnati until early the next morning—I mean early! We called home to let our parents know that we booked a flight for the next morning and would arrive around six thirty. We got comfortable in the waiting area seats to get what sleep we could until the next morning. Food was not in our expense plan since we had expected to be home by then (optimism at its best!). We barely scraped enough money to buy the military standby tickets we did get. Hungry and tired, we boarded the plane and experienced the bumpiest flight in history (maybe an exaggeration, but not to Pete and me). By the time we were taxiing down the runway to the terminal, Pete was scrambling for a second air-sick bag! By now he was making me woozy! Everyone deplaned—except for Pete and me. It took a stewardess to help me keep Pete on his feet and get him off the plane with one of us under each arm. My mom was waiting for me, and Pete's girlfriend was waiting for him. We literally dragged Pete to her car and inserted him in the back seat, where he promptly fell against the now shut door and did not move until he got home. We both had great Christmases and bought military standby tickets for our return trip directly from Cincinnati to New York.

Pete Connor was an amazing fellow in the words of his roommate Dick. He was tall and slender and an excellent athlete, particularly excelling at running. On the other hand, he hated boxing, maybe because of the large target presented by his nose! He had a memorable profile because of a large nose, which capped a large mouth. He was given the nickname of "Condor" partly because of a play on his last name as well as his profile. In addition to athletics, Pete had a remarkably sharp mind, able to retain a multitude of facts on many different subjects, which made him a natural for the Academy debate team. He also had a sarcastic, funny sense of humor, and didn't suffer fools well.

His sister, Lizz, claimed that Pete could be a party all by himself, able to tell a story and play all of the parts with the appropriate accents. One time he low-crawled into a dress store where she was working just to scare her. She claimed that he read the encyclopedia from cover to cover so Pete was never at a loss for words. On one occasion his date told him that she didn't kiss on a first date; his response was: "How about the last?" He was a quintessential Army brat, always with a hand out to make new friends. Lizz said that he was funny and outrageous, once taking cat food to a party as an appetizer and was commended for his choice. In her words, "He was smart, clever, and maddening all in one. He is so missed."

During the fall of our first class year, Pete chose Infantry branch and volunteered to go to Vietnam as an initial assignment. He wanted to go to the 1st Cavalry division, then on the cutting edge of Army organization and tactics as the first air mobile division. His dad, now a brigadier general, swore Pete and several classmates into the Army as second lieutenants immediately after the graduation ceremony. Pete, Dick McClelland, and other classmates reported to Ft. Benning for the Infantry Officer's Basic Course, Airborne, and Ranger schools, and the two of them went on to Ft. Campbell, Kentucky for a short assignment, and then left on the same day for Vietnam, Pete to the 1st Cav Division and Dick to the 4th Infantry Division. One day, Dick was on his battalion firebase when a secure call came in directing him to report to Cam Rahn Bay to escort the body of a lieutenant from 1/12 Cavalry back to the US. The name of the person he'd be escorting was First Lieutenant Pete Connor. Dick remembered that he "went berserk," throwing something against a wall and scaring everyone in the tactical operations center (TOC), to the point that his battalion commander had to calm him down. Dick remembered this escort duty as the hardest thing he had ever done.

He rode home on a C141 full of flag draped caskets, arriving at Dover Air Force Base where all casualties are welcomed home, even today, and prepared for shipment to their home of record. He somehow made it to the Connor quarters at Ft. Belvoir, where he met with them and his parents. For the burial service at West Point, Dick presented the folded flag to Mrs. Connor but was so overcome with emotion that he couldn't say anything—just presented her the flag, saluted, and backed off. Since that day, on all of his return visits to West Point, he has visited Pete's grave.

Classmate Bruce Brown was also very close with Pete. "His death shook me up more than anything that happened before or since. In a school that produced leaders, there was one of my friends who stood out. Peter Connor was a bright light among many bright lights. He was a fabulous friend. As an example, I was competing for the Brigade Triathlon Championship and Pete actually watched the final event, which was a 200-yard swim. Now I cannot imagine a more boring spectator sport than a 200-yard swim as part of a triathlon! But he was there. Later I asked him to write the essay about me for the yearbook. I should have it framed and put on the wall. I asked him 'Pete, who is this guy? Doesn't sound much like me.' But to Pete, it was me."

At one point between cow and firstie years during a two-week training course, Bruce suggested that it would be easy to substitute vodka for mouthwash by coloring it green and adding some peppermint flavor. Pete, however, counseled against that idea saying that any tactical officer (TAC) would catch that easily. He was proven right a few days later when the TAC opened mouthwash bottles during an inspection.

In the spring of 1968, just before graduation, we were allowed some freedom similar to the types enjoyed on civilian campuses. Many of the class visited the officer's club on weekdays, a new and exciting experience. One day there was a notice on the bulletin board informing first classmen that they could only use the club for meals and couldn't drink except with meals. After a classmate ranted to Pete about this for a while Pete replied, "Just relax and let's go to the club for some drinks . . . and an order of french fries."

On another occasion, one of Pete's friends was having problems with the Office of Physical Education (OPE). During Labor Day weekend his friend had a date with a very special lady. But because of having failed some earlier physical training test, the friend was due for remedial training that weekend, which meant he would not have privileges and therefore would not be allowed to have a date. The week before the date, OPE agreed to let his friend take a retest on the mile run, and if he passed, he would be free for the weekend. When his friend reported for the test, he was informed that because this run would not be in combat boots that thirty seconds would be taken off the passing time. While this was happening, Pete and other friends were on the floor of the gym playing basketball. The test was to be run on the elevated track that circled the gym. Before the run started Pete approached the OPE instructor and asked if his group could run as well. That request was approved, and the run was conducted with three classmates in front, one on either side of the one being tested, and three behind, at a pace set by Pete. With the help and pressure from classmates, the run was a success. The guy in trouble had a great date that weekend and wound up marrying the young lady in January 1969.

Another classmate, Dan Limbaugh, was in the same Beast squad as Pete, and admired him a lot as he did so well in everything thrown at them. After Beast they went their separate ways and didn't run into each other again. However, Pete left such a memory with Dan that he remarked, "One of my regrets from West Point is being so wrapped up in myself and just getting by and not valuing friendships and continuing to cultivate them."

Dan was reminded of Pete in a stark way several years later, "I was in the lobby at the JAG [judge advocate general] School around 1979. About ten feet from me stood a man that looked exactly like Pete Connor chatting with another officer! Chills ran down my back as I thought maybe I had heard wrong, and he wasn't killed after all. As I got closer, I realized it wasn't him, but I knew it had to be a younger brother. I went up to him, introduced myself, and said 'You're Pete Connor's brother.' He was. I could tell even ten years after Pete's death he was still grieving. I got the idea that Pete was a number of years older, and that his brother worshiped the ground Pete walked on."

John Hathaway spent time with Pete between West Point and Vietnam. They were in the same infantry battalion, and because of officer shortages, both commanded companies. They became very close, spending their duty days together, and most evenings at the O club with other classmates. John spoke for Pete at a memorial ceremony held at Fort Benning and met Pete's brother there. He was told that their father, a brigadier general on the major general's list, retired shortly after Pete was killed.

David Schulte might have been the last of the class of '68 to see and talk with Pete. David was a field artilleryman, and after seven months of walking with the infantry as a forward observer, was assigned to a firing battery of the 1st Cavalry Division on a firebase named LZ Grant near Tay Ninh. Pete arrived on the firebase as a platoon leader in the company assigned as base defense for a week or so before going back into the jungle. One night they sat in David's bunker listening to an Army football game on Armed Forces Network; David had hooked a transistor radio to a slice of tactical radio battery. Within days of that experience Pete was killed while on patrol. David remembered, "It was a terrible loss of a young and bright officer with a lifetime in front of him. I will always remember him."

An even more poignant story about Pete's last day was related by classmate Jon Dodson, who served in the same company with Pete. They had both joined the company in July of '69 as platoon leaders; Pete had first platoon, *Death Wing*, and Jon commanded the third. When Pete was killed on November 4, just off LZ Grant, Jon had just returned from medical treatment for a wound and was in the company HQ. A new lieutenant had taken command of his third platoon for him. When Pete was killed, Jon went out to take command of his platoon. Jon's own words best describe what happened:

> His men adored him. He was a common-sense combat leader. Fearless in firefights. Led by example. Stood up for his men. Worked well together with the other platoon leaders. He was killed doing a very dangerous act that he wouldn't let any of his men do—but which had to be done. He knew it was extremely dangerous but didn't want to risk the lives of any of his men, so he did it himself. Hence, the Silver Star for running across an open area under withering fire to neutralize an NVA position that had the company pinned down. Even though shot multiple times, he was able to neutralize the NVA threat. About six or seven NVA were in that position. He killed most of them and dispersed the rest—they ran off. He finally died of his wounds at that location.

From Pete's Silver Star citation awarded for his actions on that last day, while serving as a platoon leader with Company D, 1st Battalion (Airmobile), 12th Cavalry:

Shortly after moving from their night defensive position, the lead element of company D came under heavy automatic and small arms fire. The squad leader of the lead squad was critically wounded during the initial contact and the remainder of the squad was pinned down. First Lieutenant Connor quickly organized and led a platoon of men to assault the enemy position. He repeatedly exposed himself to the enemy fire so the assault on the enemy could be accomplished. He personally killed one North Vietnamese soldier, before being mortally wounded, which led to the routing of the insurgent force.

This story is a common thread running through lives of those from '68. Leading from the front, selfless service, putting oneself in danger to protect their men. What produces young men like this? What causes them to rise above personal fear and perform such heroic deeds? When thinking about this and pondering the experience, I believe that the answer is clear and definite: Duty! Honor! Country! Those three hallowed words molded young American men into something truly special, someone able to rise above the situation and personal safety considerations and perform acts of courage that one could never have envisioned.

As stated in this book in earlier sections, there is no finer tribute for a combat leader than the words of those he led. The following was posted by one of Pete's soldiers, Dave "Danny Duffer" Clay on The Wall of Faces:

LT Peter Connor—My friend and my brother-in-arms. I was a squad leader and point man when you came out into 'the bush' to replace LT Hawkins as 1st platoon leader, 'Death Wing' D 1-12 1st Air Cav. Even though you were a West Point grad, you knew that you were green and you wanted to learn the life of a 'grunt' in 'Nam from the 'hard dudes' like me and 'Tinker Bell' (Dale Felder). I immediately took a liking to you and I am proud to say that I helped to 'square you away'. I remember the talks we had about the war (you were gung-ho and I had come to believe it was pointless). One of my fondest memories was sitting next to you on the floor of a Huey chopper as we approached a flooded field during the monsoon season. It was a combat assault mission and you jumped ahead of me as the chopper hovered over the water. When you hit the ground and I saw the water up to your neck I froze on the chopper. You were about eight inches taller than me and I knew that if I jumped, I would probably drown. Finally, the door gunner kicked me in the ass and I hit the water and then the ground below. Turned out, you were on your knees. We both got a good laugh out of that one. I had just left the field for a rear job when I got the news that you had been killed. I cried my eyes out (as I am doing now) and felt so guilty that I wasn't with you. I thought that maybe, somehow, if I was there it wouldn't have happened. I wrote a letter to your fiancée' and told her what a good soldier you were and a good friend, as well. I hope that you are in a better place and that God is watching over you. Rest in peace, my 'Death Wing' comrade. Love, Dave.

What else can be said?

Dick McClelland, one of Pete's West Point roommates, was present at the dedication of an area in the new Infantry Museum dedicated to Pete's father's unit in World War II with the Connor kids. His comments describing that event illustrate the incredible emotions that bonds classmates together:

I think often of Pete, but this was overpowering. Pete was taller than me in lots of ways. As an Army brat, he was more mature (though younger), worldly, charismatic, dynamic, and smart. He was following in his father's footsteps. I was ready to pin stars on him when he was a lieutenant. I am grateful that I am friends with Pete's family, grateful that I can see [his brother] Bruce several times a year, grateful for my family, grateful that my pensions allow me to babysit a new generation, travel, and enjoy life. With all the knowledge, wisdom, and perspective that time has given me, one thing certainly would not change. I wouldn't trade my time at West Point and all the ensuing ramifications for anything you could offer.

As a fitting epitaph, Pete's brother Casey posted the following on The Wall of Faces:

Mom and Dad have passed away, but you have seven nephews, one niece and four great nieces (so far). One nephew is named for you, and one is currently a platoon leader in Afghanistan. You would be proud of them all. This year your niece and I will visit the memorial in Washington DC with your classmates. They are loyal to your memory to this day, especially Dick and Bruce. We have never stopped mourning.

Pete is interred in the West Point Cemetery.

The horrible November week was just getting started with Pete's death. Three days after losing him we lost another classmate when James Gaiser was killed on the seventh during an attack on his firebase. November was turning into a pretty grim month for the class. Jim was the seventh lost in six months of combat. He was a classmate that I'd never known or met, to my knowledge, but I learned a lot about him from his sister Carol St. George, as well as from classmates and men who served with him in Vietnam.

Jim and Carol's dad was a minister, and because of this they spent most Saturday nights folding the bulletins for Sunday service, while suffering numerous, "semi-fatal" (to them) paper cuts. By the time that Jim was nine they had visited all of the lower forty-eight states, and then, when he was ten, they went around the world on a preaching mission. The family visited about thirty countries, staying in missions or the homes of church members. Carol remembered that they visited Baguio in the Philippines, Guam, Pearl Harbor, Tokyo, Hong Kong, and India, among other places. Carol remembered incidents like a baby being born on the sidewalk under their window in India, a leper colony, and bodies piled up in the train station in Calcutta where they were left if the family could not afford a funeral. They were both impacted by what they saw and as a result, very thankful that they lived in the United States. Jim graduated from a small high school as a member of a class of nine, changing schools three times from the seventh grade to graduation.

Jim seemed to be physically indestructible, falling off a one-story building on his back and then shouting, "I'm fine!" He loved to swim and excelled in underwater swimming, as he could hold his breath for an inordinate amount of time. He also loved baseball, basketball, and horseshoes. Given the great number of schools he attended, and their small size, he was never able to play on an organized team. Academically he was also phenomenal and excelled in math, especially in calculus, trigonometry, and geometry. One of his high school teachers commented on how brilliant he was, as he used old math formulas that had never been taught to him.

Carol remarked on how close they were, even given the age difference. Jim had a quirky sense of humor, a slow developing smile, and a unique sideways glance. Above all, he was kind and genteel.

Jim received an appointment to West Point from the twenty-eighth Pennsylvania district after graduating from high school in East Washington, Pennsylvania. Jim was remembered by one of his high school classmates, Marion Mahoney, who posted on The Wall of Faces:

> I was thinking about Jim, because our book group is reading *The Sympathizer* which received a Pulitzer and concerns the Vietnam War. I used to walk partway home from East Washington High School with Jim, and I remember him as quiet, polite, and extremely intelligent. We are grateful for his service to our country.

After serving in First New Cadet Company during Beast Barracks, Jim was assigned to Company M-2, and eventually C-4. Classmate Jim Tanski remembered, "Jim Gaiser possessed an out sized character and bonhomie. Uniformly liked by his classmates for his attitude and self-deprecating humor, he fit in well with his company mates."

It was during his last three years at West Point that Jim developed his love of parachuting, joining the sport parachute club during yearling year, and then the Academy Sport Parachuting Team at the beginning of cow year. By the time we graduated, Jim had completed 306 freefall jumps, had earned his D License from the US Parachute Association, and was a member of the 1967–1968 National Collegiate Championship Parachute Team. During our firstie year, he chose Artillery as a branch and volunteered for an initial assignment in Vietnam. His combat tour started on March 4, 1969 and ended with his death some eight months later on November 9 during an enemy attack on FSB Dorie. During this time, he served in the 1st Battalion, 92nd Artillery (Brave Cannons), with the mission of supporting US and ARVN units in the II Corps (Central Highlands) area of South Vietnam.

Classmate and company mate Renata Price remembered Jim:

Jim was always one of my extended circles of friends in M-2/C-4. I remember him most by what Dan Gooding calls his *pixie smile*. I do not recall anything that would dampen has good spirits. But Jim was a solid guy and his heroic behavior and sacrifice in Vietnam comes as no surprise.

Jim and I shared a squad of new cadets during the second detail of Beast Barracks 1966. In the spirit of our M-2 roots, our strategy was to give the new cadets a proper Beast Barracks experience without attempting to be over the top. I recall that the Academy was toning it down a notch or two by that time. Anyway, I recall we fell into a sort of bad guy-good guy routine, with Jim naturally being the good guy.

Jim remained a good friend through the rest of our years together. I recall hearing of his passing and being deeply saddened. It seems that happened while us non-artillery types were still fooling around at schools and waiting to actually join the real Army.

Classmate David Clappier added that both Jim and Dave Sackett, both of company C-4, never took themselves too seriously nor placed their individual ambitions ahead of others; neither of them ever expressed harsh criticisms about any other cadet or officer. "This is a key character trait of a successful combat leader, as both Jim and David obviously were. Furthermore, there is absolutely no doubt that they both took being a cadet and an Army officer quite seriously and obviously made the ultimate sacrifice in the service of their country and West Point," he said.

One of Jim's yearling year roommates, Joe Javorski, had some interesting memories of Jim that really paint a picture of who he was. Jim taught Joe how to sew on buttons and repair rips and seams. To this day, when doing any mending, Joe thinks of his roommate and sends a prayer of remembrance. He also remarked on Jim's hard work and dedication when he experienced trouble with any of the academic departments, showing great pride in his turn-out stars. "He was never discouraged, he passed every [turn-out] test and had a big grin on his face when he returned to the room after taking them."

Jim Gaiser did have one claim to fame that was not duplicated by any other classmate, or probably any other cadet member of the sport parachute club. One day, on a practice jump, Jim exited the aircraft and immediately got into some trouble. There are varying accounts of the cause, either the winds were very high making it difficult to control his chute, or the handle on his reserve caught on something on the way out, causing the reserve to deploy, making it difficult for him to control his descent. As a result, not only did he not land on the drop zone, but he came down in the exercise yard of a maximum-security prison across the Hudson River from West Point.

Joe Javorski, one of his roommates, remembers Jim relating the following description: After he got out of his harness he was arrested and interrogated because the guards thought that he was part of an escape attempt! They did not , at first, believe his story, that he was a West point cadet who had trouble when he exited his aircraft that blew him off course. The authorities called the Academy to verify his identity, and he was released after being asked to sign in and sign out in the visitor logbook. Jim took great delight in retelling this story whenever asked. Whenever we wanted some entertainment, which was hard to come by in those days and under those circumstances, we would ask Jim to tell us *the story* again. Jim would oblige, grinning the whole time and laughing so hard, that at times we would have to tell him to stop laughing so much because he was consuming so much valuable time.

Classmate George Ziots remembered a telling story. After plebe year, when talking with Jim, Jim admitted that he wanted to get into West Point so bad that he had cheated on the eye exam for the incoming physical. Fortunately, this event occurred before he was subject to the Honor Code!

Carol remembered asking her brother why he had volunteered to go to Vietnam as an initial assignment, and his response speaks volumes about Jim's dedication and patriotism: "I've had four years of training, others only basic [training] . . . if I can save one life, it is worth going." He met his fiancé while volunteering at a youth summer camp and was 100 days from his wedding when he was killed.

Fred Tucker may have been the last classmate to see and talk with Jim before his death. While they didn't know each other at West Point, they quickly established a friendship when Jim arrived as a pay officer on Fred's firebase, LZ Schueller, west of An Khe on Highway 19 (in those days pay was done in cash as there was no direct deposit system). They had a great time reminiscing about their time at West Point and had a lot of laughs. Fred commented on Jim's death: "I was devastated when I learned of his death shortly after we met. He was a great guy and will be missed."

Jim was killed on the November 7, 1969, during a heavy attack from NVA forces that included rockets, mortars, and heavy small arms. He had just arrived that day with a tube (artillery piece) from his battery to better support local infantry units. According to Sgt. Gordon Claridge of B Battery, 5th Battalion, 22nd Artillery he had led a "forward raid party of one 175mm gun, fire direction control personnel, and an ammunition supply unit from their base at Ban Me Thuot in the Central Highlands to the newly established firebase near the Cambodian border." When the attack started, one account had him moving from the relative safety of his command bunker as he climbed an observation tower, the most exposed position on the firebase, to better see where the incoming fire was coming from so that he could better coordinate artillery return fire. Exposed, he climbed into that tower despite all of the incoming fire. At the top he had about a three-foot-tall sandbag wall that enclosed the space.

While surveying the area his position took a direct hit, either from a rocket or mortar round, gravely wounding Jim. A nearby medic scaled the ladder and found Jim severely wounded but responsive. The medic bandaged all that he could and got Jim on a medevac the next morning. I don't know if Jim died en route to the evac hospital or after arrival. Jim's loss was a terrible event for his classmates and family. Here again was a classmate who made an incredibly positive impact on all of those who knew him.

Once again, as with so many of our classmates, the tributes from his soldiers mean so much. Again, Sergeant Gordon Claridge, an NCO in Jim's unit, really described the feeling of loss when our classmate was killed when he posted on The Wall of Faces:

I was a sergeant, section chief for a 175mm gun. Jim was our AXO, fire direction officer. We were awake many nights together firing missions in Ban Me Thuot in support of our fellow soldiers. I just wanted to say that he was the finest lieutenant that I ever served under in my 2-1/2 years of military service. He was respected by all who knew him for his character, honesty, sincerity, and thoughtfulness. I had less than a month left on my Vietnam tour when he was taken and his presence, and loss affected my life to this day.

Sergeant Claridge felt so strongly about Jim's death that he also posted the following on Westpoint.org:

In the worst of conditions you could find Jim sharing the burden with his men. On many night fire missions, after laying the guns, he would come down from the aiming tower and stand knee-deep in mud with the rest of the gun crews, often carrying an artillery round or bags of powder to make one man's job easier; or, you could find him climbing onto the water tower to light the diesel fuel so that the men could have a warm shower; or, helping to screw the 1500 pound breach block onto the end of a gun barrel when another hand was needed; or, mediating arguments over who's horseshoe was closer to the peg; or, helping to splice the 20th break in the evening's movie; or, putting his arm around the shoulder of a man who had gotten a not-so-pleasant letter from home; or, just keeping a pot of hot coffee ready in the Fire Direction Center bunker for after the 3am fire mission. Little things that let everyone know that he cared about you and wanted to see you get home in one piece with as little trauma as possible.

We held a memorial for Jim at the main firebase on November 9. Flags in the battery were lowered to half-staff and taps was played over our never-working P/A system, made operational through the all-night effort of the commo section. We, collectively and individually, needed to salute what Jim's life meant to us all. God Bless You, Lieutenant Jim Gaiser.

This feeling of loss was also expressed by one of Jim's soldiers, who posted anonymously on The Wall of Faces:

I was their when lt gaiser was killed terrible day he was a great person.

Words and sentiments like this are the epitome of a warrior's accolade to one of their own. There is no finer tribute than this for a fallen classmate who literally, willingly, sacrificed his life so that his men might live.

I can think of no better way to end this accounting of Jim Gaiser's all-too-short life than with a poem written by Jim's Dad, Dr. James Gaiser, at Carol's request, as an incredible and appropriate eulogy:

LETTERS FROM MY SON

I've been in the Vietnam battle
And heard the mortars explode
I've listened to armored tanks rattle
Down dust and mud mired road.

I've seen the glorious sun rise
From out the horizon's rim
I've seen it set in glory
And also on battles grim.

I've seen strained looks on faces
When the battle was at its height
And pray God in heaven
To keep away the night.
I've heard the XO's praises
And his shout from the bunker, "Well done"
And the cheers from the mud-splattered faces
When our battle was fought and won.
I've fought in the terrible conflict
In times of rain and sun
Yes, I've been across the great Pacific
Through letters from my son.

Jim Gaiser is interred in the West Point Cemetery.

With the tragic loss of Jim Gaiser, the situation in Vietnam did not improve for the class, for only four days later, November 11—Veterans Day, we lost Bill Little, killed in action just twelve days short of his twenty-third birthday. This week of November 1969 was a brutal time for many of us, but particularly tough for the families of the three men that we lost.

Bill was born into a family of service to both community and nation. Bill's father, William (Will) Francis Little Jr. had graduated from Yale and then Rutgers with a law degree. He was working in this field when he enlisted in the Army in 1941. He served in the 20th Armored Division, which was one of three US divisions that liberated the Dachau Concentration Camp. For his service, he earned the rank of captain and a Bronze Star. After the war, he returned to Rahway, New Jersey, where he practiced law for thirty-five years in the firm of Armstrong and Little. In August of '45 he married Mary

Francis West, who had been an Army nurse, and they had one child together—our future classmate Bill.

Bill was called "Will" like his dad, by family and close friends. While growing up he attended a very prestigious school, the Pingry School in Hillsdale, New Jersey, founded in 1861 to offer the students academic and personal excellence. Pingry's students established an honor code and were responsible for making it an integral part of their life. In 1960, Bill's mom passed away; he had just turned fourteen. He continued to visit her family in Mississippi in the summer to keep those relationships alive.

While at the Pingry School, Bill played football, lacrosse, and especially excelled on the swim team. He enjoyed the Jersey shore, the family's beach house, water skiing, and his dog Peppy. In short, he led the *all American life* of a young male of that era. While a junior, his dad married Joyce Hulbert Simmen and the family moved from Rahway to Mountainside, New Jersey. One of his high school classmates, Emily Lyons, had a clear memory of Bill, which she posted on The Wall of Faces:

> Will Little and his family lived near our family in Mountainside, New Jersey. Will was somewhat older than my sisters and I, and we were somewhat in awe of him, particularly after he went to West Point. During middle school, my older sister, Nancy, visited West Point on a class trip; Will showed her around with her friends, which was thrilling for all of the girls, as Nancy later reiterated the story. During Christmas, we visited Will and his family at their annual tree trimming party. Will was unfailingly courteous and interested in what we were doing in our lives.
>
> My hope is that after all of these years, his family has made their peace with his untimely death. He was a special young man. As my dad once said if he'd been fortunate enough to have a son, he would have liked him to be like Will Little.

Bill Little entered West Point with the class of '68. On the twelfth of the same month, Bill's half-sister Joyce Allison was born. He probably met her for the first time when he went home for Christmas leave in 1964.

Bill was assigned to company F-1 for all four years, thought by some to have been the toughest on plebes. The class of '68 spent the year in the "old" attrition form of plebe year, where upper classmen did their best to instill pride and professionalism through stress and hardship, and to identify those who could not perform under pressure or duress. The personal qualities of Duty, Honor, Country were deeply ingrained in each cadet to handle the stress of the Academy and ultimately the stress of leading fellow Americans in combat. Reviewing his record after graduation, there is no doubt that Bill was well prepared.

While participating in intramural sports for Company F-1 like soccer and triathlon, Bill also joined the cadet mountaineering club, skied at West Point's Victor Constant Ski Area, and attended Airborne School one summer while on leave.

Classmate John Benson remembered: "My recollection of Bill's overall athletic skills comes from competing against him in Triathlon and being jealous of how he was always so consistent in all three events."

Being a bit of a Renaissance man, Bill also appreciated the arts, like photography, photojournalism, and stage production. He took photos for the Army Athletic Association and worked on the staff of our yearbook. When it came time, Bill selected Infantry as his branch and volunteered for Vietnam. Bill also bought himself a white Corvette Stingray with a blue interior.

Victor Farrugia remembered Bill's commitment to becoming an infantry officer: "When Bill selected Infantry, the North Vietnamese Army and the Viet Cong had just launched the massive campaign of surprise attacks known as the Tet Offensive of 1968. There were heavy casualties on both sides; the US Military Assistance Command Vietnam called for more US troops, and the life expectancy of an infantry lieutenant in combat certainly did not improve. None of that would deter Bill. He would be Infantry."

Bill attended the Basic Course and Ranger School at Ft. Benning before departing for Ft. Campbell, Kentucky and the 5th Battalion, 3rd Infantry. While there, he became close friends with Don Bratton, also an infantry officer in the 5th/3rd Infantry, who later posted on The Wall of Faces:

Bill, we met at Ft. Campbell, Kentucky as we served with
the 5/3 Infantry. We developed a friendship and you were in
my wedding party. You provided the sabers from West Point
that we used for my military wedding.

You were a good and caring man. It did not surprise me
when I learned your actions to save your men. I think about
you often. You will never be forgotten.

In the spring of '69, Bill departed Ft. Campbell for home and
a short leave before heading to Vietnam. While there he sold his
beloved Corvette. En route, Bill attended the Army's three-week
Jungle Warfare School in Panama, arriving in Vietnam on May 13.
Bill was assigned to another battalion of The Old Guard, this time the
2nd Battalion, 3rd Infantry, part of the 199th Light Infantry Brigade.
Since he was promoted to first lieutenant on June 5, one year from
graduation, he asked to lead the battalion's recon platoon. However,
he needed some combat experience before that assignment, so he
was given command of 2nd Platoon, C Company and quickly gained
the required experience while impressing his company commander,
retired Lieutenant Colonel Michael Lanning, who wrote in his book
A Company Commander's Journal:

I met Bill Little when he joined Charlie Company, 2nd
Battalion, 3rd Infantry Regiment of the 199th Light Infantry
Brigade as its second platoon leader in early June 1969. He
soon became the best friend I made in Vietnam. Bill, easy
going and laid back, got along well with his fellow officers
and was well liked and respected by his soldiers. I tested his
sense of humor shortly after meeting him telling him that in
College Station we considered West Point to be the Texas
A&M of the north. He laughed.

On one logistics day—to resupply units with ammunition, food,
and mail—Bill's platoon had a visitor: Private First Class Jim Hardy,
a combat artist in Army Artist Team 9. The Army's Combat Artist
Program had soldier-artists create pictorial records of activities in
the Vietnam War. Bill Little became part of that history. James Hardy

posted his sketch of Bill Little on The Wall of Faces. He remarked:

> Hardly a day passes that I do not think of Lt. Little, partially out of guilt I guess, as I do with so many others. I could see that he was very much respected by his men. He didn't say much when I sketched him, guess he had other more important things on his mind, but he dutifully held his pose for the 5 or 10 minutes it took me, a lowly PFC, to sketch him.

In August Bill developed a severe foot infection and was sent to the 6th Convalescent Center in Cam Rahn Bay. While there, he met classmate John Benson, who was being treated for a shrapnel wound in his shoulder. Both had served in West Point's Company F-1 for four years, and Bill and John were two members of the class of '68 to be awarded the Distinguished Service Cross for extraordinary heroism in Vietnam.

Upon return to the field, Bill initially returned to Charlie Company and then was given his dream job, command of the battalion's recon platoon, known as Echo Recon because they were part of E Company. These were small units, distinct from Ranger companies and long-range reconnaissance patrol teams, who worked directly for their maneuver battalions. They combined stealth, firepower, and independent operations to find, fix, and fight (when necessary) enemy formations. Many times, the mission was to find and fight the enemy while calling in major reinforcements to destroy them—classic search and destroy operations. Sometimes the mission was strictly reconnaissance, and the unit was to avoid combat whenever possible. In most infantry battalions, new recon platoon leaders were normally required to have three to six months experience in the field before taking command.

In the fall of '69, Recon operated from the battalion's rear area at their basecamp, FSB Blackhorse, originally built by the 11th Armored Cavalry Regiment. Blackhorse was well constructed and defended and offered a secure area for rest and refitting between combat missions. During this period, the 199th was responsible for security north and west of Saigon. While at Blackhorse, one of his soldiers, Sergeant Pat O'Regan remembered: "First Lieutenant Little sat with his soldiers at mealtime. He was solid, at ease with himself, friendly, good natured but in command. His leadership was smooth, flawless, and beyond question; he had the utmost respect of his men. There was an easy relationship between Lt. Little and the men of Echo Recon."

Bill's final mission began on November 10. Recon was a little understrength that day, with only seventeen soldiers present for duty. According to one of the recon soldiers, Private First Class Dave Prescott: "We know that there were several more Recon guys on roster at that time, but with diligent research of Pat O'Regan's journal notes and the combined memories of several, we think that for various reasons many guys missed this mission."

In the late afternoon of November 10, because of enemy activity developed by intelligence sources, Recon lifted off from Blackhorse to their preselected landing zone. Pfc. Prescott, who was 2nd Platoon's point man from October '69 to March '70, recalled: "I knew my squad was taking the lead that day and therefore knew I was going to be on point. I remember the heavy prep to the LZ, especially to the corner that we were headed into."

Being point man was a critical and dangerous job. He was the lead man in the formation while moving, normally a little ahead of the main body. It was his job, and that of the *slack man* right behind him, to keep the platoon moving on the required azimuth while being super observant in order to detect enemy soldiers, booby traps, or mines. It took a man with special nerves, skills, and powers of observation to fill this job successfully; every man's life, and ultimately the accomplishment of the mission, depended on the skills of the point man. I had two such soldiers in my recon platoon and rotated them as required. The job was stressful and very tiring.

The recon platoon for 2/3 was inserted into their LZ following a heavy prep by Cobra gunships firing high explosive (HE) rockets. Their mission, upon landing, was to locate the enemy and then fix him in position while calling for reinforcements. Since it was late afternoon when they were inserted, I imagine they went to ground for a while, maintaining strict noise discipline, to see if there was anyone else around. Then, at twilight, they would have very quietly moved into a night defensive position, maintaining strict noise and light discipline. They probably set up two-man positions so as to provide all-around security and then ate cold C rations or LRRPs (an acronym for dehydrated rations issued to long range reconnaissance patrols), again ensuring that they made no noise or showed any light. It would be a long night. While I don't know that anything in this paragraph is exactly what happened on that evening, it is what I've done in similar situations and seems a likely approximation of what they would have experienced.

The next morning, they probably moved out at first light, moving deeper into the jungle in search of the NVA; by early afternoon, they must have found what they were looking for. All of a sudden, they took some heavy fire; Recon returned fire and formed a tight defensive position; they had found what turned out to be the 274th NVA Regiment. Bill called for artillery and gunship support; they were so close to the NVA that shrapnel whirred through the trees and hit among his own guys. This enemy did not run but stayed to fight from well-constructed bunkers. Twice Bill paused his fire support to bring in dustoff birds to extract two wounded soldiers. They were now down to fifteen effectives. According to Dave Prescott: "Dustoff choppers picked up two wounded soldiers, Bill Mobley and George Young, by dropping a cable through the jungle tree tops. The operation required a lot of ground cover suppressive fire by Recon to keep the enemy from shooting down the dustoff birds. After all that, the enemy still did not leave or pull back."

Sgt. Pat O'Regan recounted, as if talking to Bill:

Under your direction, Lieutenant, the artillery fire froze the enemy in the bunkers and gunships raked the area with Gatling guns and rockets. Time is lost in combat, but the fight surely went on for hours. We were low on ammo and whipped on morale. But you gave no hint of leaving the area. A third man was wounded; his left arm almost severed by enemy fire. Then everything became quiet, eerily and ominously quiet. "All right," you said, "everybody hold your fire. We're going forward to check out the area." You and three men left the shelter of the bamboo mound, Lieutenant, and ventured into an open area, two men to the right flank, you and one man to the left. There was a sudden barrage of enemy fire. . .

Part of Bill's Distinguished Service Cross citation recorded what happened next:

> He suddenly saw an enemy soldier aiming at his companion. Lieutenant Little pushed the unaware soldier to the ground and, in doing so, was seriously wounded. As Lieutenant Little fell to the ground, he fired his weapon and killed the enemy soldier. Almost immediately, Lieutenant Little was subjected to a burst of hostile fire and was mortally wounded.

The NVA were well armed and protected by their bunkers, and significantly outnumbered the now thirteen men of Recon. Unable to successfully neutralize the enemy forces in order to recover Bill's body, they were forced to fall back and await reinforcements. According to Dave Prescott:

> I think all of us knew we would be going back to get Lt. Little, but we needed more resources to make that happen. In the days that followed, we went back with hundreds of Old Guard troops from two line companies, an ARVN company, and three Sheridan tanks and seven APCs [armored personnel carriers] from the 17th Armored Cav. on the ground to help us. It still took two days to clear the bunker complex. So, thirteen of us was just not enough, even if we would have had the ammo. And I have to believe our leader, Lt. Little, would have agreed.

On November 13, the Battalion Commander, Lt. Col. Burn Loeffke, was on the ground near the battlefield, with Recon as his security, while he supervised the effort to recover Bill's body. Bill's company commander, Capt. Michael Lanning, described that mission:

> On November 14, an infantry company accompanied by three tanks and seven armored carriers arrived at the abandoned bunker complex. Sweeping through the massive bunker system, Little's half-buried body was soon located along with many enemy dead. Underneath his body were

eight empty M16 magazines with six more fully loaded, a testament to his heroic stand against the enemy.

This account is very telling because it indicates that Bill, although grievously wounded, did not die immediately, he continued to fight on alone for an unknown period of time until the severity of his wounds took his life; eight empty magazines under his body, that's a lot of shooting. One can only surmise that he was trying to protect the withdrawal of his guys. Again, a classmate who rose above the immediate situation and sacrificed himself to protect one of his soldiers, and then fought on, although severely wounded, to protect the remnants of his command. We can only marvel at the bravery of such men and count ourselves as lucky and blessed to have been able to share some time with them. Duty! Honor! Country!

Dave Prescott gave more information about that enemy bunker complex:

> Cpt. Lanning and Bravo Company investigated the bunker complex for four to five days from Nov. 13–17 and reported that there were seventy-four bunkers that the army engineers blew up, and maybe a few more that were already blown up by artillery or mortars. He estimated that the enemy soldiers probably numbered over two hundred, of which thirty-three were found dead, and there were lots of blood trails from the countless wounded. And then there was the high ranking dead NVA guy that was dug up two or three times that Lanning thought might have been the commander of the 274th NVA Regiment. [It was not uncommon to dig up freshly buried enemy dead in an effort to identify high ranking personnel or recover valuable documents]. The 274th NVA Reg. had lots of men, lots of guns and ammo [Lanning recorded finding thousands of rifle rounds, RPGs, rifles, pistols, grenades, rockets, and other equipment that had been left behind] and many well-constructed bunkers from which to fight. They had the advantage that day, and Lt. Little, and our three wounded men, paid the price. But

the Vietnam War was all about *body count*, so maybe some felt a thirty-three to one kill ratio was worth it. But not me!"

First Lieutenant William F. Little III gave his life for his country— but of more immediate concern to him, I'm sure—for his men on Veteran's Day, November 11, 1969. He died leading his men in fierce combat and distinguished himself as a true hero. Sgt. Pat O'Regan has written extensively about Vietnam, and about our classmate Bill:

How should one view such a leader? As reckless and foolhardy? He was not. Though it simply must be the case that casualties are higher among the brave. As tragic? No, he was driven, but doing what he loved to do and doing it well. He would lead in the face of the enemy. With a little luck, he would have lived. As heroic? Yes, certainly that. But, likely, a lot of officers—West Point graduates, included—would have done what Recon was meant to do: "Okay, we found them. Let's get out of here and drop the artillery and air strikes on them." What was Lt. Little trying to accomplish in staying to fight against what was surely a large bunker complex?

Some of us groused at the lieutenant's obvious passion for battle, but to this day I am proud to have served under such an officer, such a soldier. If the enemy, outnumbering us perhaps five to one, had charged and we all had been killed, how would that change my feeling? From the hereafter, I would be proud.

Lt. Little heard the summons to battle more than others. His summons was irresistible, perhaps intoxicating, and certainly risky and dangerous. He scorned the risk, perhaps scoffed at it, and certainly did not pay attention to it in his battle-beset brain.

Rest in peace, Sir.

Now a retired major general, Bernard "Burn" Loeffke, who was Bill's battalion commander, still has clear memories of Bill. He had been an instructor at West Point during our time there and had Bill as a student in his Russian language classes. Then Lt. Col. Loeffke had given Bill the job of Recon Platoon leader. On November 14 he personally helped recover and carry Bill's body from the bunker complex. He reflected: "Bill Little is etched in my memories. It is not often that a commander has an officer who had been his student and then killed in combat. Bill Little exemplified true leadership by sacrificing himself while saving others. *To be remembered is to live.*"

The New Jersey's Vietnam Veterans Memorial Foundation features Bill Little. On their website is a letter from Lt. Col. Loeffke to Bill's parents:

> *The circumstances surrounding the death of your son speak for themselves. He gave his life in order to save the life of another. There is no more noble cause or greater sacrifice. While under heavy fire from enemy positions, Bill observed an enemy soldier about to shoot one of his men. In a manner above and beyond the call of duty, Bill pushed the soldier out of the way. He moved from his own position to engage the enemy soldier. The enemy soldier had his weapon positioned and was first to fire.*
>
> *The men of his platoon, the battalion reconnaissance platoon, had great respect for him as a leader and a man. Several wept openly after his death, and all of them asked me to pass condolences on to you.*

That Christmas Lt. Col. Loeffke wrote another letter to Mr. and Mrs. Little;

> *On my last day with the battalion, one of the last persons who met with me was a young specialist by the name of McKinney who said he was going to make the Army his career; that Lt. Little having saved his life had given him a mission—and that was to become an Army officer and attempt to do as well as Lt. Little and try to pay back a debt owed to Bill.*

Bill had designated half of his estate for an annual award to be presented to the captain of the ski team. On June 8, 1971, Bill's half-sister Allison presented the first William F. Little III Award. In 2014,

The Pingry School's class of '64 presented their fiftieth reunion gift of $72,000 to create the Class of 1964 William F. Little III Memorial Vietnam History Room, which was dedicated on May 18, 2018.

In 2016 the Pingry boys' varsity golf team participated in the Folds of Honor Military Tribute Program to honor Bill Little. They purchased two specially embroidered golf bags displaying *First Lieutenant William F. Little US Army*. One was presented to Allison, the other was auctioned off to raise money for Folds of Honor and was purchased by one of Bill's classmates. Bill's hometown of Mountainside, New Jersey recognized Bill by naming a quiet and elegant residential street of family homes *Little Court*.

Bill is interred in the West Point Cemetery. Annually West Point conducts an Inspiration to Serve tour for yearlings as they reach their halfway point before taking their Affirmation to Serve oath at the beginning of cow year. Bill Little's tombstone is a stopping point for the tour.

Sgt. Pat O'Regan provided this heartfelt final tribute to a fallen warrior and hero:

> Some people are designed and built—mentally, mostly— for their professions. They pursue their work with passion, pushing to the limit what people in their profession do. These men and women are shining exemplars of the human race. We owe them. But it goes without saying that such an approach to one's work is a risky proposition in certain professions, and soldiering, of course, is foremost among them. Soldiering requires that soldiers put their lives on the line when called upon to do so. Some soldiers hear that call more clearly and commandingly than others. Lt. Little was an officer of this kind to a very high degree.

After Bill's death the pain for the class of '68 paused for a few months. The last seven months of 1969 had been a horrific time, with eight of our classmates giving their lives for their country. We all knew before graduation that most of us would go to war, that we would *see the elephant* and would have to answer that age-old question of how would we react when the bullets started coming up-range. Eight of our number had given the ultimate answer, and in every case had died to protect others.

John 15:13 says: "Greater love hath no man than this: that a man lay down his life for his friends."

Jim with squad of New Cadets, Beast Barracks 1966

Pete modeling
his profile

Bill with sister Allison
and cousin Elsa Little
1968

Pete, on left, on Division
Stoops, before a parade,
1968

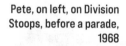

Jim with his parents
after commissioning,
June 5, 1968

Sketch of Bill in the field

Second Lieutenant Bill Little

R · JAMES A JACKSON
· WILLIAM F LITTLE III
ER · ROBERT L OAKS

"THE EMBRACE"

By Pat O'Regan, Sergeant, Recon, 2nd Battalion, 3rd Infantry,
199th Light Infantry Brigade, 1969–1970
[One of Bill Little's soldiers]

THE EMBRACE

The cold embrace of death
Stirs the heart to greater life.
They do more with their time,
Who sense they have less of it.
When death trod the jungle trails
With us at war, we paid attention,
And were never again the same.

How can these many years
Of routine living compare:
The dying enemy soldier
Tossed a grenade you had to throw back,
Like Joe DiMaggio—
To get it away from your men—
Not enough time, though,
We should have died together.
A Medal of Honor for you,
But it was a dud. That's life.

Two men sit on a listening post,
Just off a well-trod jungle trail,
Each feeling death's cold embrace.
The little pile of torn leaves and twigs
Grows steadily between the legs of one.
An enemy squad passes by in stately view,
AK's ready, but not one looked left
Or fired a burst—that's all—two bodies then.
We could see them . . .

Fire fights . . . The blast of noise, the frantic shouts,
The urgent scramble, every nerve fiber alight,
Placing shots, desperate to see and kill
The man about to kill you, the body and the mind
Twisted to the highest pitch, finally, quiet.
Numbness and exhaustion, staring into the jungle,
Mouth agape, drenched in sweat.

Forget? Through all the years
Of routine living—careers and families—
The searing moments of war are never forgotten.
Death leaves its stamp on the soul, indelible:
Awaiting the onslaught at Gettysburg,
The order to charge at Belleau Wood,
Or suffering in the Ardennes, at Chosin Reservoir
Or in the jungles of Vietnam.

Ah, men, brothers in arms,
The bond between us is indelible, too.
We each understand the others,
We've all been in the same cauldron,
And bear the same burns.
Let us live like mad, loving to the hilt,
As a tribute to those we left behind.
Let us be as just, tolerant, and peace-loving
As the Almighty made us to be.

VIETNAM: JANUARY THROUGH MARCH 1970

Donald Robert Colglazier Jeffry Randal Riek Harry Ellis Hayes

The month of December 1969 was a quiet one for our class, helped in part by the traditional stand-down over the holidays. After the mayhem of November, the class needed a break. While combat operations slowed down, they didn't stop entirely; my recon platoon started a new mission on Christmas Day. United States Army Vietnam (USARV) observed a cease fire on Christmas, the bad guys not so much, and with a week of minimal operations over the New Year's holiday, it was a time for our combat forces to rest and refit. Unfortunately, the enemy did the same, taking advantage of our inaction to move back into contested areas, and to resupply their units with men and material coming off the Ho Chi Minh Trail. My battalion moved out of our forward firebase and moved to the division rear near Pleiku a few days later, where the guys enjoyed five days free from combat and work details over New Years.

With the renewal of combat operations after the holidays, '68 began to pay a price once again. My one-time roommate Don Colglazier was the first of our ranks to be lost in the new year.

The tragic story of Don's death was relayed to me in a phone call with A-1 classmate Will Rorie, who was the last to see Don before he was ambushed and killed on January 18, 1970. Will was serving with the 173rd Airborne Brigade on LZ English, to whom Don's cavalry squadron was assigned, with Don's platoon securing a bridge on one of the major highways in the area. On the eighteenth of January, Don went to Will's location to visit with him and early in the afternoon he made plans to return to his troops. Just about that time, Will's battalion commander walked by and Don was introduced. The commander told Will and Donny to attend the afternoon tactical briefing. They couldn't understand why it was so important for them to be there, as that requirement would surely make Don's return to the bridge more perilous because the enemy usually controlled that area at night. However, they dutifully went, even though there was no tactical reason for either to be there. At the end of the meeting, the commander publicly berated Don because he had gone by the bridge earlier that day and had observed some of Don's soldiers in incomplete uniforms. After the butt chewing, as Will and Don left the briefing, it was getting to be late afternoon. Will tried to talk Don into spending the night at Will's location, but Don was adamant about getting back to his soldiers, Don called for his jeep and departed. Along the way the vehicle was ambushed, and Don and his driver were killed. To this day, it's difficult for Will to talk about this event, as he feels guilty because he wasn't able to talk Don into waiting until the road would have been safer the next morning.

I first met Don Colglazier in July of 1964 in Beast Barracks when we were both assigned to the same squad in the First Platoon, First New Cadet Company; we lived in the old First Division of Central Area. Don was a North Carolina boy from a small town near the coast named Havelock, and although he had been a tremendous athlete, he appeared to be somewhat awkward in his transition to new cadet life. He had trouble bracing and marching, and somewhat reminded one of Gomer Pyle. This, however, proved to be a very false first impression, as Don was extremely intelligent, going on to wear stars on his collar for the last three years of school, which denoted the fact that he stood in the top five percent of the class academically. He did, however, develop an ailment known as brace palsy during Beast that created a lot of pain and spasms in his neck. As I remember, he had a medical excuse from bracing for a couple of weeks, making him the envy of our classmates.

He did have problems with some of the military side of Beast. One area of great consternation to our squad leader was his difficulty in properly putting on a parade uniform that required cross-belts. His were typically twisted, with his cartridge box hanging halfway down his butt, and he was constantly getting the attention of numerous upper classmen when he fell out for formation, making the squad leader look bad to his classmates. One day our squad leader came to my room after dinner and braced me up against the wall. "Smackhead," he said, "You are now responsible to ensure that Mr. Colglazier is properly squared away before you fall out for formation. You will make sure that his uniform is correct in every detail. If you fail, I'll run your ass out of West Point, do you understand?" Naturally, "Yes sir!" was my only reply. The next day I talked with Don about my conversation with our squad leader and told him that at the first opportunity, I'd come to his room and help him with the basics; I'd spit-shine his shoes and shine his brass while teaching him how to do it properly. We then agreed that for every formation, particularly for parades, Don would come down early to my room so that I could make sure that his uniform was squared away before we'd go to formation together. Don worked hard to conquer the uniform requirements and he never again had a problem in that part of Beast. I also worked with him on marching and the arm swing requirement, which he also had some issues with that made this star athlete appear to be pretty uncoordinated and led to his nickname of "The Bird."

During the next four years, we maintained a close relationship and roomed together once. Don was always there to help me with the academic issues caused by my long absences to Walter Reed Army Medical Center in Washington, DC.

As our graduation and June Week neared, we all talked about plans and the dates who'd come up to share those special events. At that point I learned that Don didn't have a date, and I began to think back over the years and didn't remember ever seeing him with a young lady. I had a sister who was about three years my junior and who, I learned from my mom, was very upset with me because I'd never lined her up with a cadet date. So, being the sharp guy that I am, I had a brilliant idea: I would arrange a June Week date for Don with my sister, which would help Don out and get me back in good graces with my sister and family. They both agreed and both had a tremendous June Week experience. I assume that they got along well because one night when I pulled into the motel where my folks were staying, I saw Don's Barracuda already parked there, and that huge rear window was all fogged up!

When I learned of Don's death more than thirty years ago, I became physically sick. I hadn't been able to attend any class reunions or get-togethers for years because of spending so much time in Japan, so I had minimal contact with classmates for quite a while. I don't remember ever hearing that he had been killed in action. I don't remember how I first heard about it, but it was a tremendous shock, I wasn't able to do anything for a couple of days. I do remember shedding a lot of tears. After moving to North Carolina sixteen years ago for our retirement, I discovered the state's Vietnam Veterans' Memorial at a rest stop on I-85 north of Charlotte. I stopped one time to check it out and found a very well done and respectful wall with memorial bricks that had the names of all of the North Carolinians who had been lost. As I was walking along the wall, not thinking of anyone in particular, I experienced what felt almost like a slap across my face. I looked over, right at Don Colglazier's name! I guess I'd forgotten that he would be on that memorial. It was a very emotional moment. Now, every time we drive I-85 we stop so that I can visit the memorial and say hi to Don. Over the past few years, I've become close to several of Don's family because of our get-togethers every five years at The Wall. The last time I saw them, his sister Joan gave me a remembrance that I treasure, the *USMA 68* North Carolina license plate off of that infamous Barracuda. It is now on my military jeep golf cart. Don, I miss you and think of you all the time. What a life you could have had!

And what a life he lived during those few short years before his death. In communications with all of his siblings, it's very evident that Don had both the normal and not-so-normal experiences of a kid growing up in a military family. His dad was a US Marine, and his mother had also been a Marine until she married and found herself pregnant and was discharged, as it was against Marine Corps policy in those days to allow pregnant women to serve. He had three sisters and a brother, and they grew up in various places across the country. Along the way, Don excelled as a student and athlete. He had a lot of adventures both good and bad.

One of the bad ones occurred in 1955 in Solomons, Maryland one day while playing with his sister Carolyn, or Candy. They were evidently playing a game involving combat and Don found a large and heavy stick that he brandished as a weapon. A garden of tall, orange day lilies that their mom had carefully planted in the front of their house became the enemy. The two of them took turns beating back the enemy, who fell in great numbers. They were devastated when their mom came out to stop them, and they saw her cry for the first time they could remember when she saw the carnage they had inflicted on her treasured flowers. Even with the obvious gravity of this situation, only an apology was requested; there was no other punishment.

In 1961 his father was assigned to Okinawa on an unaccompanied tour, and the family moved to Wyalusing, Pennsylvania, their mom's hometown. There Don attended high school for two years from 1961–1963. During that time, in addition to excelling in academics and sports, Don volunteered to paint their two story, one hundred-year-old house. After borrowing a large, wooden ladder, Don and his sister Candy spent weeks one summer scraping, priming, and painting—a Herculean task. Don became the talk of the town.

His sister Shirley remembered Don as a friend and protector. Describing herself as a chubby little girl, she bore the brunt of a lot of harassment and kidding from her siblings. Shirley said that Don would always jump into the incident and admonish them to stop the teasing. Shirley always felt degraded and humiliated at these times, wanting nothing more than to run away and hide in a hole somewhere. Don became her hero. Don played football and basketball and was growing up to be tall and very handsome in her eyes. He was well liked by fellow students and faculty and Shirley adored him. She remembered him having a positive effect on all of those around him. She felt that Don was someone people could connect with, be comforted by, and feel peaceful with.

A football teammate, Lt.Col. Greg Johnson (Retired) had a very inspired memory of Don that he posted on Westpoint.org:

> *Don was a senior in high school (Havelock High) when I was a freshman. Don was quiet and a physically awkward kind of guy. But he was always friendly and definitely not a quitter. He worked hard and used his smarts to earn a starting position on the varsity football team. That year we ended up playing in the state high school football finals. We lost but were proud of our accomplishment. I later heard that he had died in combat in Vietnam. Don set the example for all of us to emulate. He did not die in vain. Don made a sacrifice so that all of us today can enjoy the fruits of a great nation. I have a son at West Point now. I'm confident he will measure up to the standards set forth by Don. Both are far better men than me.*

Shirley has very clear memories of the day that her brother left for Vietnam. She was sick and terrified for her brother's safety, and the world was in chaos:

> Yikes! The stairs were wheeled up to the plane! He was boarding the plane! I was heartbroken when he turned to wave as he entered the airplane that would take him away from me. It was an ominous moment. Words I never said out loud: "Will I see you again?" In that moment, at the top of those stairs, his smile was so beautiful to me! A tall, blond *God of War* still living his dream and I wanted to support him! I took comfort in that. He was doing what he wanted to do. He wanted to go. He wanted to be there.

Sister Joan provided background on Don's early life. She remembered that while the family was stationed at Cherry Point, North Carolina and living in Quonset Hut housing after their dad returned from preparing for the invasion of Japan, Don was born on January 7, 1947. In 1953, while stationed at Patuxent River Naval Air

Station in Maryland, the kids attended Solomons Island Elementary School and Don played in the first organized Little League in the area.

They moved to Great Lakes Navy Base near Chicago in 1953. Don and his brother Roy both had paper routes that required them to be up at four o'clock every morning. All the other kids also got up to help roll the papers and secure them with a rubber band; they had to be delivered in time for the boys to catch the school bus. Here the brothers ran on the track team, joined the basketball and debate teams, and were also on the wrestling and swim teams, all while participating in the Boy Scouts. They accomplished all of this while excelling in academics as well. It was during this time that the brothers also got involved with bible studies and joined the church youth group. The Presbyterian church was one block away and it was during this time that Don became quite close to the pastor. Don would continue his deep faith commitment as a Christian the rest of his life. Don also met a West Pointer about that time who came to town to practice medicine. It was probably because of his influence that Don started on the road to the Military Academy.

Don prepared himself physically for potential entry into West Point by making concoctions of nutritional drinks with protein powder and wheat germ supplements. He lifted weights and ran often, starting a regimen of running along a local highway with weights on his ankles. He was once again the talk of the town.

Unknown to most of us, Don loved music, often giving his sisters records of popular performers. He would sing to his sister Shirley; a favorite was "The Sound of Silence" by Simon and Garfunkel. He made gestures by putting his hands to his ears, listening for *the sound*, arms swinging, walking along *narrow streets of cobblestone*. Turning his collar up against his neck to protect himself from the *cold and damp* and protecting his eyes from the glare of the *neon light; Hear my words that might teach you*, holding out his arms that *I might reach you*. Shirley would watch, mesmerized and entertained. At the end he would collapse at Shirley's feet, and they would laugh hysterically. How many teenage boys do that?

During our time at West Point the family visited as often as possible. He met the family at the World's Fair in the Meadowlands in '65. They also joined him at Camp Buckner during our yearling summer and attended two Army-Navy games—in 1965 and '67. Plans for the '66 game were cancelled when Don was discovered selling women's panties with the words *Beat Navy* printed on them. Instead of attending the game, Don walked punishment tours back at the Academy!

A tribute to Don's integrity and dedication was the fact that we elected him as our A-1 class representative on the Cadet Honor Committee during our yearling year. Those selections were obviously reserved for only the best among us.

Craig Carson, A-1 classmate and roommate, shared some memories:

> Don and I were always starving. As upperclassmen, we would hang around after supper was dismissed and go from table to table and eat whatever was left, laughing the whole time. The cadet officer of the day came by once and said, "Hey you two, dinner is over." We both looked up and Donny said, "Fuck off." End of discussion.
>
> One time, we were sitting together in Donny's room discussing branch selection. The discussion was between Infantry and Armor (armored cavalry, in particular). The problem was we both wanted to go Airborne as well. Airborne armored cavalry meant jeeps. Airborne infantry meant exactly that. I said, "Donny, I am going airborne Infantry." He said, "CS you dumb shit, armored Cav is the way to go." We both ended up in the 173rd Airborne. He went airborne armored Cavalry and was killed. I went airborne Infantry, and I am writing about an old friend who I miss very much.
>
> I often think back on our conversation when we were both young and unknowing and think how thin the line is between life and death. He was killed right outside LZ English just before I arrived, and he had helped me get into the 173rd. I still have his last letter to me, and my letter to his parents.

The letter that Craig sent to Don's parents described the depths of the emotions that many of us feel even years after the loss of one of our Twenty:

Dear Mr. & Mrs. Colglazier,

I was a roommate of Don's at West Point. I was sitting with my son—now three and a half—looking at old pictures of my years at West Point and in the Army, and he pointed to Don and said "Who's that Daddy?" I said it was a good friend of mine who was killed in Vietnam. I started crying, much to the amazement of my son. I find it increasingly difficult to think of the many friends who were killed without a feeling of irretrievable loss and loneliness. As I looked at my son, I realized how trivial it must be compared to your own. I saved Don's last letter to me and as I reread it, it reminded me strongly of him. I want to give it to you. Please accept my sympathy and understanding for your loss—one that I have shared for these last ten years.

Craig Carson

Another A-1 classmate, Tom Barnes, shared some of his most important memories of Don:

From those days in A-1 with Donny as a plebe classmate, the overwhelming memory I have of him was his constant and pervasive attitude of never showing that he was intimidated or under pressure. Sure, he conformed, like we all did to avoid additional discomfort and unnecessary stress, but he never gave the impression that it was anything more than a routine part of the day. His smile and sense of humor was always there, as was his focus on the task at hand and preparation for what lay ahead.

As we slowly moved through our years at school, Donny only got better at being Donny: more proficient in his studies, always there when we needed him, more efficient in his company responsibilities, and always the loose, smiling, never-able-to-get-him-flustered Donny! We depended on him for that, although we didn't realize at the time how valuable his demeanor was to us. His word was his bond, and the Honor

Code was something he brought to the Academy with him, not something that was taught to him after he arrived. One of the photos I have of Donny was taken at the First Class Club immediately after being sworn in. I have come across it often as the years have passed and wished I had more pictures of him and that smile of his, that long, lanky frame leaping down the stairs of East Barracks on his way to formation.

After graduation, armor training took Donny in one direction and field artillery took me down another path, at least for a while. We found each other at Fort Bragg about a year later and ended up sharing a house together just off base at Spring Lake for six months before Donny left for Vietnam.

Those days with Donny at school, and those few months living together again at Fort Bragg, left indelible impressions of the character of a man for whom I would have trusted with all that I have or value. The absolute best part is that he knew who his God was and knew Him well. Because of that, I take great comfort knowing that our separation is only brief and that one day we will be together again, telling stories of days gone by, laughing and smiling together . . . forever, never again to be interrupted by a war we never asked for, but one from which we did not run. For a reason we may never know or understand, Donny was taken from us early, like Stonewall Jackson…and, like Jackson said, "Let us cross over the river and rest in the shade of the trees…" Look for me, Donny, for I will be looking for you.

After graduation Don attended the usual schools before departing for Vietnam. During the holidays of '68–'69 Don returned home and one of the highlights of that time was watching Super Bowl III when the New York Jets defeated the family's favorite team, the Baltimore Colts. A few months later it was time for Don to depart after another visit home. Joan remembered that day:

We all drove him to the New Bern airport. It was in the afternoon on a very foggy, dreary, cloudy, rainy day when

Don ascended the stairs up to the plane and through the door, waiving to us. Our mom and dad had a hand signal they would use when our dad, upon his many departures, would look out of the airplane window and hold up one finger, then four fingers, then three fingers to say, "I love you." Don signaled that to us. And we gestured back. I remember looking up at the dark, cloudy, rainy sky and thinking that perhaps the sky may never be clear and sunny again.

Don's sister Carolyn remembered a last request from her brother before he left:

Before he left our home in Havelock, North Carolina in the summer of 1969 on his way to Vietnam, he asked me if I knew the lyrics to Joni Mitchell's "Both Sides Now." I did. Her music was a favorite. He asked me to write the words down for him. He rarely asked for anything. In my best handwriting I rendered the whole lyric and presented Joni's best work to my brother, who I long for to this day:

> I've looked at life from both sides now
> From win and lose and still somehow
> It's life's illusions I recall
> I really don't know life at all.

On the evening of January 20, 1970 around eight o'clock, there was a knock on the Colglazier front door. Two soldiers had come to deliver the worst news possible. They asked for Don's mother. Don had been killed in the late afternoon of January 18. Shirley remembered:

My mother's beloved son was dead! Our beloved brother was dead! My father was not home. He was working a late shift at Cherry Point Marine Corps Air Base. The base was huge, and it was dark, but I knew how to find his office, so I went with one of the officers to get my father. As we drove down the long road lined with huge airplane hangers, one after another, the car headlights caught a man standing in the road. He was hunched over, and the glare of the headlights showed his contorted face. "That's my father!" I said, and as the car came to a stop, my father got in. He was a tortured man as he said: "I never thought you would come to my door."

The family was notified several days later that Don's remains would be delivered to Dover AFB in Delaware and his dad asked that the remains be delivered to Wyalusing, Pennsylvania, where Don would be buried in the family cemetery at Hornet's Ferry. His remains would go to the funeral home several houses down from where the family lived from 1961 until 1963. His funeral service was on January 25, 1970, exactly one week after his death, at the Wyalusing Presbyterian Church on Church Street where Don and Roy, seven years previously, were confirmed and baptized. The church was packed, standing room only, filled with aunts, uncles, cousins, classmates, and family friends. I was in Vietnam at this time and had no knowledge of Donny's death or funeral. I would give anything now to be able to set the clock back to those days so that I could have attended. His absence at all the class functions since those days is a travesty. He, like everyone else featured in this book, was taken from us much too early. So sad, as I write these words my eyes are filling, as they do every time I stop by the North Carolina Vietnam Veterans Memorial to say hi to him. My memories of him are so clear and so dear, even after all of these years.

In the 1980s, Wyalusing Presbyterian Church was renovated, and Don's parents arranged for a library and study to be worked into the plans, built, and dedicated to their son. By the same token and about the same time, a new Havelock High School was built in Havelock, North Carolina and his parents arranged for the flagpole there to be erected in Don's honor.

Another A-1 classmate, Scott Vickers, provided some thoughts that, while not intended as such, are actually a fitting eulogy for Don from those of us who shared so much time with him and loved him more than we realized during that time:

All of these years since Donny Colglazier left us have still not enabled most of us to fathom the huge chasm created by his abrupt passing. He became known to all of us as "The Bird." He was tall and when he held his arms outstretched to emphasize a point, he did resemble a bird that was readying for flight.

Looking back over the fifty-plus years since we all grew to know and care for this man is an extremely difficult task, as he was undeniably and most perfectly steadfast in his approach to God, country, and love for his classmates. His approach to almost everything that he achieved in those four years during which all of us were privileged to know him was steady, forthright, and totally honest. He calmed many of us with his witty insights into the learning process and never, ever shunned assisting anyone in need of understanding the mysteries of Calculus, *Juice* or *Nuke* [electrical and nuclear engineering].

Can any normal human being understand a person's curiosity and drive that instills in him a desire to take on four years of study devoted to the understanding of the Chinese language . . . four years? Most of us were simply overjoyed to wrestle through our paltry two years of any chosen language.

Donny was part of that elite—a Star Man—and we were, to the very last one of us, so very proud of him. Upon graduation he attended his Armor Basic Course and added Airborne and Ranger School to his list of accomplishments. One of us had kidded with Donny, asking him, "What're you going Airborne for, Donny, to jump out of a tank?" He had simply smiled that good-natured smile of his and continued on course.

When the news of his death on a remote battlefield in Vietnam spread like wildfire throughout our class, there was a sudden, numbing shock followed by a great sense of loss. No longer would we have The Bird around to help us with some of our concerns.

As the long grey line stiffens and straightens once again, we pay homage to Don Colglazier as one of our most honored and highly respected classmates. Sometimes it seems that the Almighty simply reaches down and plucks some of the very best of humanity without ever providing the rest of us (poor mortals that we are) with reason or logic for our great and sudden loss. Don Colglazier was one of the very best and he was evidently most urgently needed elsewhere.

Don's death was hard for many of us to deal with. He lost his life because he wanted to get back to his men for the most dangerous time in Vietnam—nighttime. We can never know for sure, but I suspect that he would have felt guilty and that he had shirked his duty if he had spent the night away from them. No matter the risk, he needed to get back, and he paid the price for traveling late in the day because of his devotion to duty. We all in A-1 felt, and I'm sure still feel today, the tremendous loss caused by his early departure from our ranks. We are so much the poorer . . .

Don is interred in the Homet Cemetery in Wyalusing, Pennsylvania.

A little over a month after Don Colglazier's death, Jeff Riek was killed when his recon platoon was ambushed on February 25. Jeff was one of three children—the middle child—with a younger sister Natalie and older brother Justus and was born on March 3, 1947. The early part of his life was spent on a resort owned by his parents in Chetek, Wisconsin. When the situation in Korea looked alarming, and with the resort not doing well, his parents sold the property and his dad re-entered the Army, having previously served in World War II. Their first assignment was to Ft. Benning, Georgia, followed by the Army Language School at the Presidio of Monterey to study Turkish, followed by three years in the US Embassy in Ankara Turkey. This was followed by a school at Ft. Leavenworth Kansas and then the Pentagon, and ultimately to Vietnam as an advisor.

Jeff and Justus went to Bishop Dennis. J. O'Connell High School in Falls Church, Virginia. Jeff entered as a freshman when Justus was a senior. In an unusual turn of events, both brothers began to run cross country. In his senior year Justus was running junior varsity while Jeff as a freshman was running on the varsity team. Unfortunately, Jeff did not receive a varsity letter as the school refused to award one to a freshman.

While living in Arlington Virginia, the Riek boys started their first business, mowing and trimming lawns for their neighbors. Neither liked to do the clipping, so there was always an interesting discussion about who had done it last. When their mom became a real estate agent, they solicited jobs from her customers to make their property look more attractive.

As Jeff was finishing high school in Fayetteville, North Carolina, he applied for an appointment to West Point but was initially rejected. Justus was finishing college and about to enter the US Air Force. At about the last possible minute a telegram arrived at the Riek house for Jeff and said that if he could get there in time, he could enter West Point with the class of 1968. He was given forty-eight hours to arrive and join the plebe class . . . he made it!

During his time at West Point he developed two outstanding skills—one military and one not. He established a record on the hated indoor obstacle course, which had to be run every year for a grade. For a while he held the Academy record. The other skill was demonstrated when he was home on leave, Jeff had a knack for trading options in which he was incredibly successful.

Jeff's Sister Natalie or "Muffie" to her friends had some very special memories of her brother:

> Jeff was a goof, a kidder, a loyal friend, a handsome guy, a
> dear friend for a lonesome gramma, and a pain in my neck
> lots of my life. His red shirts with white ties were horrible . . .
> and only he could get away with that kind of look. He always
> smelled good. He always had money in his pocket. He loved
> his God, but he also loved his country and his Army with a
> passion that few possess.

One of our classmates, Ross Irvin, recounts a humorous story about Jeff and the cadet glee club. During Beast Barracks we were all auditioned, as membership was a much sought-after activity, as they took multiple trips away from the Academy each year. When Ross's turn came, he was confident that he'd be selected, as he liked to sing in informal family settings. When he entered the audition room, he was given a sheet of paper with all sorts of unintelligible symbols and notes— sheet music—and was commanded to sing as the choir director played the piano. Since he couldn't read music, he failed the interview miserably.

This was one of the greatest disappointments he had experienced so far, and when he expressed this to Jeff, who had a very successful audition, Jeff had a plan. He wanted Ross to accompany him to every rehearsal, sign in, and just stand beside someone and try to mimic what they did. It worked, the sign-in sheet was replaced with a typed roster and Ross's name was on it, he'd made the cut! Ross assumed that the plebes would just be absorbed into the varsity glee club when the first class members graduated. Unfortunately, that was not the case and another formal audition was required, with the same routine as before. Applicants were given a new sheet of music and told to sing. The results for Ross this time were the same as the earlier attempt, and his singing career at West Point came to an end.

When the Riek family found out that Jeff had made the Fourth Class Choir, they were dumbfounded; of the three siblings it was felt that he had the least singing talent. When the family visited West Point, they attended a choir performance and all were glad that Jeff had so many guys around him to help him carry a tune.

Lou Pierce has a memory of an adventure filled trip to Turkey and back after our plebe year:

Jeff and I both had parents who were stationed in Ankara, Turkey. The summer after our plebe year, Jeff and I headed for Turkey. We planned to go the whole way on space available travel and left the Academy with twenty dollars each in our pockets. We caught a bus to Maguire AFB in New Jersey and went to base ops to get a ride to Turkey. They advised us that there were not really any prospects for space available out of Maguire. We caught a bus to Westover AFB in Massachusetts. From there, we flew into Torejon AFB outside of Madrid. From Torejon, we flew to Spangdalem, Germany, where our best option was catching a bus to Rhein-Main the next day and getting a flight out of there.

That night, we went to the O club for dinner. When we walked through the front door, we were met by three slot machines—two nickels and one quarter. I hit a jackpot. We weren't members of the club, so I couldn't collect until the guy sitting with Jeff at the bar said he'd sign for us. I had three quarters in my pocket, so I tried the quarter machine. On the third quarter, I hit another jackpot. The next day, we took the bus to Rhein-Main. Jeff went to base ops to see about a ride to Ankara while I stayed in the passenger lounge where it was literally wall-to-wall slots. I had a pocket full of quarters from the previous night's winnings and played the quarter machine. Yep, another jackpot. I've only hit one other slot jackpot in the last fifty years.

To continue the saga, we got a cargo flight out of Rhine-Main that was going all the way to Ankara—until they landed in Athens and the plane "broke down." The pilot said every flight through Athens has trouble because they get to spend a few days on the beach drawing TDY. We took our jackpot winnings and bought two tickets on Turkish Airlines and flew the rest of the way in luxury (another story). We arranged a return trip back to the States as soon as we landed in Ankara.

When it came time to leave, we headed to the airport. We had to be back by midnight Wednesday and were leaving on Sunday, so we weren't worried—until we landed in Chatterough, France. There had not been any space-A flights to the States in two weeks and they didn't anticipate any. They said we'd have better luck going to Paris and flying out of Orly. On Monday, we were on the train headed to Paris. We got there and got to the hotel to check in for a stand-by flight. The lobby was packed with several hundred folks looking for a ride. We didn't panic until late Tuesday when we called our folks for commercial tickets.

We got a Pan Am flight on Wednesday. We landed at JFK at ten o'clock Wednesday night. No buses. We found a cab who was willing to drive us back for every penny we had between us. We got back and signed in at a quarter after twelve, fifteen minutes late. We got written up, but I wrote a three-page B-ache [Belly ache letter explaining all of the reasons for the transgression. They were seldom helpful in avoiding punishment] explaining the circumstances. The TAC said it was the best one he'd ever read. Denied. We both got fifteen demerits and twenty hours walking tours on the Area and got to spend some quality time there with some of our friends. The next time we went to Turkey, we went commercial there and back again. I don't remember much about that trip.

After spring leave of firstie year, Jeff returned to West Point with some type of new super glue, which he thought would permanently lock the doors to the academy's computer room. He and Ross concocted a plan to leave the room at about four o'clock in the morning and head to the computer lab, figuring no one else would be out. They successfully accomplished their mission and awaited an announcement that the lab was closed. Unfortunately, that never occurred. Somehow the staff dealt with the glue; it was a great disappointment.

Jeff also demonstrated a great interest in animals and kept a turtle named Atlas, in a secret pen under the ladder closet in the hall or under the collar of Jeff's bed. Unfortunately, he met a tragic end while completing a rigorous airborne qualification test. The course involved Atlas jumping off of the roof of New South Barracks during the day, at night, in water during a rainstorm, and under combat conditions with cadets throwing rocks at him as he descended. Unfortunately, his final qualifying jump ended his airborne and cadet career when he was swept up in an unexpected gust of wind and disappeared over the top of the cadet hospital, never to be seen again.

In another escapade, Jeff and another of those classmates featured in this book, Dave Sackett, had arranged to meet some women after taps. They saw a light which, instead of the ladies, was the flashlight of the officer-in-charge, who was responsible for cadet discipline on a rotating schedule. Seeing these as examples, it's easy to see how Jeff qualified for Century Club honors (100 hours walking punishment tours in Central Area).

Ross has a great story of Jeff during our firstie year involving cadet projects. The USMA Engineering Department periodically saddled cadets with the requirement to complete a project. It was ostensibly to help cadets deal with real world problems but was always a far-out idea, like designing a space plane that would allow passengers to experience weightlessness—a fantastic idea for the late '60s. And because of the Honor Code, collaboration with others was forbidden.

As is always the case with any project like this with any college student, nothing was done in Jeff's room until the night before it was due. After supper Ross and Jeff, both *goats* sat at their desks agonizing about how to proceed. A third roommate went to bed! While attempting to get a start and also day-dreaming, Ross fell asleep. He was awakened about nine o'clock by his third roommate's alarm which caused the now awake cadet to get up, spend a couple of hours on his project, and then go back to bed. Ross worked on an idea and went to bed about midnight, at which time Jeff was still sitting at his desk with a *deer in the headlights* look in his eyes.

The next week the three roommates were able to get their grades that were posted in one of the sally ports. On a scale of 3.0, a 2.0 was needed as a passing grade. Ross received a 2.1, which was barely passing but passing nonetheless. Jeff received a 1.9, failing but not a debacle. Roommate number three came in with a 3.0. Ross felt that this confirmed the *Universal Law of Cadet Time and Effort*: reward is inversely proportional to the amount of time and effort expended.

Before graduation, Jeff selected Infantry as his branch and was commissioned by his father. As with most of the class, he attended his branch basic course and Ranger and Airborne Schools before reporting to Ft. Riley, Kansas. While there he participated in the first of the *Reforger* exercises as a platoon leader. Reforger was a massive yearly exercise where the US practiced sending large numbers of troops with equipment to Europe, as it would be required to do in case of war.

After finishing Ranger School, he volunteered for Airborne. The first week, or Ground Week, was spent learning the fundamentals of getting acclimated to a parachute harness, jump commands, and how to do a proper PLF or parachute landing fall. After Ground Week, Jeff went to the Post Exchange (PX) and started reading various Kotex boxes. A young employee asked if she could help him make a selection. Jeff started asking questions about relative absorbency among the various brands. When she asked him about his interest in Kotex, Jeff explained that he was in jump school and the parachute harness was cutting into the flesh at the top of his legs. He was looking for a thick cotton product to cushion the straps. He subsequently wore them through Tower and Jump Week and was probably the only officer to ever become Airborne qualified wearing two Kotex, with no chafing, while he completed his jumps. In hindsight, it's probably a good thing that the word wasn't spread, as there would probably have been a run on Kotex in the PX and commissary.

As a cadet, Jeff spent a lot of his time studying the stock market and his investments. He spent his graduation leave of sixty days at the Bache Company offices in DC trading commodities. He was successful to the point of making enough to pay off his car loan as well as investing in stocks and continued these efforts during his initial six-month assignment at Ft. Riley.

As Ross Irvin remembered, "In the spring of 1969, while we were both stationed at Ft Riley, Kansas, Jeff and I used to meet periodically to discuss investments. He was very interested in commodity trading. Under his guidance, I bought, on my first trade, one contract of 30,000 pounds of pork bellies. Within two days, pork bellies went up one cent, so I sold out, making three hundred dollars. In those days, this was about one month's pay for a second lieutenant. After a few other successful trades, I was hooked. Jeff and I started smoking cigars and going to the O club more often."

In September of 1969, Jeff reported to Vietnam and was assigned to 2nd Battalion, 60th Infantry, 9th Infantry Division in the delta area of South Vietnam. About five months later, Jeff was killed while leading the battalion's recon platoon. They were ambushed by a large NVA force and the four Vietnamese soldiers at the head of the formation were hit. Jeff and his RTO provided covering fire as the rest of the platoon sought refuge. While doing so, both were killed. As an indicator of his personal sense of duty, Jeff was scheduled to go on R&R leave that day but stayed behind to lead his men on what proved to be his final operation. Special arrangements had been made by the battalion to fly him out to meet a flight to his selected R&R site, Sydney, Australia, immediately upon his return from the field. Almost eerily, a battalion TOC officer monitoring the radio heard Jeff's last breaths as he clutched his radio handset. We don't know if he was trying to call for help with his last breath, or if he clutched the push-to-talk button as a reflex action. I can think of no more horrifying sound than hearing a friend die.

One of Jeff's soldiers, David Peek, had some fond memories of Jeff in Vietnam:

Before LT was killed, he came to me one day and asked me to write a letter for him because he was busy planning an operation. The letter was to his girlfriend, and I didn't have an idea what to say to a girlfriend because I didn't have one. So, I wrote a fast letter like I imagined a guy would write to his gal and put it in an envelope. LT sealed it up and sent it on the spot. I was speechless because he didn't proofread first. Mail was fairly quick and a week later he showed me the return letter. His girl thought he had broken his hand but then figured it out. She said she thought it was sweet, and for Jeff to thank me.

LT liked to think outside the box. All the other units were doing the same thing day after day and coming up with a few kills here and there. So, LT came up with what he called a *false extraction*. We made a fast insert with choppers about an hour before sundown. There were two hooches and we took over both and put all the Viet people in the bunkers. All the farmers had mud bunkers in their hooches. Just at dusk two choppers came back in and half the team rushed out and jumped on board and hauled ass. After full dark we set up claymores and trip flares. I had been sitting on a bed looking down a path when I heard all kinds of noise, so I sat on the floor and BAM, took a round across the top of my head. Next thing BOOM, the claymore goes off and we are being lit up but good. We had way more firepower and they cut and ran quickly. With a little fine tuning, LT had found a new method that was unknown.

Jeff Riek was the best officer I ever knew, the only one I have a picture of. The 4.2 mortars put twenty-one HE on deck in that spot [where he was killed] on the day of his funeral. To this day I still think of Jeff often, and always with a smile.

Natalie remembered that Jeff's passing devastated her family. Their father, by then retired, was particularly affected. He had served a tour in Vietnam and was responsible for helping in developing the tactics and logistical operations to support the war. Jeff's loss broke him in many ways. When she took her girls to Arlington to see the graves of their uncle Jeff and grandfather Justus, one sang and one saluted. A testament to Jeff's ability with the ladies is that more than one showed up for Jeff's funeral, each thinking that they were Jeff's One and Only.

Jeff was buried in Arlington National Cemetery on March 5, 1970, just two days after his twenty-third birthday. In the spring of '74 his father was also buried in Arlington about twenty paces from his son. In an emotional gesture, Jeff's mom took a bouquet of flowers from her husband's grave and placed it on Jeff's. It may have been divine intervention to have their graves be placed so close together after a four-year interval.

One of Jeff's best friends from the 2/60th named a son for him. Sadly, his son was killed in Iraq on July 14, 2001. His wife gave birth to triplet boys after her husband's death, and one of them is also named for Jeff; Jeff Riek's legacy endures.

Jeff's stockbroker, Joe Moore, and he became close friends in 1968 and '69. Some evenings Jeff spent at his stockbroker's pool, where there were always a number of attractive ladies. He enjoyed watching Jeff operate. He remembered that in his office, "there was a lot of hurt when he was killed. Even now, thirty-five years later, I occasionally see old friends and they mention Jeff Riek. Jeff Riek was a fabulous person. He had heart, character, and spirit that will never be duplicated. For his friends, the memory of Jeff will never diminish," Joe said.

Ross Irvin conducted several highly emotional phone interviews with soldiers who had served with Jeff, to include Bradley Rice and Col. Ron Pieper. They recounted that Jeff was a great leader who had a sincere interest in the welfare of his men. He was tactically proficient and good with maps—a prerequisite for any infantry platoon leader. One of those interviewed, Col. Pieper, was Jeff's predecessor as recon platoon leader and was the TOC duty officer flying overhead who heard Jeff's last breaths on the radio. That was a tough interview for Ross.

In a few short months of combat Jeff was very highly decorated, having been awarded the Silver Star, the Soldiers Medal (the highest non-combat award for bravery), the Bronze Star with V device and two Oak Leaf Clusters (denoting additional awards), and an Air Medal. Unfortunately, I could not locate the award citations.

Jeff is interred in Arlington National Cemetery.

About a month after losing Jeff, '68 was hit again. This time it was Harry Hayes on March 31, Easter Sunday of that year. Harry was the eleventh of our ranks to fall in ten months; we were really paying a price. And once again our classmate was leading from the front, as we all were trained to do. It was the position from which we could best direct the action, but a perilous place to be. His loss was staggering to all his friends and family.

Harry was born on November 10, 1945 in Lafayette, Alabama. In fact, Harry spent most of his childhood in Alexander City, Alabama where he graduated from high school in 1964. His dad was a WWII veteran, and his younger brother Jim is now a retired Marine Corps lieutenant colonel. At the time of his birth, his dad was serving as a B-29 mechanic instructor in Texas and his wife had returned to Alabama for Harry's birth. Shortly thereafter his dad left the service and joined the family. Some eighteen months later, little brother Jim arrived, and the family moved into a duplex where they would remain for Harry's lifetime.

As they were growing up, they spent a lot of time at their grandparents' farm in Five Points, Alabama. Here they learned how to milk cows, churn butter, and slop the hogs—skills that were important for any soon-to-be West Point cadet.

Their mom stayed at home until both boys were in school and then took a job at a private school established by a mill company, a common practice in the Southern fabric industry. In 1957 their dad died from brain cancer, leaving their mother to raise the kids. The two boys went to public school even though their mom kept her job. When the weather was good, they could walk to school with the boy who lived across the street and the girl next door, who was a couple of years older and a regular playmate. During this time, they learned one of life's lessons when the girl was no longer allowed to go shirtless with the boys when they were playing together in the summer—something they just couldn't understand!

As he was growing up, Harry learned all of the skills that most guys of those years acquired. He was given a sixteen-gauge, single-barreled shotgun and was introduced to hunting by his uncle. He played the coronet through about the eighth grade. And then, of course, he needed to learn to drive. The boys learned on the neighbor kid's father's old *three on the tree* truck.

As was expected, sports was an important part of school and growing up. Harry lettered all four years of high school in football and baseball, and two years in basketball. He was selected as an all-star for several years in both football and baseball. With all of this he was also a superb student, elected president of his class for two years, including his senior year, and was also a member of the National Honor Society. In his senior year he was selected by the Kiwanis club as their athlete of the year. After his death the award was renamed the Harry Hayes Athlete of the Year.

Harry was the punt returner for his high school football team. During one game he signaled for a fair catch, but a defender hit him at full speed, knocking him out. When he woke up, he had no idea who they were playing but that was okay since he'd get no more playing time. While he and his brother Jim were cleaning up after the game, he asked his brother if he had a date for that night. When Jim told him that he did indeed have a date, Harry asked his brother to point the girl out to him! Jim was worried about Harry, but Harry said he was okay and would get home that night after his date, and he did.

One year they both helped the assistant football coach work on a cabin on Lake Martin. That was where Harry learned to water ski and those skills then transferred to snow skiing after he entered West Point.

Bob Brace met Harry in the summer of '63 when they were both taking the entrance exams for West Point at Fort McPherson, Georgia. They met again a year later as they were about to start the journey into their future. After Beast they were assigned as roommates in company I2 with Jim Harter. To escape the rigors of plebe life, he and Harry discovered a way to temporarily escape the misery of

West Point. Every night after studying, they'd turn off the overhead lights, leaving only the desk lights on and thus created *atmosphere*, or what passed for it in a plebe room. Jim would go to bed, Harry would read his Bible, and Bob would try to write to his sweetheart. Then, before they went to bed, he and Harry would have the last cigarette of the day, which they called their *reflection cigarette*. At that time, they'd talk about anything other than West Point, like girls, God, and their past, and with this a deep and lasting friendship was formed, based on what Jim described as a "mutual dis-admiration and dislike for West Point's obnoxious and somewhat senseless ways," and a growing mutual trust and admiration for each other. With this as a basis, they committed to getting through West Point to graduation. I believe that only those who have lived through those "obnoxious and somewhat senseless ways" can understand the depths and strength of the male bonds of respect and love that were formed between roommates, and on a larger scale, most classmates. It's a bond like no other and is timeless. I can meet a classmate this year, after fifty-three years, for the first time and the bond is already there, to be nurtured and strengthened as we go forward. It's remarkable, it's supportive, and it's somewhat mysterious, but it sure is there.

Bob and Harry roomed together a couple of more times, but they each also went into their separate lives, Harry to 150-pound football where he was an incredible running back, and Bob to benchwarmer status, or so he humbly claims, on the Army soccer team. During yearling year, Harry convinced Bob to take up skiing, which he reluctantly did, and found it to be a new passion and one which further strengthened his ties with Harry.

During cow year the two somewhat disgruntled cadets decided on another gambit in complete and total violation of every West Point regulation, short of the Honor Code. Screw West Point, they'd go *over the wall*. They figured that if they got caught, they'd pay the price; if they were successful, they'd have the immense satisfaction of having beaten the system. On one dark and snowy night after taps, they ventured out to hit a backstreet bar in Highland Falls, the town just outside the southern gate, for a few beers and a burger and fries. They stayed in wooded areas until they broke through a couple of blocks off Main Street. There weren't many people there, and they huddled in a booth and had their burgers and beer, really enjoying their temporary freedom.

The trip back was a little rougher than the one out. It was late, and they may have had one too many beers. They approached a cut through the woods where the underbrush had been somewhat cleared, leaving spikes of saplings similar to the punji stakes they'd later see in Vietnam. Harry lost his shoe, so Bob told him to get on his back and he'd carry him back. Suddenly Bob tripped and one of the stakes just punched him in the gut, knocking the wind completely out of him. Harry was afraid that he was seriously hurt, but as Bob slowly got his breath back, he assured Harry that he was neither dead nor dying. As Bob related, "By the grace of God" they made it back to their room undetected and Harry escaped frostbite on his shoeless foot. Mission accomplished! They had beat the system in a big way.

One classmate remembered that he and Harry got *slugged* on the first class trip. Getting slugged was the punishment meted out for a gross violation of a regulation or requirement. It usually included a lot of demerits, many hours walking punishment tours, and confinement to one's room for a month or two. Because of this punishment, the two started first class year as cadet privates rather than as cadet officers or non-commissioned officers. For parades the latter carried the famous West Point saber, the *sluggees* were cadet privates and carried their M14s with bayonets as they had the first three years. For the first saber drill practice of senior year the two of them fell out with their classmates wearing their web belts and bayonets. The two cadet first class privates were not authorized to carry sabers, so they used the next best thing, a bayonet and scabbard on the webbed field belt. They could draw their bayonets on the command to "draw sabers!" and practice the saber manual of arms with their short bayonets, thus participating in the drill with their classmates. Highly irregular! Their TAC saw them and went berserk, banning them from participating. Maybe they got another slug?

There is a common thread that runs through the memories of other classmates when you mention Harry's name. He was unflappable, never intimidated, lived with integrity, and was a great friend. One dedicated a book to him. Harry was much loved and admired by all with whom he came in contact. Bob Shimp remembered:

If you were lucky to be Harry's roommate, you knew what it was to have a true friend. Harry learned quicker than most that to survive plebe year, you had to help each other. Do you remember the time you had laundry duty? The first time I was laundry carrier, I realized that there is no way one person could get all the laundry delivered in the allotted time. Harry saw that it was my turn, jumped in, grabbed an armful of twine-tied brown-paper packages, and headed up the stairs, no questions asked.

After graduation a group of about five classmates traveled across the country from Jacksonville, Florida to go to various classmate weddings. It was a time of great camaraderie and lasting memories. They started in Florida, visited the Air Force Academy, and ended in the state of Washington. When they arrived in Florida for the Shimp wedding, they showed up at the church on Saturday afternoon for the rehearsal. When the minister looked at this gaggle of unshaven, sun-burned, laughing guys he said "Let us pray. Dear God, please don't let this motley crew spoil this special occasion for Carol and Bob." They spent a great time in a beach house with massive amounts of beer and alcohol with a lot of bullshit and horseplay thrown in. They tried to pick up women and were occasionally successful. It was during the final wedding in Washington State that Harry met Gretchen, who would later become his wife.

When the trip ended, they all separated to go to their required schools. For some of those who went to Ft. Benning, including Harry, a ritual developed. After every night-training exercise, they'd meet at the Steamliner Diner and eat a T-bone special for $3.69. After Ranger School, Harry and Steve Marcuccelli volunteered for Airborne School because it was only a five-day work week, and they'd draw a lot of extra money, as temporary duty pay was $4.60 a day with an additional $110 a month for jumping out of airplanes. And they'd have a chance to spend Christmas at home. Their feet were wrecked from Ranger School and Harry's mom suggested they use corn oil to cure them, which worked like a charm.

Just before Christmas, Harry called classmate Bob Brace and convinced him that they needed to go to Seattle because the skiing was great and the girls wanted to see them again. So right after Christmas, they caught a red eye out of Atlanta for Seattle. It was a very special week, filled with good times, great skiing, and many adventures. At the end of the week, after a harrowing drive to the airport through a blizzard, they got to the airport to find that their flight was delayed. Of course, they had no option but to spend the time in the bar. They eventually boarded their plane, ordered another drink and Harry announced, "Ya know what Brace, I'm going to marry that girl!"

Harry's first assignment was in Germany with a group of classmates, including Bob Brace and his bride Carol, who decided they wanted to see what the Army was like before heading off to Vietnam. One of their favorite memories of Harry occurred during that assignment when Harry was invited over for dinner. While eating Harry got a strange look on his face, and when asked if everything was okay, he replied, in all seriousness, "I think a leaf flew in from outdoors and got in my stew." He had never seen or heard of a bay leaf before, and we all fell out with laughter!"

About halfway through his assignment in Augsburg, he flew home to marry Gretchen Klinkert, returning with her to Germany to finish his assignment before his inevitable Vietnam tour. Harry had met Gretchen in Seattle at the Curran wedding where she was the maid of honor and he was the best man.

Gretchen was kind enough to share some warm and personal memories of her relatively short time with Harry. During Harry's trip to Seattle after Christmas it became obvious that her relationship with Harry was deepening and becoming more serious. That was confirmed when Harry went to her father and asked permission to marry her; the family was elated. Harry shortly left for Germany and Gretchen started her student teaching. One day she was informed by the post office that she needed to sign for a package. It was a small package and the folks in the post office had a good idea of what it was. She opened it with her roommate after returning home and found a beautiful solitaire diamond engagement ring. Planning began right away, and the date was set for August 2, 1969. Gretchen remembered, "Then wedding day came! It was a day to never be forgotten and I can't believe it has been fifty-one years."

After the wedding, they traveled to Alexander City to meet Harry's family and friends. There were many good times and Gretchen was introduced to the famous Southern hospitality. "I was also introduced to some great new Southern dishes and even spent an evening with Harry, his brother Jim, and a couple of others on their front porch with a bottle of Everclear! What can I say? It was clearly a unique experience, but I don't recall how clear it was the next day!" [Everclear was a tasteless distilled grain liquor that could be as much as 190 proof].

After this trip they departed for Augsburg, Germany where they were for approximately four months, during which time Harry was in the field for about eight weeks. During that time, they explored Germany as much as possible, and Gretchen was introduced to skiing. They spent Christmas in Stuttgart with close friends. In January they left Germany to visit friends and family back home before Harry left for Vietnam. One of the highlights for her was an overnight stop at the Grand Canyon. They made some wonderful memories on that trip. Harry left in mid-February and Gretchen drove to Sacramento to spend the time with her sister. They wrote as often as they could, but Harry didn't share details about what he was doing, as if he wanted to protect Gretchen from all the bad stuff. Shortly before he died on March 31, he wrote about his concern for the lack of NCOs in his unit. Harry was lost to Gretchen and all of us just over a month after his arrival in-country. What a terrible loss to her, to his family, to his country and Army, and especially to his classmates that loved him. Six months of marriage and six weeks of combat . . .

On Easter Sunday, March 31, 1970, only weeks after arriving in Vietnam, Harry's platoon, with a scout dog team, was on a reconnaissance mission along the spine of a ridge when it came under heavy enemy fire. From Henry's citation for the Bronze Star with V Device:

While serving as a platoon leader in company B, 2nd Battalion (Airmobile), 506th Infantry, Lieutenant Hayes' unit was on a reconnaissance patrol when it came under enemy small arms fire. Moving to the point of contact, Lieutenant Hayes repeatedly subjected himself to hostile fire to supervise and encourage his men. Displaying excellent leadership, he directed the return fire of his men until he was mortally wounded. His efforts allowed his men to gain fire superiority and thwart the enemy ambush.

He directed his men until he was killed in a heavy fusillade of small-arms fire, which killed two others and the dog. There abruptly ended the life of an incredible young man before he even had a fair start. He was doing what he was trained for, and what he believed in—leading from the front. His loss was a heavy blow for many of us.

After graduating from Airborne School, Steve Marcuccelli never saw Harry again. Between phases of flight school, Steve went to Alexandria, Alabama to see Harry's mom and to visit the cemetery. When he went to pay his respects, he reflected, "I remember thinking what a waste it was to lose someone who enjoyed life so much. He was a good one."

Bob Brace provided a fitting epitaph for this remarkable young man:

> Like so very many others who knew and loved Harry well and deeply, I will never, as long as I live, forget the day I learned of Harry's death.
>
> Like Harry, I was a young infantry first lieutenant eight months into a twelve-month Vietnam combat tour. We were in a jungle resupply position *logging-up* for the last leg of a lengthy reconnaissance-in-force and search and destroy mission. The mail came, the first in several weeks. There was a thick letter from my mom. About halfway through she had drawn a line across the page, as if having stopped writing for a while and about to continue anew. It read something like:
>
> "My Dearest Son, It is with the heaviest of hearts and great sadness that I must tell you we have received word that your very best friend from West Point, Harry Hayes, has been killed in Vietnam . . ."
>
> There I sat in the middle of my men stunned to the core . . . unable to breathe, my heart feeling as if it was being

torn out of my chest, and the tears started streaming down my face uncontrollably. I didn't, or couldn't, read anymore. I stuck the letter inside my fatigue shirt and simply wandered off into the jungle, face in hands, where I could sob alone until I wore myself out and the tears ran dry. It was perhaps the darkest moment of my life, and my emotions were as raw as I can ever remember. Losing Harry still hurts my seventy-five-year-old heart even today. His friendship meant the world to me. He was my best buddy and a dear brother! Harry was a very special guy to me and many, many others!

Harry is interred in Hillview Memorial Park in Alexander City, Alabama.

Don and his mother after graduation parade

Jeff in his backyard—1961

Harry Hayes—150 pound football

Harry and his Mom at
West Point, Plebe Year

Jeff with Dad, Ankara Turkey

Jeff as the Recon Platoon Leader, 2nd/60th INF, 9th Infantry Division

Don on an ACAV, Vietnam 1969

Second Lieutenant Harry Hayes

Jeff's headstone in Arlington National Cemetary

Don's license plate on author's golf cart

VIETNAM: MAY 1970

Richard Aspinall Hawley Jr.   John Edward Darling Jr.

April 1970 was a safe month for us, despite what I'm sure was some heavy combat for some of '68; we lost no one, which is remarkable as April was the beginning of the incursion into Cambodia. Then came May and the loss of two more of our brothers; Rick Hawley was killed on the sixth, and John Darling on the eighteenth. The horrible costs of the war continued to rise for '68.

According to W. Killian in his post on The Wall of Faces,

Firebase Henderson was a US Marine Corps and US Army firebase located south of Ca Lu in Quang Tri Province, RVN. The base was occupied by elements of the 2nd Battalion, 501st Infantry Regiment; 2nd Battalion, 11th Artillery; 326th Engineer Battalion and ARVN units supporting Operation Texas Star when it was attacked by the North Vietnamese Army's 33rd Sapper Battalion at 5:05 a.m. on May 6,

1970. The attack began with rocket-propelled grenades, small arms, satchel charges, recoilless rifle, and mortar fire followed by a well-organized and coordinated ground attack. The NVA employed flamethrowers, which started fires causing approximately 1000 rounds of 155mm artillery ammunition to explode. The enemy withdrew at 7:20 a.m. Company B, 2nd Battalion (Airmobile), 501st Infantry, moved by air to reinforce Company A. An ARVN unit assaulted the south of Henderson to locate and destroy the remainder of the enemy force. A number of friendly casualties were caused by the exploding 155mm artillery ammunition; twenty-three Americans were killed, thirty-three wounded, and two were missing in action. The lost Americans included First Lieutenant Richard A. Hawley Jr.

Little first-hand information is available on Rick's early life. A glance through his 1962 yearbook, *The Non Pareil* from Nether Providence High School of Wallingford, Pennsylvania, shows that Rick had a typical experience for kids of our time. The book is filled with best wishes from guys and girls reminiscing about past good times and extending best wishes for the future. Rick played football, was a member of the varsity club and was the business manager of the school newspaper *The Bark*. Much of the information that follows is from classmate Mike Brennan, a company mate, roommate, inspired admirer, and close friend of Rick's. They were truly brothers.

Rick's father had been an infantry lieutenant at the famous Battle of the Bulge in December 1944. The Germans broke through his division's lines, causing many of its soldiers to flee in panic. Lt. Hawley and his men stayed and fought but were pushed back to Bastogne. There they linked up with units of the 101st Airborne Division and repulsed many attacks. During those actions Lt. Hawley was wounded in the leg, which had to be amputated. He was finally able to be evacuated, and before he left a trooper took out his knife and cut the 101st patch off his own uniform and presented it to Lt. Hawley in thanks for his bravery and fighting alongside the division. Rick's dad treasured this gesture and after the war made a shadow box for the patch and his own combat infantry badge.

As the son and nephew of World War II veterans, Rick heard many such stories growing up that instilled in him a deep sense of love of country and respect for the US Army. Like many of us, Rick saw the movie *The Long Gray Line* in 1955 and watched the TV series *The West Point Story* from 1956–1958. He decided that he wanted to attend West Point and serve as an infantry officer like his dad.

Unfortunately, Rick's grades and test scores were not high enough to qualify for admission and he was rejected. He then attended Birmingham Southern for a year, and with improved grades applied again. He was rejected again. So, not to be denied, Rick enlisted in the Navy and graduated from their nuclear submarine qualification course. During December 1963 he resubmitted an application again, this time from the USS Nautilus, deep in the waters under the North Pole. This time it worked, and Rick was admitted with the class of '68.

After the completion of Beast, Rick, Mike and a soon-to-be third roommate, Eric Thomas, were all assigned to Company C1, US Corps of Cadets. What a trio they proved to be. Eric was an academic, especially a math hive. Mike had real problems with math but could squeeze by because he was good in liberal arts. However, Rick fell further and further behind because he had no real academic strongpoints. As his academic problems continued to mount, Rick was taken out of the room and moved in with Jack Cochran, who became his good friend and tutor for the rest of the four years. Later that December, Jack, Eric and Mike all voluntarily returned to school early after Christmas to work with Rick to prepare him for the turn out exams that awaited him. Several other classmates were in the same situation as Rick, but just gave up and left West Point. Rick refused to do that. He spent every waking hour preparing for the exams, and took and passed them all; he remained a dedicated member of the class.

During plebe year *gloom period* (after Christmas and before spring break—everything is gray; uniforms, buildings, snow) when there is not much to do outside, Mike decided to visit the West Point Cemetery, figuring that there wouldn't be any upperclassmen there to harass him. It became his favorite hideout and as he walked the rows of headstones, he thought about the guys they represented. They had been cadets as well and had survived their time at West Point. If they could do it, so could he.

One afternoon as he walked the cemetery, he saw another cadet ahead of him; it was Rick. Rick had a real contemplative side to his personality that many of us were not aware of. Mike discovered that Rick had been making similar pilgrimages for the same reasons. As they walked together, they shared their frustrations about the stresses and strains of academics and of being plebes in First Regiment. They talked about the men buried there, wondered what their lives had been like as cadets and officers, and realized that they had survived West Point, so they sure as hell could as well. This day raised their spirits and they continued visiting this inspirational place even as first classmen, although not together. "The cemetery, its graves, and the mental images of the men of the Long Gray Line who had gone before us kept us grounded and sane." They truly *gripped hands*.

In Mike's words:

> Our classmates respected him for his tremendous moral courage and tenacity, for his steadfast dedication to hanging in there in spite of all adversities, and for his dogged refusal to quit. But I was luckier than most, because I was one of the few classmates who was privileged to know Rick as a roommate, good friend, and personal inspiration. In many ways that really mattered, Rick was an exemplar of dedication to being a West Point cadet, of devotion to serving his country as an infantry officer, and of both moral and physical courage.

At the start of firstie year, we were allowed to sign up for one elective course. Mike decided on an Age of Enlightenment course on eighteenth century European history, and because Mike was his tutor, Rick signed up for the same thing. Rick did well on the exams but had no inspiration for an end-of-term paper. Mike suggested the topic of how the lifestyles and sexual peccadilloes of the rulers of that time period affected their style of governing. Needless to say, Rick jumped into the research that was needed.

During this time Rick was doing so well that he was afraid of losing his *class goat* status so Eric and Jack pulled out their slide rules to see how many tenths he needed to stay eligible for weekend passes but not lose his cherished status. During a conference with his *P* (how we referred to our professors) Mike was asked how Rick was doing. All of the instructors really liked Rick and were pulling for him, so Mike explained Rick's conundrum; he needed a passing grade—but just barely. The P said he understood. On his departure the P said that he wanted to see Mike the afternoon of the day the papers were handed in.

When Mike arrived, he was told to sit in the P's cubicle while he went to talk with the officer grading Rick's paper. There were several other officers there and Mike could hear them discussing Rick's paper. Rick's P finally said that it looked like a passing paper, but only just barely. Mike's P returned with a large grin and told Mike he could return to the barracks. When Rick was told the news he was pleased, but a little taken aback because he didn't realize that the instructors would care enough to go to bat for him. He was both proud and humble.

There's another very special story about Rick, and his ability to relate to, and be friends with, everyone with whom he came in contact. Like most institutions, West Point had a custodial staff who was responsible for the general upkeep, cleanliness, and maintenance of the buildings. At our alma mater they were referred to as *BP*s or *barracks policemen*, instead of janitors as they were known in most other places. Unbeknownst to most of the cadets there was a special BP who had an office in the sinks of East Barracks under company C1. This gentleman's name was Bobby Brown and he had become good friends with Rick. What made this guy so special was that he was a Medal of Honor recipient from World War II who had received a battlefield commission in North Africa. In addition to the MOH, former Captain Brown was also the recipient of two Silver Stars, the Bronze Star with V, and *eight* Purple Hearts. In 1971 he tragically took his own life due to his constant pain and inability to cope with his memories, and subsequently received a hero's burial in Arlington National Cemetery. During Rick's four years they maintained a close and personal relationship because he knew that Bobby was more than just a janitor.

During branch selection firstie year, Rick had a profound effect on the process. There came a time in the proceedings when all branches had been filled except Infantry, and the guys left had no choice, they were *ranked* (couldn't select anything else because they ranked so low on the order of merit list) into that branch, which included Rick because of his standing as last in the class. Those ranked would not have the option to stand and select their branch. The following was provided by Mike Brennan:

> At that point, Rick stood up and stated, "Sir, Mr. Hawley requests to be recognized." The tactical officer knew Rick and wasn't sure what would come next, but he agreed to listen. Rick then made the following comments. "Sir, Mr. Hawley requests the right to select Infantry as his branch of choice. Sir, Mr. Hawley's father was an infantry officer at the Battle of the Bulge. He lost a leg fighting alongside the 101st Airborne Division. All Mr. Hawley has ever wanted to be since he was a little boy was to be an infantry officer and to serve in the 101st Airborne. Sir, Mr. Hawley demands his right to select Infantry as his branch. Sir, Mr. Hawley has earned that right.
>
> Seeing how serious Rick was, the officer agreed. He stated that he would call each of the names of the last men in the class and allow them to verbally select Infantry as their branch. And so, one by one, when each man's name was called, he stood and stated, "Infantry," sometimes resignedly and sometimes proudly. When it was Rick's turn, he stood up as proudly as if he'd been the first man in the class and shouted out, "I choose Infantry. MOS 11B, the combat infantry's the branch for me." At that point, all of us who had volunteered for the infantry jumped to our feet and gave Rick a standing ovation. He had said, in just a few words, what we felt to our depths.

Classmate Tom McConnell had some very special and very emotional memories of Rick, who was a great friend and truly a brother. They spent four years together in Company C1. Rick was a great outdoorsman and reintroduced Tom to deer hunting and fly fishing.

One weekend, they spent the time on Long Mountain on the West Point reservation. They got up early in the morning and went to their deer stands a couple of hundred yards apart. Tom saw a beautiful buck come out of the tree line in Rick's area so didn't shoot. Rick didn't either, which really confused Tom, so he went over to ask what had happened after the deer had disappeared back into the woods, and why Rick had let that beautiful buck walk away. Rick looked up and said that Tom had obviously not seen the doe and two little fawns that were with the buck. "That statement told me so much about Rick."

The Rick that Tom knew was, well, a passive soul. In plebe boxing class, Rick had absorbed far more punches than he landed. So, what happened one day when both of them were spending the weekend at Rick's home near Philadelphia gave Tom a deeper, more accurate insight into what his friend Rick was all about. Tom and Rick were enjoying conversation, drinks, and music at a yard party in the neighborhood when they noticed a young man at the other end of the yard, about half a football field away, getting ready to set fire to an American flag. Rick handed Tom his drink, told him to meet him at their car, and then took off in a sprint toward the unaware flag-torching protester. Rick hit the culprit at full speed, launching him sprawling in a daze. Rick got up, picked up the rescued flag, and walked calmly out to the car. He and Tom drove off, the point having been made.

And another memory from Tom:

During the academic year I was one of Rick's tutors trying to get him ready for exams. I had another experience that also told me a lot about Rick in a different setting. I had spent a long time getting him ready for an exam firstie year in, I think, thermodynamics. When the results came back Rick had flunked it convincingly. I couldn't believe it and asked how that could have happened as we'd been over all of the material, and I knew that he knew it well. He didn't say anything but just looked at me with that little shit-eating grin again. I guessed then that Rick was determined to be the class goat.

At the graduation ceremony in Michie Stadium, Rick was the last to walk across the stage and receive his diploma. When it was presented, he proudly held it over his head and the whole class roared our congratulations. A light memory from Ken Hauk:" Rick Hawley bought a blue Camaro convertible as his graduation car. I bought an Infantry-blue Corvette convertible. He wanted a Corvette in the spring of 1969, and I wanted out of the Corvette, which had a problem with vapor locks. We switched for the cost difference. Rick never told me if he had problems, and if anyone still has the car, they are pretty happy with the value now."

There is a story of Rick and Ranger School that needs to be shared. He and many classmates were *winter rangers,* who really suffered from the cold weather. One of the last requirements of the Benning phase at Camp Darby was held at Victory Pond. The Ranger candidates were required to climb a tower, walk a narrow plank, shimmy along a horizontal rope, hang from that rope near a large metal Ranger tab, and ask permission to drop. When that was received, the candidate dropped into the water and then exited the pond. That was the normal procedure. Rick, however, hung from the rope and recited a very demeaning poem alluding to the family history, sexual orientation, and general depravity of the cadre. Rick then asked for, and was given, permission to drop whereby the enraged cadre exacted their revenge. The rest of the class, meantime, had erupted into howls of laughter, many rolling on the ground. For those guys, Rick's complete lack of fear and incredible sense of humor will live forever.

After completing the normal schools, Rick served his stateside six months, and in the summer of '69 boarded a plane for Vietnam. Because his orders did not assign him to the 101st Airborne Division (Airmobile), Rick went AWOL from the replacement battalion in Long Binh and reported to the division anyway at Camp Eagle. Somehow, as only Rick could accomplish, he was accepted, without accompanying orders, and assigned to the 2nd Battalion, 501st Infantry because the division needed Infantry lieutenants and Rick was volunteering. When his unusual assignment was detected, it was overlooked, as Rick was certainly not shirking combat duty. He had finally realized his boyhood dream of serving in the division.

On May 5, Rick, as the battalion's recon platoon leader, was ordered to move to an abandoned Marine Corps firebase named Henderson to augment the security force, A Company/2-501st. Alpha Company had been battered in previous contacts with the NVA and arrived on the hill with sixty replacements who could be integrated into the company in this "quiet" area. Also on the firebase was an ARVN 105mm battery and the 155mm howitzers of B Battery/2-11 Field Artillery. There was also a regimental TOC of the 1st ARVN Infantry Division. It took all day for A Company and recon to establish their positions and set up their claymore mines. There was no time to clear fields of fire or establish a concertina wire perimeter. There were no security patrols run or listening posts established. An hour before dawn on May 6, NVA sappers cut two paths through the inadequate wire and led NVA assault troops into Henderson's perimeter. Either a flame thrower or a satchel charge ignited a fuel fire which detonated the ammunition in the storage area where over a thousand rounds of 155mm ammunition were stacked. First Lieutenant Rick Hawley and most of his men were killed in that blast. Rick's parents received the news of his death on Mother's Day. Inadequate defensive measures and preparation made Henderson an attractive and easy target for the NVA, who had obviously been scouting it for a while.

Those in the class who learned of Rick's loss were devastated. He had been such an inspiration, taking on all problems while never losing his love of being a cadet and his love of West Point. Eric Thomas, Rick's best friend, escorted Rick's body home. Chaplain James Ford, who was the cadet chaplain during our time there, and who Rick had befriended, officiated at Rick's funeral and internment in the West Point Cemetery. Rick's father and inspiration was buried in Arlington National Cemetery in the fall of 1984. James Ford, then the chaplain of the US House of Representatives, officiated at that ceremony as well.

One of Rick's soldiers, Wesley Wieghmink, wrote on the Vietnam Memorial Wall of Faces:

Captain Hawley, I have thought about you often in the last 35 years. How, when we were in the bush talking about country music, plans after Vietnam . . . I was always looking forward to getting out of the Army while you looked forward to your career IN the Army. I served under your leadership in September, 1969, when you were a 1st Lt. You were a super nice guy and I saw you more as a friend than an Officer. We got along very well even though I was only a Corporal and two years older than you were. Your integrity and bravery will always be remembered. . .. From a friend.

At least four classmates or other friends named their sons after Rick. Mike Brennan told Rick's mother, "I didn't name my first son Richard Hawley Brennan just because Rick was the best guy in the world; I named him after Rick because Rick just didn't know how to quit."

An anonymous classmate posted the following tribute to Rick on Westpoint.org:

THE LAST SHALL BE FIRST . . .

You anchored the line for us in '68; thanks to you there was
no one left to graduate.
With your crossing the stage, we all began life
on a new page.
History has written the story for all;
Some short, some long, some good, some we can't recall.
But your life is remembered, though short in days,
For it was one of distinction in many different ways.
Each of us in front of you did not envy your fate,
Yet the last showed us all that there was no task too great!
You made it!
You are remembered!
We shall all join you someday as the Long Gray Line
continues as a Corps of Brothers.

Classmate Bill Miller has some fitting words for Rick:

I didn't know Rick personally but knew of him as a classmate. I always admired his determination and effort to graduate, even though he had many chances to fail. Several years ago, I was walking through the cemetery at West Point, looking at classmate's tombstones and when I saw Rick's I was moved in a way I have never been. To think of all the effort that he gave to earn the chance to serve in Vietnam as a West Point graduate and to be killed less than two years after graduation marked him as a distinguished graduate in my mind. Every time I return to the cemetery, I make a point of spending a few quiet moments at his grave. I never knew him, but I feel a strong admiration and respect for this distinguished graduate.

I suspect that these days, there are cadets who walk through the cemetery seeking solace and inspiration as Rick and Mike Brennan did in 1964, and they might stop at Rick's grave and marvel at the fact that he gave his life for his country such a short time after graduation. Like many others from the class of '68. If they knew of the incredible obstacles he overcame to graduate, and how proud he was to serve in the 101st Airborne Division (Airmobile), they'd be even more impressed.

And from his sister Meg:

Now in our 60s and 70s, we are all the same age, but as children, eight years is a huge gap and that was the number of years between my oldest brother and me. That gap made me somehow interesting to him. Perhaps much younger siblings are interesting because they are available and willing participants. The legacy wants to know who Ricky Hawley was before West Point. There was Ricky Hawley without West Point but there was no Ricky Hawley without the army.

When one realizes the determination and sacrifices of young men like Rick one can only wonder and marvel at their dedication to West Point, the Army, and most importantly to their country. It is indeed sad to see such promising lives end so soon after years of struggle to be where they were when they died, where they wanted to be, leading American soldiers in combat. Men like Rick, and the others in this book, never had a chance to realize their true potential or to live a complete life. This is the true meaning of the word tragedy.

A fitting epitaph to Rick's unjustly short life is offered by Mike Brennan:

Courage—Determination—Unbreakable Spirit
Classmate, roommate, and friend
Rick Hawley had a dream:
To become a West Pointer and member of The Long Gray Line
To serve his country as an infantry officer
To be a paratrooper and Army Ranger
To serve as a rifle platoon leader in combat with the 101st Airborne
Rick was a wonderful guy, a fun-loving and loyal friend
A determined and resourceful young man
A cadet of unbreakable will and guts
An infantry officer by choice
Number 706—our last man standing
An officer who talked his way into Airborne School and the 101st Airborne
A combat infantry officer who led from the front and respected and loved his troops
A soldier who did his duty, courageously and valiantly

DUTY, HONOR, COUNTRY—
It is one thing to say it, but another thing to live it.

Mike wrote in Rick's Memorial Article for the Association of Graduates:

> We realized then [when Rick was killed in action] that none of us had worked as hard as Rick had throughout our years at West Point, and none of us was more deserving than he of the opportunity to fulfill his ambition of a career of service. Suddenly, that opportunity had been snatched away from Rick forever. Yet, in giving up his life for his country, he made the greatest sacrifice a soldier can make, and in that sense he had fulfilled all that his country could ever ask of him.

Rick Hawley is interred in the West Point Cemetery.

❖ ❖ ❖

Some twelve days after the loss of Rick, on the eighteenth of May, with the class still reeling from that news, an Army Huey helicopter from company C, 158th Aviation Battalion, was flying a resupply mission to LZ Ripcord when the aircraft was hit by enemy ground fire and attempted to make a forced landing. The attempt was unsuccessful, and it crashed and rolled down a hill into a triple canopy area. Three crewman and two passengers were later found to have died, the crew chief jumped clear and was rescued on an adjacent ridge the next day. He had no knowledge of the exact location of the crew members or wreckage. One of the passengers who was missing was First Lieutenant John Darling Jr, the signal officer for the 2nd Battalion, 506th Infantry Regiment. The class of '68 had lost yet another phenomenal member from our ranks.

On May 19, the aerial rifle platoon of Troop B, 2nd Battalion, 7th Cavalry was inserted into the area to search for the bird. They were unsuccessful and were extracted as night fell. The downed aircraft was finally located on May 31 after almost two weeks and remains were recovered, confirming that everyone on the aircraft had died but the one crewman thrown free.

John was raised in the town of Fremont, Michigan where he was an outstanding student athlete. Today, his high school presents the John F. Darling Jr. Award for Wrestling annually and states "This is awarded each year to the wrestler who best exemplifies the character of the soldier who gave his life in Vietnam." In addition to school achievements, John also became an Eagle Scout. Some of the scouts remember him as a kind and thoughtful leader even at an early age. Not only was he an outstanding scout and an accomplished wrestler, but he also played football and was a member of the high school varsity club. A fellow alum remarked that he respected John for his leadership and dedication.

Reading anecdotes and stories from classmates about John, he comes across as a big tough guy who loved to wrestle, sometimes moody and temperamental as he strove to make weight before a match, a party lover, and a carefree non-conformist, dedicated to doing the best that he could, but most of all, a dependable and loyal friend.

During Beast Barracks, John was assigned to First New Cadet Company, living in old Central Area. On the first day a roommate happened to glance over his shoulder as he was writing a letter home; it started with "THIS PLACE IS HELL!"

John was one of many of our classmates who I've learned played musical chairs with company assignments during our four years. After Beast he started in Company M-1, which became F-3 when we reorganized into four regiments, and firstie year he wound up in H-3. It happened to John even in Beast. On the second day, just as the roommates were getting acquainted and getting their room arranged, their squad leader came in and announced that the company was being reorganized and that they were being assigned new rooms with new roommates. So, the three struggling new cadets put all of their worldly possessions into their mattress covers and trudged off to their new assignments. The three short- term roommates did not meet up again during the ensuing four years, although they did all graduate. One resigned from the Army as a conscientious objector, one served for his initial five-year obligation, and John was lost in combat.

When Beast was completed, John was assigned to Company M-1, and again experienced some roommate turmoil. John and one of the guys couldn't get along with the third and this came to the attention of the company chain of command. Subsequently the source of friction was moved, and Tom Margrave became the new third. Tom had quite a change as well, as he had been living with a fellow corps squader (varsity athlete). Tom remarked on his new environment; "Gary and John were quite the pair and I remember spending a lot of time trying to keep the room straight and avoid special attention from our tactical officer."

Early on, John exhibited his love of parties. One night during plebe year, John disappeared, returning just before taps. He had obviously been drinking . . . a lot. Unfortunately, John slept in the bunk bed above Tom, and in the middle of the night hung his head over the side and barfed. This could have been catastrophic on a couple of counts. The room was obviously not in inspection order, which could have caused untold misery for its occupants had an upperclassman or officer been around, and John's obvious state could have resulted in a huge slug (major punishment of demerits, punishment tours and room confinement) and dismissal from the wrestling team because he had been drinking. The roommates cleaned up and lucked out.

John's love of partying was exhibited again at the Army-Navy game of our first year. The entire Corps went to Philadelphia by train and had to report back to the train for the return trip around midnight, resulting in a few free hours in town after the game. Classmate Pat O'Keefe remembered that John managed to arrange for several kegs of beer to be delivered to a hotel room, where it was iced down in the tub. Somehow John had arranged for plenty of food and drink for all, resulting in a great party. No one knows how he was able to pull this off, particularly as a plebe. John was a natural leader and very charismatic, and people wanted to be with him and follow him.

One of John Darling's most memorable escapades was when he reported to Camp Buckner with dyed-blond hair that had turned a shade of orange. Reports are that he was written up by a TAC for destruction of government property!

Paul Joseph recounted a weekend yearling year when John took a bunch of classmates camping. His Eagle Scout skills were on display, as John did everything from making the fire to cooking and cleaning up. It was a great night away from campus, as well as provided a great bonding opportunity for several classmates. Once again, John was the leader.

Paul had another experience with John when he visited John's home in Michigan, a real eye-opening experience for Paul. They would go out every night, and on one occasion they went to a dance hall on the outskirts of town. At some point in the evening, John found Paul and told him that he was leaving with someone for a while but to not worry, as he'd return before the club closed to pick up Paul. By five o'clock the next morning, John had not returned, so Paul called John's parents, who said they would pick him up. Before they arrived, as the sun was rising, John showed up. When told that Paul had called his folks, he was not real happy. Without waiting on his folks, John pulled out of the parking lot just as they were arriving. He wanted to face the music at home, figuring that it would go down easier since Paul would be there. They survived this adventure and wound up as roommates again when school started.

Academics and wrestling practice started in the fall, and the roommates had to deal with John making weight. One morning, as Paul was trying to get the room straightened out before class, John got irritated and roughly grabbed Paul. Fearing for his wellbeing Paul lashed out and punched John; Paul was a good boxer in his own right being brigade champion later that year, but he thought that John would kill him at that point. However, John, stunned that Paul had actually hit him, just let him go and walked away. Even with that discord, John and Paul remained good friends.

The third roommate, John Cruden, remembered how difficult John was to live with as he strove to make weight for every weigh-in. At one point, it got so bad that John and Paul moved all of their roommate's belongings out into the hall and prohibited his coming back in—a subtle message to say the least. Eventually, things improved and John was allowed back. John also remembered an incident in New York City when they attended the New York World's Fair, where of course they found the beer tent! On the subway after they left, John was sitting next to a comely young lady. Wanting to impress her, and give her something from West Point, he took off a shoe and handed it to her. She smiled and kept it!

The next year, on opposite sides in a volleyball match, John remembered jumping to spike the ball. It bounced off of John Darling's head, and with his follow through, John Cruden broke John Darling's nose—something that John never forgot. The next year, during intramural lacrosse, John got his revenge. John Cruden was playing attack for Company H3, John Darling was on defense for F3. As John Cruden was running in for a shot at goal, he was blocked and then John Darling *cleaned his clock*. John continued for a few minutes and then passed out. He discovered at the hospital that he had split a thigh muscle, maybe revenge for a broken nose?

Classmate Joe Dooley recounts another story of John Darling the partier in the spring of '68, shortly before graduation. John had asked him to help him with a few "minor" details of planning for a party in a New York City hotel suite. The details included cosigning for the suite and procuring and transporting the beer to the hotel. He soon found himself driving his shiny new Pontiac into Manhattan following

John's directional guidance. They went past the northern end of Central Park and into Harlem. As they had no idea where they were, John kept asking people on the sidewalks for directions. The streets kept getting narrower until they ended up in an alleyway with no signs or numbers on the buildings. John said, "I think this is it." He got out of the car and banged hard on a closed metal door until someone came out. After a few words, several big men came out and somehow loaded the beer kegs into the trunk and back seat of the car. With a sagging vehicle, they were off to the hotel, more than eighty blocks to the south. Don't ask how they got the kegs up in the elevators—that was more of the Darling magic. The rest of the party was easy because John had personally arranged for food and supplies to be delivered to the suite. He kept an eye on everything and everyone, always the welcoming host. The party was another huge success for John. The aftermath and clean-up were altogether different matters.

Julie Heck (Heckman), the widow of classmate George Heckman Jr, had some fond memories, as John and George were the best of friends. In her mind they were not friends but rather brothers. Sometimes they were rivals, sometimes teammates, but they always had each other's back. They were close through West Point and Ranger School, until their final goodbye in Michigan. Through thick and thin, good times and some not so good, their friendship flourished and deepened. To Julie, John was very dear, good looking, and again, a fun-loving rebel. She was always glad to see John, as he always made her smile.

While George and John were the best of friends, so were their girlfriends, and eventual wives, Julie and Cathy. During June week the two intrepid young cupids had plans for a final success over the tactical department. John got the girls a room at the on-campus Thayer Hotel. The plan was that the guys would sneak out after taps, meet the ladies behind the hotel, and go up to their room for a party. John had once again arranged for drinks and snacks, and the two would leave early the next morning to be back at the barracks for the days' events. What the heck, they were being commissioned in a few days, what could go wrong? Things went well initially, they ascended the back staircase, and were about to sneak into the room when confronted by an MP (military policeman) who had been stationed on the floor to prevent just such escapades. The dejected guys slunk back to the barracks.

As Paul Joseph remarked, "He was an individual that lived life to its utmost. He was a character with a booming personality with a bent for mischief! If you were hanging with John, you were going to have a good time!" He felt fortunate to have roomed with John and George. They were two big, tough guys but they knew where they were going.

Chuck Canella seemed to follow John through those early Army days. In '69 Chuck went to his first assignment with the 82nd Signal Battalion as a platoon leader. John was already there and in the same assignment with a sister battalion and had been there for a couple of months and therefore was well-seasoned. John took Chuck under his wing and made sure that he knew what was going on and what his requirements were. They were certainly comrades, but also became great friends; Chuck was often invited to dinner at the Darling's. John left for Vietnam and was assigned as the signal officer to the 2/506 Infantry in the 101st Airborne (Airmobile) Division. Chuck arrived a couple of months later and was assigned to the same job in the 2/502nd Infantry, and again John reached out to help Chuck learn the ropes. They communicated frequently by radio, field phone, or personal visits.

The two battalions were operating in the same AO, so Chuck learned almost immediately of John being shot down. He remembered that in their last conversation John had told him that he was to leave the next day for Hawaii to meet Cathy on R&R.

From John's Silver Star citation:

> On April 1, 1970, while serving as communications officer for the 2nd Battalion (Airmobile), 506th Infantry, during a combat assault on abandoned Fire Support Base Ripcord, Republic of Vietnam. As the elements of the assaulting unit were inserted, the firebase came under intense hostile mortar fire. The tactical operations center received a direct hit, wounding the executive officer and several other men, and Lieutenant Darling immediately assumed command, then administered emergency treatment to the casualties. Braving the impacting rounds, Lieutenant Darling carried a wounded man to a medical evacuation helicopter, then returned to the command post to direct armed helicopter support of

extraction operations. His actions under fire enabled the prompt evacuation of casualties and forced the withdrawal of the hostile force.

From all of the stories related by classmates, there is no doubt that John Darling Jr. was an exceptional man. From the very beginning he made indelible impressions on all with whom he came in contact. I didn't know John any more than to know who he was when I saw him, but there was no doubt that he had a presence about him that basically separated him from everyone else around him. As is the case with all our fallen, it's impossible to read the memories and stories without having a really sad feeling that they left us much too soon. The devotion and love of classmates who related memories is obvious for all to see.

Sometimes the most poignant accolades and memories come from those who served in combat with the man we're honoring. Such was the case with John. Several have posted tributes on Wall of Faces:

> You will never be forgotten you were a great leader and a caring officer. I had the privilege to serve with you in Vietnam and will never forget the nights we spent playing cribbage with only 2 weeks left in country. I wanted to come on that flight but you would not allow it since I was about to return home. You were everybody's best friend you were not as west point as the stiff shirts wanted you to be.
>
> —SGT Paul Donalds 2ND BN 506INF 6/69 to 6/70.

> 44 years have gone by, and every May I remember you are the reason I got to come home. May God bless you forever John.
>
> —SP 4 Terry Betts

> WE SERVED OUR TIME IN THE VALLEY—Lt. Darling was my platoon leader in Vietnam. Sometimes you meet someone, and you automatically know they are exceptional people. Lt

Darling was this type of a person. He had an air of confidence about him and he was a natural leader. All of the men in our platoon would not have hesitated to follow him through the gates of Hell if he deemed it necessary. From a comrade in arms in Vietnam.

　　—Jerry Lampier

THE FINEST YOUNG OFFICER—My cousin was the aircraft commander of the slick you were riding in on 18 May 1970, and he died with you. My research of his service brought me in contact with one of your men, and I learned from him that you were an outstanding young officer. You provided great leadership and motivation to your men, and they would have followed you into the depths of Hell if you led them there. Learning about you has taught me that, in war, we lose the very best of our young leaders, because they are most needed where the danger is greatest. Thank you for your service and sacrifice. May God Bless you and your family.

　　—Dean Gabriel

As a final tribute to our classmate, and a lasting honor to a soldier who gave everything for his country, the US Army Signal Corps dedicated a building in memory of First Lieutenant John Darling Jr. On June 8, 1994, the US Army Signal Center and Fort Gordon, GA dedicated the new Darling Solider Service Center. The building, called Darling Hall, is a high-tech general purpose office building. Military, civil service, and non-appropriated fund personnel are in-processed and out-processed through this building, and a variety of services will be available for those personnel through their period of service at Fort Gordon. John's picture, awards, and medals are hanging on the wall. This building will be a lasting tribute to Lt. Darling and serve others who share in his dedication to the United States of America.

Classmate Major General Chuck Mahan ends this chapter with a fitting tribute to John that he posted on The Wall of Faces:

John Darling was a great athlete—one of West Point's best wrestlers. More importantly, he was the kind of individual that we, his fellow cadets, wanted to be. He was a dynamic leader, but with a caring attitude that reflected his unmatched ability to get things done through his strength of will -- and character. Those of us who knew him remember him still— and always will.

John is interred in the Maple Grove Cemetery, Freemont, Michigan.

Rick and date, high school prom

John and his new GTO—
Spring 1968

Darling Hall, Fort Gordon

Rick holding last seat at graduation

Rick somewhere in Vietnam

Lieutenant John Darling

VIETNAM: JULY THROUGH NOVEMBER 1970

Donald Renay Workman   David Thornton Maddux   Douglas Terrell Wheless

A fter the death of John Darling, the class did not lose another member until July, a two-month reprieve. In the last half of 1970 we lost three more: Don Workman on the twenty-first of July, Dave Maddux on the ninth of August, and Doug Wheless on the twenty-second of November, four days before Thanksgiving.

Don Workman was another of the giants of the class of 1968. He entered West Point from the US Military Academy Prep School at Ft. Belvoir, capping a couple of years of enlisted service. Although not academically gifted, he was hard working and a superb athlete. The '64 *Challenge*, the Prep School yearbook, says of Don, "This fellow has shown himself to be an excellent athlete and quickly became the boss of lacrosse," a skill that would follow him to West Point, where he would eventually captain the academy team. He was the man of many nicknames, known as "Weezerk" at Ft. Belvoir, "The Troll" at West Point and "Ranger" in Vietnam. From very humble beginnings where he had to work to help support his mother during high school, to enlisted service in the Army, to being one of four regimental commanders at West Point in 1968, and at the end, a commander of an infantry company in the 101st Airborne Division (Air Mobile), Don's life was full of achievement but tragically all too short. In fact, the personal traits of leadership and courage that he demonstrated all the way through would probably have marked him for achievement of the highest levels in the Army had he survived Vietnam. His death was a tragic loss to the country, the Army, West Point, and especially to our class.

Don's sister, Karin Loke, provided some great insight into Don's early life. He was born on April 14, 1943, in Albany, California, neighboring Oakland, to Marion Eugene Workman and Faunlee Ferrell. Don's father was working in the shipyards in the San Francisco area when Don was born and spent twenty-seven months overseas afterwards in service to his country during WWII, including Italy and Northern Africa. The Workmans divorced in 1950 and Don and his sister Karin went to live on a farm with their maternal grandparents in Missouri near Springfield. Their dad lived in the same area but only saw his kids on weekends because of his work and the fact that he had remarried. Even though their grandparents took great care of them, the kids moved to Florida after six years to be with their mom. Don was thirteen at this point and worked mowing lawns to help his mom financially, as she now had two kids to support.

The family moved back to Missouri after the kids' grandfather passed away and lived in the Kirkwood area of St. Louis. Don entered Nipher Junior High School and then later Kirkwood High. Because he continued to work after school to help his mother with the family finances, he couldn't go out for any sports. Working at the gas station, however, he developed a life-time love of cars and bought a 1937 Chevy Coupe.

Karin remembered a special story about Don from those early days:

> On our grandparents' farm he and I decided to go to an old barn that was seldom used. We were told by our grandmother

to *not* go there since it probably had snakes in it. So, what did we do? We went to the old barn! We had to cross over the barbed wire fence to get there and I got tangled up in the barbed wire and tore a big hole in my shorts. I was crying that I would get into trouble with our grandmother and Don came to my rescue. He went back into the house without being seen and got a new pair of shorts for me to wear. Problem solved. The torn shorts were buried in the field, never to be seen again and our grandmother never knew the difference. Big brother to the rescue!

Don's high school years were remarkably innocent and carefree. We were living in an era of peace and prosperity under the leadership of our aging World War II hero Dwight Eisenhower as president. While we were living in the Cold War, with things like Sputnik and the prospect of nuclear war with fallout shelters in our backyards, the main impact this had on us was the threat of the military draft. Vietnam was totally beyond our comprehension.

Classmate Jerry Hansen remembered Don on Westpoint.org:

Don and I went to the same high school – Kirkwood High School in Kirkwood, Mo. I never knew him there, though, because he graduated before I started. We were interviewed by our local Congressman at the same time. I was a skinny 17-yr old almost ready to graduate from HS. Don was a man – a Sergeant in the Army and much more qualified than I; I knew he was in a different league. When we were both accepted to West Point, I knew that he would be a role model and pacesetter for the rest of us – if not in academics, then in every other endeavor.

Although we were in different regiments and I never got to know Don as well as I would have liked, I never lost the respect, almost awe, I felt for him. He always seemed a bit bigger than life. I was tremendously saddened to hear that he was killed, lost so soon. He would have been a great General. The Lord will have to explain all of this to me in time. We miss you Don!

Don graduated from Kirkwood High in 1961 and went to night school at the University of Missouri while holding down a full-time job at a medical device supply company. He saw that it would take too long to get a degree with this schedule, so he enlisted in the Army on the twenty-ninth of November 1962. He underwent basic training at Fort Leonard Wood, Missouri and then went to Sandia Base in Albuquerque, New Mexico for Nuclear Weapons School, where he graduated on May 29, 1963. His first duty assignment was in Germany, where his commanding officer noticed that Don had some outstanding leadership qualities and recommended that Don apply for the United States Military Academy Preparatory School (USMAPS) at Fort Belvoir, Virginia.

Karin remembered that in 1963, as he was about to start at USMAPS, she and Don went to a Chevrolet dealer to look at the new 1963 Corvettes. He told her that he'd have one someday, and so he did, buying a blue '68 Corvette his firstie year that he named "Blue Bird."

It was at USMAPS that Don developed his skills and love for lacrosse and where I really got to know him as I learned the game there as well. While at prep school, Don studied hard and received an appointment to the class of 1968 from Congressman Thomas B. Curtis. He entered West Point as an *old vet*, being three years older than most of his classmates and with two years of active duty already under his belt.

Our classmate Charlie Lieb had the great and unique experience of being close to Don during the entire four years at West Point, and then again in Vietnam. As he related:

Don and I were both in Company L-1 and C-3 together. Plebe year he was my roommate and saved me from many tours on the Area! I was a seventeen-year-old recent high school graduate from Minneapolis who had no idea what I was getting myself into by going to West Point. Luckily for me, the grizzled twenty-one-year-old Army veteran, Don Workman, was my first plebe year roommate after Beast Barracks. He taught me how to *dress off* my uniform, to make my bed to military specifications, and he tried to teach me how to shine my shoes. Unfortunately, I failed Shoeshine 101, so often that he would shine my shoes for me. He was always willing to help when asked and his stellar advice kept me out of a lot of trouble!

He also introduced me to drinking. On a trip to New York City for a football game plebe year, Don somehow managed to get to a liquor store and purchased a bottle of bourbon. He was of legal age and snuck it into the luggage room back at West Point and hid it in his suitcase. On one of the next weekends Donny, Greg Unangst (our third roommate), and I slipped into the luggage room and put a serious dent into his bourbon supply. Being underage and an athlete, I was somewhat of a Goody-Two-Shoes in high school. I had never had hard liquor before and although I participated, I didn't really like bourbon and still don't. This clearly showed the resourcefulness and leadership of Don Workman.

During our four years together at West Point, Don and I shared many great experiences. We did not room together after plebe year, but we were in the same company and played lacrosse together. I had never seen a game and knew nothing about it. He would go with me to the squash courts and teach me how to catch and throw the ball. He explained the rules and helped me learn the game. That was the kind of man Don was, always willing to help! Because of his age and maturity, he was often consulted by other cadets on the ways of the world and willingly provided advice and counsel. He always scored high in military aptitude and that led to his being selected as the Third Regimental commander our firstie year. I served one detail on his regimental staff and witnessed his leadership qualities up close and personal.

Classmate Rick Fetterman had a remarkable experience with Don while we were away from West Point on our first class trip that illustrated Don's selfless commitment to his classmates:

While we were at Ft. Benning, a group from C-3 decided to take a trip to Panama City. Don was the only one old enough to rent a truck. He had the back outfitted with a bunch of old car bench seats. He took the gang to Florida, doing all of the driving down and back, and none of the drinking, while his classmates sampled bubbly liquid and played cards. They arrived at the beach drunk and crazy. They slept on the beach, swam a lot, and had a ball. Don got them back to Ft. Benning in time to continue on the trip.

Don had a superb record at West Point. Even though he was not academically gifted, and had problems through all four years, his devotion to his classmates, his leadership qualities, and his physical prowess as a lacrosse goalie made him a *star man* of a different sort.

During the class trip, he encouraged classmate Dan Nettesheim while Dan was serving as the class commander. While all the installations we visited went out of their way to welcome our class and provide entertainment and celebration, there were some incidents that resulted in heavy punishment for the cadets involved, like one that ended in a US-Mexican border incident, a missed flight to the next post, and a high-level embarrassment to one post command. Several classmates received slugs, and a few confronted him with the belief that it was unwarranted to be that harsh with classmates and that Dan was carried away with his position. Don went to Dan and reassured him that he was doing the right thing, commenting that there is nothing more difficult than commanding peers.

While Don struggled with academics, there is no doubt that he was a natural leader. It was no surprise when Don was selected to serve as the commander of the Third Regiment, United States Corps of Cadets during our firstie year. In addition, he excelled at lacrosse as the team goalie, and was elected team captain our first class year. He set several records as goalie that lasted for years.

Charlie Lieb and Don wound up on the same plane going to Vietnam. They sat together on the flight and talked about memories of West Point, playing lacrosse together, and what they thought would happen once they arrived in Vietnam. After in-processing they were both assigned to the 101st Airborne Division; Don went to D company of the 1st/506th Infantry and Charlie to C Company of the 2nd/506th Infantry. They rode to Camp Evans together and then separated to go to their respective units.

They had no contact with each other for most of their tours until Don, now as the company commander of D Company, 1st of the 506th Infantry, was attached to Charlie's battalion for the intense battles around firebase Ripcord during July of 1970. He had spent the entire year in the field, first as a rifle company platoon leader, then as the battalion's recon platoon leader, and finally took command of D Company on April 14—his twenty-seventh birthday. Between that date and his arrival for duty attached to the 2nd/ 506th, his company had suffered many casualties in tough fighting. When the battalion commander selected Don's company for the assignment to Firebase Ripcord, Don had been scheduled for a change of command ceremony since he'd been in the field for more than eleven months and was scheduled to return home in about three weeks. However, Don, the consummate combat leader, didn't want to send his company into a dangerous mission with a new commander, so he postponed his change of command and accepted the mission. His incredible concern for the welfare of his soldiers, plus his confidence and leadership ability, defined Don's commitment to his job and how he lived his all too short life.

Charlie didn't see Don after his arrival into the second battalion's AO because he was wounded two days after Don's arrival. He does know that Don's company was in heavy contact until he was killed four days later. Charlie was in the hospital and was devastated when he learned of Don's death. The battles around Ripcord were the last major engagements by US troops in the Vietnam War. The fighting was so fierce that there were three Medals of Honor and several Distinguished Service Crosses awarded there.

Classmate John "Tony" Dodson was very close to Don and was in the area when the Ripcord fight was raging. A month before this battle, John and classmate Jim Llewellyn met Don at Cam Rahn Bay before his last R&R to Hawaii to meet his wife. Don had just come off an ambush patrol that had engaged an enemy force and was still wired. So, John and Jim drank a lot of beer with him that night to help him transition back to a semi-normal state. It was the last time they saw him. It is believed that Don got married either just before he deployed or while on R&R, but no one knows anything about his wife, where she was from or even her name.

The division commander ordered the evacuation of Firebase Ripcord on July 21, 1970, and it was during this evacuation that Don was killed. As the company was being evacuated from a hot pickup zone, a helicopter was shot down and Don was killed when hit by its rotor blades. Of the ninety-five soldiers in Don's company on the seventeenth of July, only twenty-five were evacuated. The remaining troops on the ground left the LZ and moved overland, leaving the dead behind, as they couldn't be carried, and enemy fire was too strong to attempt landing another helicopter. Don's body, along with the others killed on that ill-fated LZ, was finally recovered on the third of August. During the intervening time, Don and his men were listed as Missing in Action. This was unquestionably a tragic end for such an outstanding man and officer. Don was awarded a Silver Star for his actions during that time period. Jim Llewellyn escorted Don Home.

An excerpt from the citation for Don's Silver Star describes his heroic actions on his last day:

> . . . during a combat assault near Fire Support Base Ripcord, Republic of Vietnam. Soon after insertion, Captain Workman's unit came under intense hostile mortar fire followed by an assault by an enemy ground force. Subjecting himself to small arms and automatic weapons fire, Captain Workman moved from position to position directing his men in placing suppressive fire on the insurgents. When medical evacuation helicopters arrived, Captain Workman continually braved the hostile fire to assist the wounded personnel aboard the aircraft, placing accurate rifle fire on the hostile soldiers during the entire operation. Captain Workman was directing the extraction of his unit from the landing zone when a helicopter, hit by enemy fire, crashed, pinning him underneath and mortally wounding him.

There were several books written about that battle, one of them being *Ripcord, Screaming Eagles Under Siege, Vietnam 1970* by Keith Nolan. A classmate sent me a copy while I was living and working in Tokyo. I have never been so affected by a book as I was by this one because it recounted the stories of, and deaths of, several classmates, to include John Darling, Rick Hawley, Harry Hayes, and Don Workman. In addition, there were accounts of Chuck Hawkins and Charlie Lieb. Up to this point, I'd had little interface with classmates or West Point since retiring from the Army in 1991. Reading this book had an effect on me that can only be described as debilitating. I didn't—couldn't—go to work for a couple of days. I had no idea that we had lost so many classmates during that operation. I was in turn stunned, angered, and incredibly saddened as I read through the book. Even though I didn't know some of them well, they were classmates, brothers, warriors. My personal sense of loss was almost overwhelming and brought back a sad and guilty memory of Don.

In July of 1970, after returning from Vietnam, I reported into the 1st Battalion, 3rd Infantry (The Old Guard) at Ft. Myer, Virginia as an Assistant S-3. In early August, I received a phone call one day from Casualty Branch in the Pentagon. I was told that a classmate had just been brought back to the US and was asked if I'd accompany him home. I asked who the classmate was and was told that it was Captain Donald Workman. I was stunned, I hadn't heard of the fight at LZ Ripcord and didn't know that Don was in-country. I remember having trouble mentally processing the news, and I'm sure there was a gap in the conversation with the pentagon. When I had recovered, I told them that of course I would be incredibly honored to escort Don home.

I immediately went to the S-1 (battalion administrative officer) to let him know that I was going to get rush orders for an escort detail. He went into the BN commander's office and when he came out, he told me that the colonel wanted to see me. When I reported to him, he curtly told me that I would not be released for the escort duty. That was my second time that day to be stunned. When I asked him why, I was informed that because I was in the middle of the Old Guard Charm School, required of all newly assigned officers to learn about Old Guard standards, to learn saber manual (as that's what we carried in ceremonies), and the Old Guard Glide (a way of marching that prevented bobbing up and down), and because my records were then being processed for my White House clearance, which might require a personal interview, that he wouldn't release me. We had a rather heated discussion about this decision, and I was then invited to leave his office. Calling the officer in Casualty Branch to tell him that I couldn't be released to take Don home was one of the hardest things I've ever done. I have felt guilty about that dereliction of duty to a classmate, bother, and good friend to this day. It still bothers me today more than I can explain when I think back about that time. I failed Don.

Several soldiers from Don's company posted accolades to him on Westpoint.org, as well as tributes to him on The Wall of Faces. The comments include assertions that his soldiers would have followed him anywhere, and the fact that he continues to inspire them so many years later. They also admired his example of leadership under fire. Classmate Jeff Wilcox, also involved in the fight around Ripcord, has met many soldiers who served in Don's company, and they all sing his praises as an outstanding company commander. And of course, there is grief that he died way too soon and statements that he is thought about every day, even now. His memory will live in their hearts forever.

Classmate Greg Unangst remembered when he heard about Don's death:

> I first met Don Workman on the first or second day of Beast, as we were assigned to the same squad. We also were assigned to the same company for the duration of our four years at West Point. We were frequent roommates and became close friends. After graduation, we were on separate schedules for the usual training at Ft. Benning and we had separate initial assignments. We lost track of each other. I went to Ft. Wainwright, Alaska and Don went to the 24th Infantry Division and was eventually assigned to the 101st Airborne Division in Vietnam. In September 1970, I had just arrived in Ban Me Thuot, Vietnam and was pulling the night shift at the division tactical operations center of the 23rd ARVN Infantry Division. It was a slow night in the bunker, and I found a stack of *Stars & Stripes* newspapers. The *Stars & Stripes* typically had a listing of recent KIAs, WIAs, and MIAs, and it was there I saw Don's name under KIA. I briefly hyperventilated and then spent most of the night and early morning pacing the floor with mix of disbelief, anger, frustration, sadness, and a deep sense of loss, not only to myself but also to the Army and the country.

Classmate Stott Carlton has carried his memories of, and commitment to, Don Workman through to the summer of 2020 with an incredible story of devotion to Don's memory. He also has an interesting theory about the recovery of Don's remains. Don became very close to Col. Alexander Haig our first class year, as Col. Haig was the regimental tactical officer for Don's Third Regiment. When Don was listed as missing in action, Stott thinks that his mother contacted then General Haig, who contacted Secretary of State Henry Kissinger, who contacted President Nixon regarding recovering Don's remains. Stott had heard that the 101st had no intention of returning to Ripcord.

Stott and Don were on the same flight to Vietnam and together were assigned to the replacement battalion in Long Binh, from which they went their separate ways to their units of assignment. They stayed in touch until about Christmas of 1970, when they were both transferred to jobs in the rear and they lost contact with each other. Stott didn't know what Don was doing or that he had been given command of a company around that time. By chance, as he was changing jobs in-country, he ran into Harry Hayes in an officer's club and spent the entire night with him there. Stott had agreed to extend his Vietnam assignment for six months to take a job as a general's aide and was on his extension leave when he heard of Don's death. Stott made a hasty trip to West Point and got there in time to be a pall bearer at his funeral. "I don't think a day has passed I haven't thought of Don," Stott said. "On May 4, 2020, I began walking across the bridge that separates our town from the one across the river. I walked back and forth with our flag and my dog in the memory of Don and the others who made the ultimate sacrifice for our country and our freedom. On the bridge I felt free and had many great talks with Don. We will all be together again soon."

Don is interred in the West Point Cemetery.

About three weeks after losing Don, the class suffered another loss. This time it was Dave Maddux who was killed on August 9 by an exploding land mine. Once more, friends, classmates, family, and soldiers experienced a tragic loss of an incredible young man and officer who was just starting out in life.

Dave's sister Sheila gave me insight into his early life. By the time Dave entered West Point he had lived in six states as well as Germany and France. His dad was a career Air Force officer and afterward moved his family again as he was pursuing advanced degrees for his next career as a college professor. Dave also lived with a family in Denmark as an exchange student during high school. Dave had attended four different high schools before graduating from Park High in Racine, Wisconsin. Dave, and his best friend James Lassiter, USAFA '68, both wanted to attend the Air Force Academy, but Dave's eyesight disqualified him, so he went to West Point.

Dave loved to travel, using vacations to visit Spain, Japan, Brazil, and France. His dad became a professor of French and Dave became fluent and always professed a love for all things French. In many ways he seemed older than his years; he loved opera, ballet, classical music and played the accordion.

Dave and Sheila's Aunt Kathleen provided other information that shows what the young Dave was like:

> How many times over the last fifty or so years have I wished he still walked this earth! Passionate about discovering what he could in life, indeed with life itself. Very funny kid, and as a young man, usually caused me to convulse with laughter at his humor. Witty. Prankster. Always interested, wanting to learn, intelligent. A leader. I always felt he would become a leader of importance. Loved his grandmaw, in his somewhat southern drawl, and his granddad. Loved Montana fiercely and planned to build there, perhaps with his father, on land our family owned, rich with history. Loved exploring underwater, whether a mountain lake or the sea surrounding an island. I believe he was a scuba diver. Loved riding the horses at his grandparents' ranch in Montana or swimming in the large irrigation canal with neighbor kids. Liked helping do ranch chores involving animals of all kinds. Precocious. Letters from him after West Point and overseas I have kept and reread many times, enjoying this outstanding young man once again.

As his aunt observed, he loved the outdoors, particularly land in Montana that had been in the family for years. It's not surprising that he loved to ride horses and to help with ranch chores involving animals. He was a leader and always thought that he would become a leader of importance. Kathleen used a very descriptive word in describing Dave Maddux; he was precocious.

Classmates remember Dave's dedication to the fencing team and scuba club. I met Dave briefly, only through the context of fencing, when I decided to take up the sport plebe year, since at that time he was in Second Regiment and those of us in First Regiment didn't have a lot of interface with the others. I had visions of swashbuckling pirates and the Three Musketeers. He was also a part of the outdoor sportsman's club and the chapel choir. With his love of swimming and exploring underwater, he was an integral part of the scuba club, progressing to completion of the instructor certification program. The club met all year, primarily visiting local ponds and other bodies of water, sometimes diving through ice, with an occasional weekend trip. And while he enjoyed the hijinks that are a traditional part of cadet life many remarked on his unusually high level of maturity and focus.

Classmate John Blevins had a memory of Dave that really illustrates his tenacity and dedication. We spent yearling summer at Camp Buckner undergoing some demanding military training. The most grueling portion was a several-day exercise called Recondo. One hot, sweltering day with both the temperature and humidity probably in the nineties, we had spent the morning in hand-to-hand combat training, which had been exhausting, and were double-timing up a dirt road in the woods to the next training session. There was no relief, no breeze, and it was hard to breathe. Dave was running beside John and struggling with the run and the weather. At one point he asked John to hold his rifle and went to the ditch on the side of the road to vomit. Then John heard David say, "Give me the rifle back." He looked over to see Dave running beside him again. John never forgot that incident and remarked that many times in life when he felt that he couldn't go on, he remembered that, and it still inspires him. "If Dave could do it, so could I," he said. "Thanks Dave, I'll not forget you."

Renata Price and Dave were roommates during plebe years. She remembered them all being in a daze and focused on surviving every day while mastering military requirements along with some daunting academics. However, there was time for practical joking in which they all joined. She always felt that Dave was a solid friend. Dave was probably more focused and mature, but at the end of the day they were just college students trying to survive.

In 1969, classmate Bob Merritt remembered Dave "blitzing through Wiesbaden, Germany looking for another classmate who was on a trip. So, Bob and Dave went to hear a Russian choir that was performing downtown. Bob remembered it as being one of the best choir performances he'd ever heard; a couple of years studying Russian sure helped. Bob is grateful for that night; Dave had class!

James Lancaster Jr., USAFA '68, provided a great account of his friendship with Dave before, during, and after the military academies. "Like many of you, I have reached those years in life in which I can reflect on things past—good, and bad. It is a wonderful thing to have this gift given to me, even though it also comes with pain. I treasure my memories as the most valuable assets I have." He was very clear that, "This was not just a friend, though. This was the best friend I had in my entire life."

Dave and Jim had been friends since 1958 when they were eleven years old. Jim's dad was also career Air Force and had been assigned to the North American Aerospace Defense Command (NORAD) at Ent Air Force Base in Colorado Springs, Colorado. In the middle of sixth grade, Jim was escorted into his new classroom, feeling uncomfortable, as do most kids entering a new school. That first day during lunch, a skinny, freckled guy came up to him and asked in a deep voice if he could join Jim. Jim offered to share half of his peanut butter and jelly sandwich and an enduring friendship was started. Jim remembered that the Maddux family was very tightly run by Dave's dad. They were not allowed to watch much TV but, instead, were told to read, learn a foreign language, and to be prepared for intellectual discussions at dinner. They were devout Episcopalians; Dave was an altar boy and sang in the adult choir because of his deep voice. So, the Dave I came to know was profoundly serious about things from the onset of our relationship.

Jim found Dave had a great sense of humor and a razor-sharp wit, with a phenomenal vocabulary. He also proved to be exceedingly brave, never backing down from a fight or standing up for his friends. He also had a knack with the girls. He wasn't shy around the fairer sex, using a degree of formality and charm to have the prettiest girls at a dance talk and dance with him. Jim referred to him as a regular chick magnet! When asked how he pulled this off he responded, "It's simple. Never lose eye contact, compliment her on what she's wearing and listen and respond to what he has to say." Jim said that the girls absolutely loved him.

Dave and Jim had a lot of adventures. They'd build snow forts and lob snowballs like artillery shells at passing cars, aiming for the roof. They'd go hunting and fishing in the mountains with Jim's dad, who Dave really liked. They played baseball together, with Dave as a catcher. He had some huge crashes at home plate as opposing runners tried to score on him. After some of the worst, he'd stand and just stare at the guy who tried to score on him as if saying "you can't get through me!" They'd also play touch football in the park against bigger and stronger high-school kids. These quickly degenerated into full contact, and afterward Dave and Jim would ride their bikes home, nursing black eyes and bruises, but satisfied that they'd given as good as they received.

Because rockets and missiles were just being developed, they decided to build a rocket. When it was done, complete with an electronic ignition system, they invited their families to come watch the launch at a school playground. They built a command structure and had a handheld loudspeaker. With great drama they counted down to ten and pushed the ignition button. Success! The rocket ascended about 1,500 feet and then deployed a small parachute. For those times this was quite an accomplishment.

Growing up in the Cold War they both decided that they'd serve their country as their fathers had. Soon after the rocket event, Dave's dad retired and the family moved to Racine, Wisconsin. Even though far apart, they kept in touch while attending their respective academies. Jim observed that Dave was gung-ho Army even though he felt that a lot of what went on at West Point was total B.S. In 1966, after each had completed his summer training, they decided to try Air Force space available flying and go to the island of Mallorca. They got to Torrejon, Spain in a freezing USAF tanker and started looking for ways to get to Mallorca. While waiting, they went to a bull fight in Madrid and watched the famous matador El Cordobes fight two bulls. They felt that they learned a good bit about staying calm when in great duress by watching him. They finally caught a Spanish prop plane flight to Mallorca; the pilot flew wearing sandals. They had a great time while there, staying in a pension filled with a bunch of Swedish young ladies. They found a lot of free sangria at the local cafes and the night clubs were generally inexpensive and open air. It was a summer to remember!

The last time they saw each other was during our sixty-day graduation leave. They decided to go diving, this time somewhere in the Caribbean. They caught a couple of Air Force flights and wound up at Ramey Air Force Base on the north shore of Puerto Rico. With help from the local scuba club, they had a great thirty days, sometimes going to depths greater than 100 feet, and each day got their limit of spiney lobsters. These they sold at a local fish market to get money with which to repay their host. After thirty days they decided to go home but could find a flight only to Recife, Brazil. It was a long, hot, and bumpy ride. When they finally got there, they were dissuaded from diving because there were a lot of sharks in the area. After ten days, they were able to catch a C-141 going to Patrick AFB in Florida, and not wanting to waste a stop, they did spend another week diving off of Key Largo. There they parted company, Dave to Ft. Knox for armor training and Jim to Selma, Alabama for pilot training.

They would write occasionally, and sometimes speak on the phone. They knew that their lives would be forever intertwined, they'd marry with the other being the best man, and the families and kids would enjoy each other as much as Dave and Jim did. However, in August his folks told him that Dave had been killed in action; Jim didn't even know that he was there, thinking that Dave was still in Germany. Jim was shocked, mad, and "truly pissed . . . at somebody . . . at everybody." It's now all a blur, but he somehow managed to accompany his life-long best friend to West Point and acted as a pall bearer. Jim attempted to be strong for the family, "and outwardly I was, I think, but inside I was truly crushed." Every year on Dave's birthday, and Memorial Day, Jim thinks about all of those who have given their all for their country. "Dave was everything that West Point stands for and more. The United States Army should be proud of its son. America lost a valuable treasure that August day in Vietnam, and so did I."

Classmate Reverend Tom Margrave was assigned to the same unit that Dave joined, the 1st Squadron, 1st Cavalry Regiment, the reconnaissance and quick reaction force for the Americal Division then in southern I Corps in the northern part of South Vietnam. When Dave arrived, Tom was preparing to move to a troop command and Dave succeeded him as the squadron assistant S-4 (supply officer) and custodian of the beer and soda fund, with the responsibility of sending those drinks out to the troops in the field. This is one of the distinct advantages of serving in an armor unit—you have room to carry that stuff! It was almost as good as being assigned as an advisor to the Vietnamese Airborne and eating lobster thermidor in a restaurant in Vung Tau, their headquarters, on the beach at the Army in-country R&R site.

Later that summer, the squadron returned to its former basecamp at LZ Hawk Hill north of Chu Lai; their mission was to participate in a major division offensive operation. At that point two troops plus an infantry company were in heavy combat with NVA in fortified concrete bunkers in the infamous Ashau Valley. About that time, Dave came forward from the rear and the two bunked together until he took command of C Troop. With that assumption of leading soldiers in combat, Dave developed a great reputation; the squadron commander liked his aggressive but competent work.

On August 9 a report came into squadron headquarters that there had been an incident with C Troop and that there were casualties. An ACAV, (an up-armored M-113 armored personnel carrier) had become entangled in some barbed wire; the vehicle was evacuating four men he had personally rescued who had been wounded earlier by a mine. David went over to help when a mine blew up, killing Dave and wounding one of his lieutenants and others. He apparently didn't want any of his men doing that dangerous job, so he jumped in to do it himself. Some reports describe the mine as a Russian made *Bouncing Betty*, designed when tripped to fly up to about waist high before detonating. Earlier that day Dave's company had unknowingly entered an extensive minefield. Their first knowledge came when a mine exploded, wounding several soldiers. Then a second mine detonated, wounding more. Dave then directed his track to enter the blast area, where he assisted in loading the wounded onto his track for evacuation. Several times Dave put himself at risk entering uncleared areas to rescue his soldiers. It was during this process that Dave's track became entangled in barbed wire, and he jumped down to clear the vehicle's track.

When Dave had been evacuated, Tom Margrave went over to the morgue and made the identification. When the attendant unzipped the body bag Tom saw the guy he gone to school and served with. All the damage was to his lower body.

Renata Price remembered Dave and Doug Wheless showing up at her TOC (3/4 Cavalry, 25th Infantry Division) during the Cambodian Incursion. Her basecamp was a staging area for units headed for Cambodia, to include the 11th Armored Cavalry Regiment. Both were killed later that year.

In keeping with my belief that the finest accolades for a combat commander are those from the soldiers he led in combat, I'll offer a few here. One of Dave's soldiers, Bill Nelson, posted the following emotional tribute to Dave on The Wall of Faces:

> **Never forgotten, forever remembered. If you are able, save for them a place inside of you . . . and save one backward glance when you are leaving for the places they can no longer go . . .Be not ashamed to say you loved them . . . Take what they have left and what they have taught you with their dying and keep it with your own . . . And in that time when men decide and feel safe to call the war insane, take one moment to embrace those gentle heroes you left behind . . .**

The excerpt quoted above is from a letter sent home by Maj. Michael Davis O'Donnell, recipient of The Distinguished Flying Cross and killed in action March 24, 1970. He was shot down while attempting to rescue eight fellow soldiers surrounded by attacking enemy forces; Nelson was so taken by the quote that he dedicated it to Dave in his post.

And, from several others, all Dave's soldiers:

We Nam Brothers pause to give a backward glance, and post this remembrance to you, one of the gentle heroes lost to the War in Vietnam: Slip off that pack. Set it down by the crooked trail. Drop your steel pot alongside. Shed those magazine-ladened bandoliers away from your sweat-soaked shirt. Lay that silent weapon down and step out of the heat. Feel the soothing cool breeze right down to your soul . . . and rest forever in the shade of our love, brother. From your Nam-Band-Of-Brothers.

—Staff Sergeant Seagraves

Always on my mine. My capt. i think about you every day. i remember aug 9, 1970. i was there. you were a leader of men. i had respect for you and i hope i will be with you some day with our Lord.

—Just one of your troopers.

thanks for getting me out alive. we lost so many in are year together. ill never forget you and the others.

—Anonymous

A final example of Dave's admiration and love for his classmates comes from Clare Barkovic, widow of Bill Ericson, who recounted, "Sometime before the end of 1969, I received a beautifully written note from Dave's mother." Totally unexpected and received several months after Bill Ericson's death, Dave had written to his mother that Bill had met an early death in Vietnam, and he had asked that she write to Clare to offer sympathy and consolation. "A warm and kindly woman, both on her son's behalf and mine. I wrote back, thanked her sincerely, and said I was thankful to hear from her and appreciated the kindness of Dave to ask her to do so," Clare said.

As is so often true when dealing with these memories, it's sometimes difficult to come up with the correct words to describe their impact on other classmates, and friends and family members who loved them. How do you put into words the successes and accomplishments achieved in their short lives? However, classmate Tim Carpenter has an eloquence that far exceeds anything that I'm capable of:

> As a member of company C4, I knew Dave Maddux, Jim Gaiser, John Darling, and Ken Cummings. Like many of us, they were just trying to survive four years and graduate. We were young and really had no idea of our grand plans for the future. But all were outstanding young men, the best of their high school classes. All were wonderful classmates, teammates, and roommates. Most of us went on to survive Vietnam, then find our true callings either as career military leaders, captains of industry, medical or legal professionals, or in other endeavors. But these four and others never got the chance to become the ultimate leaders West Point produces. They never got the chance to have fifty-plus-year marriages, children, and grandchildren. They never got the chance to affect and influence hundreds of others with their intellect, leadership, and judgment So, unlike most of us, they were denied the opportunity to make close relationships over the years and have a long and prestigious biography told and printed. They were instead the true heroes who, while not glamorously intending to, gave the ultimate sacrifice so that we, the survivors, might do all the above things they were denied. I am personally honored to have known each of them, even briefly, and salute their memory.

Dave is interred in the West Point Cemetery.

Some three and a half months after Dave's death, we lost our last classmate in 1970, Douglas Wheless, on November 22, on the seventh anniversary of President Kennedy's assassination—a sad way to end the year 1970. It had been a tough one, now with the eighth classmate to be lost during that time.

Doug was born in Shreveport, Louisiana on July18, 1946, to Mr. and Mrs. Wesley E. Wheless Jr. and lived there until his entry into West Point with the class of 1968. Robin Rankin was a very close friend of Doug's throughout his life, the two having met in first grade when they were members of the same carpool. She would later marry Gary Willis, a year ahead of them in high school and a 1967 graduate of the US Air force Academy. As time went on, she and Doug became extremely close friends with never any romance, although some thought they would make a cute couple. Robin was convinced that their two mothers just knew that they would fall in love and eventually marry. As Robin described it, they "upset that apple cart" and became the best of friends instead. Their friendship persisted and grew throughout their school years, surviving junior high acne and Arthur Murray dance classes.

Doug spent a good deal of time at Robin's house, and her mother always had a freshly baked cake for him. In some sort of cosmic payback, he once baked a cake for her, chocolate, with chocolate icing. On visitor's day, he brought it to the girls' summer camp where she worked as a counselor. They shared a number of classes, as they both took all of the Latin classes plus honors math and English. They always sat as far from the teacher as possible so that they could pass notes to plan for their double date on the coming weekend and to make each other laugh. They double dated through much of high school, gave each other birthday cards, shared problems with girlfriends/boyfriends, and cried on each other's shoulders when breakups occurred. Doug drove his family's *terribly* uncool station wagon; she and her date occupied the back seat.

Doug had a unique and funny laugh; his whole upper body would shake without making any noise. Robin's laugh usually ended in an unladylike snort audible throughout the classroom. There's no way the teachers missed all of this, but they never got into any trouble. Then one day their Latin teacher told Robin's mom that "they were such a cute couple." Her mother laughed and told the teacher that Robin was going steady with someone else, that she and Doug were just close friends. The Latin teacher immediately separated them! Robin remarked at the end of her contribution, "After all these years, I still wish I could talk to him."

Doug's brother Steve explained that the three Wheless brothers were not very close. Doug was the middle brother and very different from the other two. Steve was the youngest, Wesley the oldest. Doug was the shining star of the three, an Eagle Scout, National Merit Scholar, commander of his JROTC unit, could build his own amp or short-wave radio, and then to cap it off, went to West Point. Steve realized that they weren't close, Doug being accomplished while the other two just kind of skated along. As they grew and became college students, they began to get closer. Steve regretted that an improving relationship was cut so short.

Doug certainly was an achiever; he was a member of the National Honor Society and earned a scholarship to Michigan State but turned it down to enter West Point. He was also a life-long member of St. Mark's Episcopal Church. Robin lovingly said that everyone who knew Doug also knew that he was hard working, talented and "smart as a whip—a Renaissance man who could quote Virgil and build a stereo amp." He was very serious about his position as commander of his JROTC battle group, was a member of Patton Platoon Drill Team for three years, but at the same time had a devilish sense of humor.

While at West Point, Doug continued to excel. He was a member of the Judo club, becoming its president firstie year. He was also the class historian as part of the *Howitzer* yearbook staff, and was active in the Russian club, the Math forum, and the military affairs club. He was also a Sunday school teacher. A member of the West Point English faculty wrote his parents after his passing to say that they had hoped he would return at some point and be an instructor.

Classmate Jeff Rogers had a very special memory of Doug Wheless. His character, generosity and commitment to classmates was clearly demonstrated during yearling summer. As Jeff related:

> As new yearlings at Camp Buckner in July of 1965, right after plebe year, our Buckner company went in the early cohort to Fort Knox for tank gunnery and combined arms training. Our company arrived late in the afternoon, at which point we were told we would be given privileges right away for the evening.
>
> As it turned out, my dad happened to be stationed at Fort Knox with my mother and siblings living in quarters a

few blocks from our barracks. Of course, my plans were to visit family that day. Unfortunately, as I was getting ready to leave, a firstie from the Buckner detail announced that there would be a guard detail that evening and I somehow ended up being one of the *lucky* ones selected.

Needless to say, I wasn't happy and asked the firstie if I could change it. He said the only way was to find a classmate willing to trade with me for a guard duty at a later date. Doug Wheless, from another platoon in our Buckner company— who was unknown to me from the other side of the Corps— overhead the conversation about visiting my family and immediately offered to take my guard duty.

Doug was willing to give up an opportunity for an evening of privileges at Fort Knox for a classmate he had never met by taking my guard duty in a swap for a future guard duty of his I'd later take at Camp Buckner where privileges were much more constrained. I, of course, thanked him profusely, but other than taking a guard tour of his later, never really came in contact with him the rest of our time at West Point. Doug Wheless, however, is etched in my memory. I will always remember his unsolicited kind and generous act that day in 1965. Doug was a very special guy. Well Done, Doug. Be Thou at Peace.

One of Doug's favorite pastimes at West Point beginning plebe year was participating in the debate club. His sharp mind, breadth of knowledge, and witty personality made him a perfect fit. This club enabled him to periodically leave the cold gray walls of our alma mater on club trips and venture back into civilization and normal college campuses. One of the club's primary attractions for any plebe is that it had its own table in the dining hall. Here plebes were allowed to fall out and eat a regular meal. This meant no bracing at the table or requirements to recite plebe poop.

Upon graduation Doug attended the requisite schools, Ranger and Airborne at Ft. Benning, as well as the Armor Officer's Basic Course at Ft. Knox. With these courses completed, Doug departed for Germany and the 3rd Armored Division, where he served as a platoon leader, maintenance officer, and company executive officer. On the fifth of June, he was promoted to first lieutenant and subsequently awarded an Army Commendation Medal for his service in the division. In early 1970, he was assigned to the 11th Armored Cavalry Regiment (ACR) in Vietnam. He had confided in his mother that he didn't feel that Vietnam was our war, but that as a professional, career Army officer, he felt that he had to serve there. He told his brother Steve that he wanted to go.

When he reported to the 11th ACR in March, he initially commanded a platoon in L Troop, 3rd Squadron until June 1970. During this time, he participated in the Cambodian Incursion during May and June, engaging Viet Cong and North Vietnamese regulars. In addition to some heavy fire fights, his unit destroyed bunker complexes and supply points in the Fishhook area of Cambodia. He was promoted to captain on June 5 and served as a staff officer for several months before taking command of I Troop in October.

Doug's buddy, Gary Willis USAFA '67, had a special memory of Doug in Vietnam. Gary was in-country as a USAF forward air controller (FAC) supporting the Vietnamese Airborne Division. Doug wrote in April 1970 that he had seen an L-19 Bird Dog (the same aircraft Gary flew) providing air cover while his troop escorted convoys. Doug said the plane swooped low from time to time and buzzed the convoy. He assumed Gary spent his days in the same sort of barn-storming shenanigans. Both units played significant roles in the Cambodian Incursion beginning May 1, 1970. The Vietnamese Airborne air assaulted into two LZs in the Fishhook as the 11th ACR attacked across the southern border of that region. That first day, the 11th surprised the NVA and engaged in several fierce fire fights. On day two, the 11th passed through the Airborne positions and proceeded north to a major crossroads at the village of Snoul.

Gary remembered:

> Throughout the operation, Doug commanded a platoon in the 11th, and I flew support missions for the Airborne from Quan Loi. Coincidentally, the ACR used Quan Loi as its

tactical operations center and for its Hueys and gunships. Doug learned that our FAC detachment was flying from Quan Loi and on June 6 showed up unannounced at their temporary quarters. I never learned why he was back at regimental HQ . . . maybe just getting a day or two off after a month in the boonies. But the date was significant, and Doug planned it that way.

Doug and his class graduated from USMA on June 5, 1968. They became first lieutenants a year later and pinned on captain's bars after another year. Gary's class graduated from USAFA on June 7, 1967, almost a year ahead of Doug. The Air Force grads pinned on silver bars eighteen months after commissioning, rather than after a year and became captains in another eighteen months. Consequently, on the date of their meeting, Doug was already a captain and Gary was still a first lieutenant, one day short of promotion on the seventh . . . exactly as he had figured. Gary got to give him one of his first salutes in his new rank, and they had a good laugh at his cleverness. They shot the bull for an hour or so. It was the last time they saw each other.

On November 20, Doug, while commanding I Troop, was severely injured while attempting to disarm a booby trap, suffering a serious head wound. His unit had found some Chinese claymore-like mines and was attempting to destroy them with demolitions. Doug and his squadron commander had taken cover prior to the detonation but somehow one of the mine's projectiles penetrated Doug's helmet. The squadron commander, right next to Doug, was unharmed. A couple of days later, on the twenty-second, the day after Thanksgiving, he died of his wounds. The class lost another incredible classmate who was cut down early in life before he even had a chance to begin to live up to his potential. He was awarded three Bronze Stars (two posthumously), two Army Commendation Medals (one posthumously), the Purple Heart (posthumously) and the Combat Infantryman's Badge.

As a final tribute to Doug, Gary Willis and Robin drove to Shreveport in October of 2020 to deliver in person a copy of our thirtieth reunion class print to Byrd High School. The painting is of the old West Point, our West Point, looking from The Plain toward the old barracks with the cadet chapel in the background. Superimposed is a facsimile of The Wall, The Vietnam War Memorial, containing the names of the Twenty we lost. I have number sixty-three of sixty-eight numbered prints. Attached was a letter describing the print and detailing Doug's history. Significant parts of the letter follow:

> On behalf of the Wheless family, I present to C. E. Byrd High School this framed print honoring my brother Douglass Terrell Wheless, who died in Vietnam November 22, 1970. Doug was a 1964 graduate of Byrd and a 1968 graduate of the United States Military Academy.
>
> The West Point class of 1968 commissioned this print for its thirtieth reunion, ordering sixty-eight numbered prints signed by the artist Paul R. Mitchell III. The earliest prints in the series were presented to the next of kin of the deceased classmates. One of the presenters was Captain Henry Riser, Byrd 1963 and Doug's West Point classmate. This print, number sixteen of sixty-eight, is inscribed:
>
> IN LOVING MEMORY OF DOUGLASS T. WHELESS
> "BE THOU AT PEACE"
> FROM THE CLASS OF 1968
>
> Douglass was an outstanding student at Byrd and a courageous leader in the military. I hope this print might be displayed in a place that honors Douglass, his sacrifice, and his service to the country fifty years ago.
>
> Sincerely,
> Stephen F. Wheless, Byrd '66

The principal assured Stephen and Robin that the print would be proudly displayed in the main hall of the JROTC area.

A friend and fellow officer from the 11th ACR posted a moving tribute to Doug on the Wall of Faces:

A FELLOW OFFICER Time has dimmed the clarity of events on that fateful day, almost thirty years ago when Doug paid the supreme sacrifice in the service of his country. My memories of Doug, however, remain bright and clear. As I write this remembrance, Vietnam Veterans of the 11th Armored Cavalry Regiment are gathering in reunion in Buffalo, NY. Doug, along with 766 fellow Blackhorse Troopers who died in Vietnam, will be remembered for their courage, friendship, love of country, and devotion to our regiment. May God bless my friend as he rests in eternal peace. Until we meet again, ALLONS!

—Thomas H. Reese.

Doug is buried in Shreveport in the Forest Park Cemetery East.

And so ended the Year of Our Lord 1970; eight more classmates had lost their lives, bringing the total to that date to sixteen. What a price!

Brothers Doug, Steve and Wesley

David high school yearbook—1964

Senior picture from Byrd high
School, Shreveport, LA

Don in high school
with his '37 Chevy

Stott Carlton (L) and
Don after graduation
parade

David enjoying
winter scuba at
West Point

Don, center with radio handset, in Vietnam

VIETNAM: 1971

William Francis Reichert   David Lee Alexander   Louis John Speidel

As the new year dawned, troop withdrawals from Vietnam continued at an accelerated pace. Combat with the NVA could still be intense and deadly, but new, internal enemies were raising their ugly heads in the troops remaining in Vietnam, particularly those in rear areas. Racism was becoming rampant, and there were numerous incidents of violence between White and Black soldiers. Incidents of *fragging* also increased wherein disaffected soldiers would roll an armed hand grenade into a room or area in which the intended target was living or present. Normally, enlisted men were the perpetrators, and sergeants and officers were the targets. These incidents could often be coupled with the use of illegal drugs, which was also becoming more widespread.

My one experience with this phenomenon was in 1969, in the division rear at Camp Enari near Pleiku. I was back there for one night for some type of administrative requirement, I don't remember what it was now. In the middle of the night, as I slept in the bachelor officers' quarters building, we were awakened by an explosion outside of where we were sleeping. Fortunately, the building was surrounded by a blast wall of fifty-five-gallon drums filled with sand and topped by two layers of sandbags. For those of us inside, we had no idea whether the sound may have come from enemy mortars or maybe rockets. Everyone scrambled for their weapons and proceeded outside. What we found was horrific—the remains of a mangled soldier. At first, we thought that maybe he had been caught by the mortars or rockets we first suspected, but a closer examination of the scene, and talking with the battalion adjutant, revealed a different possibility.

The adjutant was not a popular man with the soldiers, particularly those coming back from units in the field for some purpose. The adjutant, who was a captain, was renowned for hassling these guys over dirty and improper uniforms, haircuts, or a myriad of other things that the troops considered to be chickenshit. That night he reported hearing a thud on the tin roof over his room and the sounds of something maybe rolling down the roof. As best as could be determined by the investigation, the dead soldier had decided to frag the captain. We think that he had taken a grenade and had then low-crawled around the building, stopping where he knew the captain's room was. He pulled the pin, thus arming the grenade when the spoon or handle flew off, and then threw or maybe overhand lobbed it at the building as he lay on the ground. Maybe he thought that the force of his throw would cause the grenade to puncture the screens along the side, penetrate into the captain's room, and kill him when it detonated. Or maybe he thought that the grenade would explode on the roof and kill the room's occupant with all of the shrapnel generated, Instead, the grenade landed on the tin roof and rolled off right back at him, and exploded, killing him instantly. Maybe the guy wasn't very smart with his plan, but his end was a truly terrible loss of a life of a soldier who didn't need to die.

Our first loss in 1971, on January 25, was Bill "Ace" Reichert who was brazenly killed by one of his own soldiers in full view of the entire unit. Death in combat is to be expected, but this kind of loss was senseless, needless, and tragic to his soldiers, classmates, and family.

William (Bill) "Ace" Reichert was born on February 18, 1947, in Valley Stream, Long Island, New York. Bill attended Shaw Avenue School, Memorial Junior High School, and Central High. He played football in both junior and senior high school and was a devoted member of Blessed Sacrament Catholic Church. He was well known and well liked in school and effortlessly earned outstanding grades. With this background he had no problem in obtaining an appointment to West Point and entered in July 1964.

All of the stories and accolades that I received from numerous classmates in putting Bill's story together attest to the fact that, just as in high school, Bill was well liked and respected by all. As with the others that we lost, Bill was an exceptional cadet, officer, and man.

Bill was a big guy and had a distinctive gait, described by some as *lumbering*. This invariably attracted the attention of upper classmen, much like in Don Colglazier's case, and provided some respite to the other plebes. He was a good roommate because he was so easy going and possessed a great sense of humor. And much like our classmate John Darling, Bill enjoyed a good party, often accompanied by his close friend Johnny Walker. Because his family lived so close to West Point, they often hosted Bill and many of his classmates whenever they could get away. They'd go to Bill's house, sleep on the floor, go to a local pool hall, and thoroughly enjoy his mom's cooking.

Bill's parents provided a home away from home for many who lived hundreds, if not thousands, of miles away. Most of these guys had no military affiliation or background, so the tribulations of West Point were difficult to adjust to. The Reicherts were a welcome support providing a warm home atmosphere. Mrs. Reichert provided counseling on troubles with girlfriends and behavior, while Mr. Reichert assisted in their transition from teenagers to men. There were two younger brothers, very interested in what was going on, but polite and loving.

If Bill had a weak spot, it was his inability to swim; he was relegated to the infamous *Rock Squad* for similarly challenged cadets. The PE instructor was well known to bellow "There are no walls out there!" if a floundering cadet tried to make it to the side. He was also known to stomp on the hands of anyone who managed to get a hold. When class started, everyone was commanded to get in the pool; Bill would just sink to the bottom. After what seemed like a cruelly long time the instructors would get a hook on a long pole and fish the poor guy off of the bottom. Being a Rock Squader was certainly not fun.

Bill had a distinctive New York accent. According to his classmates, he would play it up to make them laugh. John Strand said, "On a bright March day, and at our urging, a reluctant but game Ace Reichert, in his exaggerated New Yorker accent would say 'Spring is sprung, the grass is riz, I wonder where the boidies is? They say the boid is on the wing, but that's absoid, the wing is on the boid!' to our mutual applause and laughter."

Bill could give the impression of not being too smart, but his roommates and others knew better. They spent many a long night, sometimes with some Johnny Walker, studying for exams. During one firstie history class, Ace appeared to be gazing out the window and not paying attention. So the P asked a complicated question, similar to "What started WW I?" Several hands were raised, but hoping to catch Ace unprepared, the P called on him, who then proceeded to give a five-minute, impromptu speech on the causes, showing he knew more than what had been in the book. The P held his gaze for a minute and then nodded and said, "Very good."

Classmate John Strand met Ace's parents during the first weekend that parents were allowed to visit their new cadets. They were going to have a picnic and John was invited along. Bill's parents made John feel welcome and part of the family, and they remained close from then on. John spent a lot of time at the Reichert's, and he and Ace would spend time with his high school buddies, often playing pool at a local pool hall. On one occasion they felt that each was good enough to have his own break-down cue. With these, they would often sneak into the firstie club in Old North Barracks to play pool and relax.

During firstie year, emphasis turned to girlfriends and max time away from the Academy. The amount of freedom was dependent on grades, the more proficient (passing), the more time away. So, the three roommates, John, Ace, and Pete Bonasso decided they would develop a new study system. They broke academics down into an area of specialty for each: Pete with engineering and math, Bill on history and law, and John on literature, English, philosophy, and the soft sciences. Every night they would all study for the next day, and then when appropriate, the subject matter expert would teach their specialty area, identifying what they thought were the key points of the lesson and identifying what they thought would be on a pop quiz or exam. At the end of the session, they'd all toast with Johnny Walker.

Ace graduated with a high class standing and was commissioned in Armor with a first assignment in Germany. After graduation on June 5, many guys, with their girlfriends, went to Bill's house to celebrate. They *partied hardy* late into the night and departed the next day to start the next phase of their lives. We all had a sixty-day graduation leave, and Bill and many of his friends convoyed around the country to attend weddings— from California to North Carolina. After the completion of leave, everyone went to their required schools and then off to their first assignment.

Along with his swimming difficulties, Ace may also have been somewhat challenged with driving. Classmates report seeing his new Triumph Spitfire arrive for a wedding with a front bumper newly shaped into a V almost in the center. This may have been the result of a slight interaction with a telephone pole. The gathered classmates came up with a solution since Ace couldn't afford a replacement—they cut the V out of the bumper at the nerf bars and all was good. There are also reports from classmates in Germany that Ace, then driving a Porsche, invariably showed up with a new door, or new hood, or some new fixture . . . some think he may have gone through two Porsches.

Classmate Gordy Sayre recounts the last time he saw Ace, at the officer's club in Grafenwoehr. Ace's battalion had just finished tank gunnery and Gordy's was about to begin. They got together to swap stories about what had happened since the basic course at Ft. Knox, and started off drinking beer, they then switched to Nicholaskas (a shot glass of schnapps, with a lemon slice on top which had half sugar and half ground coffee on the top). The objective was to put the lemon in your mouth with the condiments on top, then drink the shot while filtering it through the lemon, then eat the meat of the lemon and its condiments, and then pull the rind out of your mouth. He who accomplished this first was judged the winner and did not have to buy the next drink. The two traded losses and wound up with terrible hangovers the next morning. This was to be their last meeting.

Another classmate, Ralph D'Allesandro, recounts another story of Ace's lack of luck with automobiles. Ace's Spitfire was a magnet for automobile repair shops. It didn't last too long, and Ace was transitioned into an older family sedan for attendance at the Armor Officers' Basic Course that finished just before the 1968 Army-Navy game in Philadelphia. He loaded up a classmate in the big vehicle and headed off to the game, and from there was going to make his port call for transportation to Germany. Unfortunately, on I-74 outside of Cincinnati he dozed off and awoke just in time to see the car headed for the median. The car was launched about fifteen feet into the air and came down right-side up with a thud. Fortunately, the two guys were fine; the same could not be said for the car. They missed the game, but Ace managed to make his port call to start off on the next adventure.

While in Germany, Ace visited with old friends and roommates for camaraderie and good meals. In the summer of 1970, Bill visited the Trollingers and wanted them to accompany him on a trip to Italy before he shipped off for Vietnam. Unfortunately, they couldn't go but took him to the train station in Augsburg. He got out of the car, and they said their goodbyes, Mike hugged Ace's neck, telling him to keep his head down. He said, "aw, they won't get me." Mike said, "My last memory of him was when he turned and walked into the station. As he got to the door, he turned and waved, and that was it."

With orders for Vietnam, Bill returned to the US and headed for Ft. Lewis, Washington for travel to Vietnam. While en route, he met a young lady on the airplane named Diane Egan. They became fast friends while Ace was at Ft. Lewis. Diane was teaching first grade and had her students send Ace letters and artwork; they hoped to meet on R&R. Unfortunately, that never happened. Diane posted on The Wall of Faces years later:

> I met Bill on a flight from San Francisco to Seattle. We dated a few times before he shipped out and then corresponded until I learned of his death from his father. I will never forget that letter as it was so filled with a parent's grief and love. Bill was so full of life and laughter.

Upon arrival in-country, after finishing the initial in-processing at the replacement battalion, Captain Reichert reported to the 4th Infantry Division in Camp Radcliff, An Khe. From the division, he was further assigned to division's cavalry squadron, the 1st Squadron, 10th Cavalry Regiment. This was a unit with a long and storied history dating back to the Indian Wars when it was constituted at Ft. Leavenworth, Kansas in 1866. The regiment was nicknamed the "Buffalo Soldiers" by the Cheyenne Indians. The 10th was initially an all-Black regiment and one thought concerning the origin of the nickname is that the Indians thought that the hair of these soldiers resembled the hair of the buffalo. The other thought is that the unit was given the name because of the ferocity with which they fought, much like the buffalo. In either case the troops knew how much the Native Americans honored the buffalo, and thus felt honored themselves. At one point in their history, the 10th Cav garrisoned West Point in barracks and stables near the current Thayer Hotel. The large, grassy area across from the hotel is known as Buffalo Soldier Field and a new statue honoring those troopers was recently unveiled.

Initially, in late summer of 1970, Bill was assigned to D Troop, which was formed with both air and ground assets, but he was frustrated because he was in a staff position, not leading troops in combat. In December Bill took command of C Troop, equipped with both M48A3 tanks and armored cavalry assault vehicles (ACAVs). Bill's combat missions included road security for convoys and jungle reconnaissance. C Troop had an incredible amount of firepower and was a formidable force to move against enemy bunker complexes. When not in the field, the troop was assigned perimeter guard duty in the defensive positions around Camp Radcliff.

While on the surface C Troop appeared to be a force to be reckoned with, internally it was torn by drug and racial problems. Drug use was increasing as the Army drew down its combat forces and it became obvious to even low-ranking soldiers that there was no plan to actually win the war. Who wanted to be the last man to die in that environment? Bill recognized the problem immediately and asked for command level support, which never happened. A clear indication of the problem was provided by John Sloan, who served in the 1/10:

A short time before the senseless death of Capt. Reichert, I had returned from the field to find some of my personal possessions had been stolen, and the person who stole them was in Charlie Troop. I went to see Capt. Reichert to see if he could help me to get my belongings back because the man was under his command. I gave him a list and descriptions of the stolen items and the name of the witness that saw the theft, and the following day he had my things back. I was afraid to confront the person myself about the theft because of the racial problems we had and what could have happened [physically] to me over the whole incident. About a week later he was gunned down. I didn't know him well, but I know he was well liked by his men and hardly a day goes by that I don't think about what happened to him.

The problem was so severe that in the short time Bill had been in command of C Troop, both he and the troop first sergeant wrote sealed letters and left them with the squadron headquarters—with instructions to open them only if something happened to either Bill or the first sergeant. The letters named the soldiers who were ringleaders for problems in C Troop. The sealed letters were left for safekeeping with classmate Jim Stefan, who was the commander of HQ Troop, 1/10 Cav.

On January 29, 1971, classmate John Keane, assigned to the 21st Signal Group, had travelled to An Khe to coordinate a communications terminal in the same area in which C Troop was based. He was there to resolve any issues that might arise because of signal corps soldiers working in the cav area. John did not know that the C Troop commander was Ace. They were happy to meet, as they'd been friends in the Fourth Regiment during cadet days. John said that Bill was on top of the situation and concerns were resolved quickly. John was the last classmate to see Ace alive.

Later that same day, the discord in the troop erupted. They were to begin a jungle reconnaissance mission that day, and the tanks and ACAVs were loaded to begin the mission and lined up to move out. Sergeant Robert Dorriss was sitting on top of his vehicle and saw two soldiers standing off to the side when they should have been loaded on their assigned vehicle. Bill approached them to find out why they were holding up the unit departure. One soldier, Private First Class James Moyler, took offense, flipped the safety on his M16 and, in broad daylight in front of the entire unit, shot Bill at point blank range. Captain William "Ace" Reichert fell dead in front of his orderly room. Robert Dorriss and the rest of the troop were shocked, and I'm sure enraged. He posted on The Wall of Faces the following tribute to his commander:

> **Still In My Heart as a Real Soldier in Vietnam. It's the 49th anniversary of the tragic event that took Capt. Reichert's life and took it away from C Troop, 10th Cav. in Vietnam. I remember him today and that day as if it were yesterday. Taken from the soldiers who depended on his leadership, his style of command was not duplicated for the rest of my year in Vietnam. He was respected for his courage in the face of an unresolvable challenge, and his life was forfeited in the cause of military duty and honor. Again, I salute Capt. Reichert this day.**

Moyler was quickly arrested, jailed, charged, court-martialed, convicted, and sentenced to a fifteen-year prison term. He was released in 1975 after serving only four years. A childhood friend and fellow Buffalo Soldier, Larry Cutrone, posted on The Wall of Faces:

> **I grew up with Billy in Valley Stream, NY. Billy was always one of the nicest kids in our crowd. We both served in 1/10th Cav, even overlapping our tours slightly, but never saw each other in-country because we didn't know. Finally, after all these years (43), and thanks to John (Jack) T Sloan, I finally learned the truth about Billy being a kind, compassionate, well-liked soldier, and the truth about his senseless death at the hands of a COWARD, over 'stuff'! I don't believe it was the stuff at all, but rather a hatred of authority and racial differences. I salute you today, Billy, on Veteran's Day 2014. You will NEVER be forgotten.**

Mark Stolz, who was in Bill's command that day wrote his recollection of the events of Bill's death on The Wall of Faces:

> I was there on January 27, 1971, and saw it happen. I want to share my story, of that eventful day, after 38 years. I was the driver of the lead half-track, 31D. One man [Pfc James D. Moyler] was holding up the whole unit from going to the field that day, because he refused to get a haircut. As he walked up to Captain Reichert, they stood there talking. I could only wonder what they were saying, when the soldier in question, cut loose with a short burst. I too was sorry and mad for such a waste of life that day. Captain Reichert had a good reputation with the men.

Pete Bonasso recounted how he felt when he learned what had happened: "Somehow John Strand told me—I can't remember if it was a sat phone or a letter, but I recall being on a firebase south of Phu Bai when I got the news. I remember at that moment everything becoming surreal—the firebase, the war, what we were fighting for— and the sadness that I'd never see Ace again."

The final chapter of this terrible event was provided by another classmate, Jim Stefan:

> When this trial took place in Vietnam, I was at Fort Knox teaching at the Armor School, following attendance at the advance course and was ordered to return to Vietnam as a proposed witness at the trial. One night prior to my flight back to Vietnam my wife received a phone call at our quarters, while I was teaching a University of Kentucky history class, from a man who told her that "they knew where I was and had me in their sights." He said that I would be a dead man if I returned to Vietnam to testify at that trial." She was smart enough to call the MPs and two showed up in my classroom to escort me home. They wouldn't tell me what had happened, and I was pissed. When we got to our quarters, there were three MP cars there. Short story—I went to Vietnam; I waited there for four

days and was never called to testify. My wife and the kids had a constant MP presence at the house the whole time I was gone.

Mike Trollinger provides a poignant memory to the tragedy that befell Captain William "Ace" Reichert:

> In May of 2000, my mother and I went to Fort Lauderdale, Florida, to be with other classmates [Gordy Sayre and John Strand] to present Mrs. Reichert with a framed class print entitled *Bond of Brotherhood*. We shed a lot of tears and told stories about Bill. His mother, bless her heart, couldn't understand why none of his classmates came to the funeral. All these years, she had wondered why no one came to honor Bill. We had to explain to her that we were all in Vietnam or en route to Vietnam and couldn't come. When she found this out, she was greatly relieved. Bill's nickname was "Ace." It fit him perfectly to all of us. I have four grandchildren now, and the youngest was born on October 3, 2009. His name is Ace Everett Trollinger, in memory of Bill. So, Bill's legacy goes on with this young boy. May God rest Ace's soul. Please God, let him know that we love him and that we will be with him one of these days. I hope God has helped you learn how to swim by now.

Bill is interred in the Long Island National Cemetery in Farmingdale, New York.

Only about two weeks passed between the death of Bill Reichert and the loss of our next classmate in February. The year 1971 was starting out to be as costly as the last two years had been. Dave Alexander died on the sixth of February in what may have been an aircraft mechanical failure.

It was a hot humid day on the February 6, 1971 when Captain Dave Alexander steered his Army Chinook helicopter CH-47B, from 178th Assault Support Helicopter Company, and approached LZ

Siberia in Quang Tin Province. The huge twin-engine and twin-rotor helicopter—one of the Army's largest and most difficult to fly—had been ferrying water, munitions, and supplies among bases for three hours. It had several large water tanks and a generator slung below it. The helicopter had descended to about 150-200 feet on its approach when two loud noises were heard, and the helicopter's rotors quieted. It is unknown whether the helicopter's loss of power was caused by enemy fire or mechanical failure. The aircraft dropped out of the air, breaking apart and killing all five crewmen and two passengers. Rick Rhoades summed up the loss. "That crash took the life of one of '68s most beloved classmates and brought unbearable pain and suffering to his cherished wife Louise, his parents, brothers and sisters, and all who had ever known him."

Dave's West Point Association of Graduates memorial article, written by family and classmates, starts with:

> Captain David Lee Alexander will always be remembered as "Dave," a name like those his mother gave all her seven children...Linda, Anne, Tom, Mike, Joe, Jim ...and to her oldest son. A name that was solid, easy to pronounce, and didn't get lost when he offered his hand with that ever present infectious grin to anyone who needed a friend, be it a plebe roommate, a yearling struggling with the decision to stay at the Academy, or young Army officers en route to Viet Nam stopping by his and new bride Louie's San Francisco pad.

Dave was the eldest of seven children born to Esther and Hubert Alexander. The family worked a 180-acre farm in Pennsylvania, and the parents held second jobs to support their families. Dave filled a starring role at Central Dauphin East High School. He was an A student, class president, an outstanding three sport athlete, captain of the football team and marched in the school band. His coach described him as "the most honest, reliable, and respected player I ever had contact with." His classmates created a special award in his honor for the school's outstanding scholar-athlete.

A high school classmate remembered learning a lot about Dave during the summer of 1963 when they were both selected to attend Kiwanis young leaders camp. A select group of new seniors was selected from across eastern Pennsylvania for an intense week of leadership activities, including case studies, problem solving, role playing, and team building challenges. During this time, the classmate gained greater insight into Dave through discussions on current events, issues and their futures. He also was able to observe Dave's interaction with other attendees. It was obvious that he had incredible interpersonal skills that were readily transferable to larger organizations. This particular high school classmate also went to West Point with the class of 1969. Dave had a lasting positive impact on him.

Dave entered West Point in July 1964 with almost a thousand other incredible young men. At the end of four years his write up in *The Howitzer* read:

> Coming from the Pennsylvania farming area, Dave entered West Point and turned in his plowshare for a sword. He excelled in the engineering portion of the curriculum and barely gained a working knowledge of English. Dave was cursed with high aptitude, but he never let that hinder him in the pursuit of his one objective . . . pleasure, which included the Sandhurst exchange trip to England. This wild earthy farm boy will always be remembered for the loudness and length of his laugh coupled with an all-knowing grin.

As hinted at above, he was well known for his action-packed adventures with his fiancée Louis Waltman, affectionately known as Louie. Many classmates have fun memories of Dave sprinting across Thayer Road, rushing to beat the time limit for turning in a term paper that he'd worked on all night. Many also remember him thumbing rides back from a weekend trip to get back before bed-check.

Gus Lee remembered a time with Dave off campus:

> Several other guys and I were at a small Greenwich Village party after the Notre Dame game. More girls were clustered

around Dave's magnetic personality. Respectfully, he was as attentive to the less noticeable girls as to the head turners. Considerately, he invited some of us into the inner circle that had formed around him. Loyal to his girlfriend, instead of leaving with someone, he sensed that his large and generous presence would help the conviviality of all. His many talents could cultivate arrogance, pride and egotism in a lesser man. Not for Dave, whose helpful spirit endures.

Jim Madora shared some clear memories of Dave and Beast Barracks:

Dave, Tony Ambrose, and I were roommates during Beast Barracks in Third New Cadet Company in Central Area. Dave was a great roommate. Always kept his sense of humor, never got flustered. He was smart and quick witted. He was always a team player and we all helped each other to survive during that stress-filled time. Dave offered us help with anything that we needed to do during Beast Barracks. We met his wonderful parents when we had privileges.

Classmate Rick Fetterman shared a story of his trips home with Dave for Christmas leaves, a true bonding experience:

For two Christmas leaves we got picked up by my father and driven down to Reading accompanied also by my fourteen-year-old brother. We didn't go straight home, as both years it just happened that the Reading Aviation Service (my dad's employer) was holding their annual Christmas party. This was a slam-bang affair held inside the main hangar and consisted of hangar doors laid out on wooden horses and covered with all the Pennsylvania Dutch food you could eat and all the liquor and beer you could drink. My dad would then drive us the mile and a half home to our house, completely inebriated. One of those years my dad missed our driveway and my brother, who was the only one sober, yelled out "Dad, here's our house!" My dad made a quick *Broderick Crawford Highway Patrol* turn and drove right thru our shrubs, knocking them all flat! Dave and I laughed about that for years. The next day we'd get up and I'd drive Dave to his farm.

One of his most famous escapades was the infamous overnight *Thunder Run* to Florida from Ft. Benning, Georgia while on the first class trip. Dave was the only one in his group of friends deemed mature enough to rent a van to haul a bunch of classmates down to the beach. Having just completed airborne orientation the day before, many motorists were slack-jawed at every stop light when the occupants would run around the vehicle singing airborne Jody cadences. There's also a story of an all-night diner that took down its *come as you are* sign after the departure of this strange crew. They had no civilian clothes to wear so they spent the weekend in West Point gym shorts, tee shirts, and khaki pants—certainly a ragtag group. They spent a cold night on the beach amidst all of the bugs and made their way back to Benning the next day, bedraggled but happy.

Classmates have a lot of fond memories of Dave Alexander. One remarked that Dave was the finest guy that he had ever known. During Beast Barracks he always maintained a sense of humor and never got flustered. He was a team player and was always willing to help anyone out who was having problems. He lived the plebe adage *cooperate and graduate*. He invited friends to meet his parents when they came to visit when plebes were allowed their first privileges during Beast, a first trip to the Boodlers (the candy and ice cream store in the sinks of Central Area) when everyone bought and ate so much that they had trouble eating supper. The upper classmen were well aware of what was going on and unmercifully hazed the new cadets at supper, making them eat incredible amounts of food—someone remembered the meal was ham steaks—and then made them pay again even later in their squad leader's rooms.

Dave led a camping trip of several classmates into the woods one weekend during our yearling summer at Camp Buckner. Not only did he showcase his fishing skills, but his cooking ability as well, and all enjoyed the fresh fish. Rick Rhoades remembered an incident, also yearling year, when he arranged blind dates for his two roommates. Evidently the dates turned out to be less than satisfactory because when he returned to their room Rick found that his bunk had been moved out into the hall.

As the class became upperclassmen, Dave was selected for the most prestigious exchange trip possible. Selected cadets went to another academy for a semester to help forge interservice awareness and cooperation. Dave was selected to attend Sandhurst, the British Royal Military Academy, which was a tremendous honor. He was really making his mark on West Point.

Firstie year, Dave was the company commander of Company D3. Other classmates were right across the hall and could look down on Thayer Road in front of Grant Hall. One night they observed a cadet talking with his girlfriend from an open window. A major and his wife were driving by when the car stopped, the major was outraged that a cadet was talking with a girl from the barracks window. He got out of his car and started to berate the cadet in front of his girlfriend. Dave heard what was going on and hurried out of the barracks and assured the officer that as company commander he would deal with situation. The angry major got back in his car and drove off. Dave's maturity and command presence were put to good use that day. As the company commander, Dave was a role model for everyone who might be struggling with West Point, whether in academics, athletics, or military aptitude.

Classmate Hank Gregor had a very clear and telling memory of the man who was Dave Alexander:

> One memory I have of Dave that stays vividly with me is of a trip we took to his family's farm. On a late arrival to a small local airport, we sat drinking coffee and a having a snack while, as I recall hazily, awaiting a pickup from a family member or friend. A very tired looking, let's make that a very, very tired looking, waitress, had taken our orders and very cheerfully and attentively served us. She went out of her way to comment on our USMA status, offering compliments and thanks for our being in service to our country. Afterward, Dave very

thoughtfully noted how tired and obviously hardworking she was, and that while we all could gripe and complain with the best of the Corps about rules, regulations, restrictions, etc., we really had so much to be grateful for. Specifically, he noted the often unsung, unappreciated efforts of very hardworking, taxpaying, certainly not wealthy, but great folks who made it possible for us to be at a place like USMA, enjoying compliments and privileges we probably hadn't really earned. I thought then and now, it was a window into his character and who he was, to have been that observant, considerate, and appreciative.

Sometime between yearling and cow years Dave got reacquainted with a high school classmate who was then living in Boston. Louise "Lou" Waltman captured Dave's heart and after a whirlwind romance, they were married soon after graduation. Lou was a perfect match for Dave, enjoying adventure and a good party. They were the perfect couple.

After graduation Dave, who had always wanted to fly, had to serve a year in a combat branch assignment, so he selected Air Defense Artillery (ADA). He also received a choice assignment to Ft. Baker, an air defense site in the hills above the Golden Gate Bridge. First, he had to attend the ADA Basic Course at Ft. Bliss, Texas. Dave really wanted Lou to accompany him, so they decided they would elope. This worked well when Dave learned that they could get married in Texas without being a resident and without a waiting period, so just the two of them went to the San Antonio courthouse and were married on August 8, 1968. Second Lieutenant and Mrs. David Alexander then reported into the basic course.

In September they left Ft. Bliss and headed for San Francisco. On the way, they stopped to see the Grand Canyon, hiking down to the river, spending the night, and climbing out in the morning. While on the road they talked about where to live, and Lou pressed for finding a place in the city. Dave insisted that they could not afford the rent, so if they were going to live in the city, Lou would have to get a job. She found one as a salesgirl in an upscale department store. While there she actually waited on Janis Joplin, who bought a hat and asked Lou how it would look on her while riding around in a convertible. After six months on the job, and with no desire to join the union, she was asked to leave. Three days later, she was hired by the public relations office in the new Bank of America world headquarters building. They could now afford rent and enjoy San Francisco a little.

One day, in walked a young girl looking for a job. They became close friends when Lou found out that that the young lady was a first cousin to a classmate, Bill Little. They have remained close friends for more than fifty years. During this time, Dave's adventurous spirit convinced him to buy a Triumph motorcycle and they loved crossing the Golden Gate Bridge and camping in the Sierra.

Classmate Mike Mears remembered serving with Dave at the same missile site. Whenever his fiancée joined him, they teamed up with the Alexanders and tore around San Francisco. Some of their best memories are the jesting and laughing on day trips and camping in Desolation Valley.

They both enjoyed working together, swapping stories about what was going on. Every morning at ten o'clock, Dave would drop by Mike's place to drink a cup of coffee. That site, SF-88, became a national recreation area and is open every Saturday for tours. You can see the missiles and hydraulic systems, and the place where they drank coffee every morning.

In September of '69, Dave started flight school, first at Ft. Walton in Mineral Wells, Texas, then to Ft. Rucker, Alabama, and then to Ft. Sill, Oklahoma. He finished in the fall of '70 and in October departed for Vietnam. Lou said, "I joined my parents, who by that time had moved to Florida. Dave loved the flying, but he was not enthusiastic about the war. Then, after only five months, came February 6 . . . what I would give to relive those years. There isn't a day that goes by that I don't think of him."

Rick Fetterman also remembers Dave's loss and its effect on him:

We went our separate ways after graduation, got caught up in training programs and the war, and never communicated again. He lost his life in a helicopter crash on February 6, 1971.

I learned of this shortly afterward, and, along with many, many others, was devastated. His was a short life but one of great fun, value, and achievement. He will never be forgotten.

Mike remembered hearing the terrible news. "In February 1971, I learned about Dave's death, and I escorted his body back to Pennsylvania for his funeral. It was my saddest day. The world lost one of its greatest. When my son was born, Pat and I named him Alexander. As an adult, my Alex firmly stepped into Dave Alexander's shoes as a positive force in the world."

Mike has a very meaningful postscript to Dave Alexander's story. In the initial volume of *Both Sides of the Wall: Reflections of the West Point Class of 1968,* he finally confessed to leading the team that stole the West Point reveille cannon some forty years earlier. After his confession, classmates began to contact him and fill him in on some information he didn't know:

I learned that the West Point Commandant Bernie Rogers was outraged. Of the many pranks of the class of 1968, this was the one he viewed as a crime. If he had caught us, he had intended to bring felony charges. That was chilling to learn. Our arc welder expert had taken his gloves off to check the cannon frame temperature during the theft. Late the next day, as I walked from Ballistics class, I noticed a team from the Criminal Investigation Division taking fingerprints off the frame. I also learned that earlier that morning, Dave Alexander had walked out to Trophy Point to see where the missing cannon had been. He picked up several of the rags we had hastily abandoned and wiped down the frame before the criminal investigators arrived. Thirty-seven years after his death, I learned that a man I didn't know at the time but who would become my best friend, had saved me from expulsion from West Point and a prison term. If he hadn't done that, I would never have met him, I would never have married Pat, and we would never have named our son in his honor. During the time I shared with Dave and Louie, the cannon theft topic never came up.

One final story comes from classmate Mark Hansen, who didn't know Dave until Vietnam. Mark was commanding the Ranger company for the Americal Division. Their compound was on the beach at Chu Lai. Next to it was another compound housing the division's heavy helicopter support company to which Dave was assigned. Both the Ranger and aviation companies shared a common mess hall, which was natural because the men in those two units shared a strong bond. Mark met Dave one day in the mess hall and formed an instant liking for him. Because he was unassuming and sociable, and possessed a quiet dignity, everyone liked him. They coordinated mealtimes each day to spend time together and learn about each other's worlds. Dave's best buddy and hooch mate was a short and gregarious pilot who went by the nick name "Stump." The two were inseparable but had never been assigned to fly with each other until that terrible day. "David Alexander was one of those people who everyone loved, just an all-around great guy. I think of him often."

The athletic complex at Central Dauphin East H.S. in Harrisburg, Pennsylvania, is dedicated to David Alexander. The following is the write-up that accompanied the dedication.

ALEXANDER SPORTS COMPLEX

Construction of the new entrance gateway, identifying the athletic fields as the David Alexander Sports Complex, is the culmination of events growing out of the desire to remember and recognize David Alexander, president of the first class to graduate from East High in 1964. David was an honor student and lettered in football, wrestling, and track. He was also a member of the band, Key Club, and student council. David was a friend to all, a person of sound character, and an exemplary leader. He was chosen as the first recipient of the Robert W. Wentzel - John W. Bolton Outstanding Athlete Award.

David attended the United States Military Academy at West Point where he continued to exhibit extraordinary leadership skills, humility, concern and care for others, and love of country. David graduated with the class of 1968. He served in Vietnam, where he lost his life in service to his country.

The Outstanding Athlete Award, having been established in 1964, continued to be awarded in subsequent years. Upon David's death, the name was changed to the David Alexander Outstanding Athlete Award. Presently, the award is called David Alexander Memorial Award. Young men graduating from East High are recognized for their character, leadership, academic, and athletic accomplishments in the mold of David Alexander.

In 2016, David was recognized by the Panther Ram Foundation as a Distinguished Central Dauphin School District Alumni. High school classmates from Central Dauphin High School in Harrisburg, Pennsylvania, West Point classmates, family, and friends, as well as former David Alexander Memorial Award recipients, gathered to celebrate the occasion.

The Central Dauphin East High School graduates of the class of 1964, family, friends, and West Point classmates of David wish to thank the Central Dauphin School District Directors, CD East Administration, and the Panther Ram Foundation for their support and encouragement of this fitting memorial to David L. Alexander.

At least three West Point classmates named a son after Dave Alexander. They are Alexander Gregor, Alexander Mears, and Alexander Wilhite.

In conclusion, perhaps what we remember most quickly are his zany antics. But more importantly we remember Dave's deep concern for the people around him, his wisdom, insights, thoughtfulness, and leadership. For all those reasons he remains a cherished memory of one of the finest people we have ever known.

The AOG memorial article quoted in the beginning of Dave's story ends with a very fitting epitaph for this remarkable young man:

He remains in our memories nearly four decades later as though it were yesterday . . . young, happy, mischievous, and full of life, with Louie at his side. Everyone wanted to be on his team, whether it was sibling competition, intramural sports, pick-up games or just learning to play guitar. All knew that inside his happy-go-lucky exterior was a smart, rugged Pennsylvania farm boy with grit and an unassuming natural leader with a huge heart who you wanted to follow because he cared. We all loved him . . . and he loved us. Dave—all of us are better for having known and served with you. Thanks.

Dave Alexander is interred in the Hershey Cemetery, Hershey, Pennsylvania.

For four and a half months the class was spared any more losses. That grace period came to an end when we lost Louis John Speidel III on the twenty-fifth of June.

After I asked her about contributing to this book, Ellen Johnson, John's widow, responded:

> My main goal since 1971 has been that John never be forgotten and Greg [Camp], Dale [Hansen], and Lou [Schlipper], among others, have certainly seen that that will never happen. Gretchen and I are profoundly grateful for that. Gretchen has shared the father she never knew with our grandson, Andrew, since he was very young (he is 13) and Lou's gift of his West Point experience with his grandfather has certainly augmented that. I am humbled by the outreach many in your class have shown to us, as, in many ways, it seems it would have been so much easier to just move on after Vietnam.

These words from Ellen describe the very reason that I undertook putting this book together. Thanks to a group of dedicated classmates in the Washington, DC area, the class of 1968 has worked hard to not only assure family members, but those of our class who were fortunate enough to come home from that war, that we will never forget our classmates who gave their lives in Vietnam. In many ways we have been able to "move on" from the war in that we've led successful and rewarding lives, but I would bet that the experience of Vietnam is seared forever in the hearts, minds and memories of all of who served there, as is the knowledge that not all of us did come home. To be able to totally move on from that war, to completely flush it from our memories and lives, and to forget those whom we honor, would be to do an incredible disservice to them, for it is imperative that their service never be forgotten.

Even after all these years, Ellen has difficulty with the memories of life with John, and I am so thankful that she decided to add her thoughts and recollections to his legacy. Because many of us in '68 didn't know many of those who were lost because of serving in different regiments, this is an effort to introduce all of them to all of us. And so begins the story of Lou or John Speidel as he was known by either name among his friends.

John was born in London on the twenty-third of April, 1946 to a British woman, a war bride, and an American Army captain, who married in England in 1944. At the end of World War II, John's father had returned to the US and had left the service, working as a chemist at the Drackett Company. His wife had to wait on the delivery of their son before she could come to the States and join her husband. Ellen has provided us great insight into Lou's early life:

> He was one of the finest people I have ever known in my life, one of the gentlest people I have ever known. He had such a wonderful sense of himself. By that, I mean he didn't have the need to impress anyone, although he had accomplished a lot by the young age of twenty-five. He was a very quiet person, at least with most folks, but he was very comfortable with that—I used to think he was shy but realized with time that he just didn't talk to fill voids in the conversation; he talked only when he had something to say.
>
> I fell in love with John Speidel when I was fourteen years old. I was a freshman at Milford High School and he was a junior, and I had a huge crush on him. We went together for part of our high school years but broke up before his senior year. He was in the class of 1964, and I was two years behind him in school. In high school, he was very active—track team, band, advertising manager of the *Droflim* (yearbook),

circulation manager of the *Reflector* (newspaper), vice-president of the senior class, third in the state in biology in the state scholarship tests, Spanish, Latin and English Clubs, National Honor Society, intramural basketball, senior class play, etc.

Those years of growing up for both of them were idyllic. They spent a lot of time together with John's family, sharing fun times and Sunday dinners, sharing a lot of joy and laughter. John Sr. by then owned a nursery business, which he loved, and which involved the whole family, including Ellen. Their budding romance came to a temporary halt when John entered West Point in July of 1964, although they did date occasionally when he came back to Milford, Ohio on leave.

John and classmate Dan Robinson met before entering West Point when they took their final SATs, physicals, and physical fitness tests at an Army base in Ohio in March of 1964. They wound up in the same lettered company at the Academy and were roommates several times during the four years. They also shared several of the cadet clubs and activities, one of the highlights was a Rocket Club visit to the US Army Missile Command's George C. Marshall Flight Center at Redstone Arsenal in Huntsville, Alabama. John was really impressed with the gigantic size of the Saturn V rocket and took an elevator all the way to the top. Dan suspected that John's desire to go to flight school was really because he wanted to become an astronaut, many of whom were West Pointers and frequently returned to the campus to talk with cadets.

After graduation the two friends lost touch, with John going Armor and Dan to the Signal Corps. Dan's tour in Vietnam was earlier than John's, and he had been back for a while when he learned of John's death. "I was back almost six months when I heard of John's tragic loss. It was a great shock, and his loss still haunts me. Such a great leader and dear friend gone so soon." Dan has stayed in touch with Ellen, her daughter Gretchen, who never met her dad, and her grandson Drew. Dan also stays in touch with John's sister Sandra, who is an accomplished artist.

Dan has lived and taught in England for many years, and didn't talk about Vietnam, partly because of the sacrifices of many like his roommate John. However, he was often asked to give talks about the war in schools and even on the BBC. He has since become an avid student of the Vietnam conflict. Every year on Remembrance Day (England's Memorial Day), people gather in churchyards, parks, and town greens and recite the following words, which are certainly appropriate for John and the others that we lost:

> *They shall grow not old, as we that are left grow old:*
> *Age shall not weary them, nor the years condemn.*
> *At the going down of the sun and in the morning*
> *We will remember them.*

In keeping with these thoughts, classmate and roommate John Stallings shared these remembrances about John on The Wall of Faces:

> July 9, 2003—To John, My Roommate at West Point. John, you were a great friend. You were a gentleman, and a gentle man. We served together in the 101st. I remember we talked about going home after the war, just three days before your chopper was shot down. I think about you often and wish we could talk again now. You lived by the motto of "Duty, Honor, Country." God bless you for your service to your country. "No task too great for '68."

As so many of our classmates have done, Dale Hansen maintains close contact with Ellen and Gretchen. Dale considers John to have been his best friend at West Point, and the two were roommates during firstie year. That was a fortunate thing, as John always worked hard to keep the room prepared for inspection, thus helping to ensure that the roommates would be able to enjoy some weekend freedoms. John and Dale played a lot of squash during free times, and also became avid golfers, playing a lot of near-by courses. John was always willing to drive because he truly enjoyed his new red Pontiac GTO.

John Speidel was Dale's Best Man when Dale married. After the wedding they both went their separate ways in their different branches, and Dale was shocked to learn of John's death. He immediately reached out to Ellen with a letter of condolence and has maintained contact with Ellen and Gretchen since those days.

When the class decided to personally present copies of our thirtieth anniversary print entitled *Bond of Brothers*, Dale and classmate Greg Camp teamed up, and with their wives went to see Ellen, Ellen's husband Randy, Gretchen, and other members of the extended family at Ellen's home. Even though Dale had not seen Ellen since 1970, the camaraderie was as though no time had passed. They had a great and rewarding evening. Dale summed up the experience and the bonds that have developed since:

> It's been a pleasure knowing Ellen and Gretchen over these past years, seeing Gretchen grow and mature into a daughter and mother who would have been a source of pride for John, and then seeing John and Ellen's grandson, Drew, grow into a fine young man. It is easy to see John's resemblance in his grandson, along with the same fine qualities that we all saw in John Speidel.

John did ask Ellen to join him at West Point during June Week for graduation and commissioning. All of the festivities and parades, culminating with the class throwing our hats into the air as a last joyous traditional action as a cadet, were great events for her as she remarked that she'd never forget the sight of all of those hats. Immediately after graduation leave, John went to the Armor School and Ranger training. He then departed for his first assignment in Kitzingen, Germany and an armor unit.

Classmate Sam Wyman had not known John at all while at school. They met for the first time in Ranger School when both of them, despite receiving a maximum score on the physical fitness test, fell out on a one mile run because of Georgia's heat and humidity. They were joined by another classmate who had suffered the same fate. They spent the next weeks running and acclimating themselves and reported to the next class when they had no more problems.

They were the only West Pointers in that class and so formed a three-man Ranger team. In Dahlonega during the mountain phase, they had a night so cold that the lane grader allowed them to build a fire. John went down to a nearby farm and liberated some apples that were left on the ground and corn left on the stalks. The lane grader allowed them to be cooked and gave John a good spot report for his initiative. After graduation, John and Sam drove together to Cincinnati, stopping in Columbus, Georgia for a steak and Atlanta for a roast beef feast at Sam's mother-in-law's house.

Both lieutenants were going to go to Germany for an initial assignment and wound up not too far from each other. After returning to the States, they both went to flight school at about the same time and arrived in Vietnam around the same time as well, to different units in different parts of the country, although they were in close proximity to each other in February '71 when both supported Operation Lam son 719, the huge south Vietnamese incursion into Laos. Sam recounted: "When I returned home from Vietnam, I called Ellen and paid my condolences and offered any assistance. John was a great guy and friend, would do anything to help someone, and a real leader."

When John returned home for Christmas in 1969, he asked Ellen to marry him. Knowing that Vietnam was in their future, they planned the wedding for right after Ellen's graduation from Ohio Wesleyan and were married at the Milford Methodist Church on June 20, 1970. At this point, John went through his flight training schools and finished in November. In early December they took a delayed honeymoon trip to Bermuda. John left for Vietnam from McGuire Air force Base on December 28, 1970. Ellen remembered, "I flew to New Jersey with him, and we stayed with my aunt and uncle near Princeton. Saying goodbye at McGuire was one of the most difficult things I have ever done in my life. I lived in an apartment on Laurel St. in Milford and just tried to stay busy with friends and prepare for our baby's birth in May. I took childbirth classes at Our Lady of Mercy Hospital in Mariemont. We hoped to be together in Hawaii for an R&R in June. We were able to talk by telephone a couple of times through two-way radio operators here in the States, but mostly communicated by letter and cassette tapes."

John's assignment was to B Troop, 2nd Squadron, 17th Cavalry, 101st Airborne division (Air Mobile). He first flew light observation helicopters (LOH) whose main missions were recon or flying low to attract enemy fire, which could be pinpointed for a US counterattack.

Ellen knew that would be a difficult and dangerous job. She felt safer when he was reassigned to Huey's (UH-1H) used for ferrying troops and supplies. However, on April 25 she expected bad news was coming when her dad and brother arrived at her apartment unexpectedly. John had been shot down on his twenty-fifth birthday, April 23. His downed bird was in an inaccessible area filled with NVA troops and getting him out was a long and costly operation. He was severely wounded and after ten days, he was transferred to a hospital on Okinawa, where he lived for a few more weeks. Unfortunately, the gravity of his wounds was such that he passed away on May 24 (already May 25 in the States). While he was never to meet his daughter, he did hear her cry on the telephone.

From John Speidel to his wife Ellen, written on April 15, 1971, eight days before he was shot down, expressing his pride in his job and in the Cav:

I don't expect you to write as often now as I know you will be busy. I hope the time is going faster for you now. I know once the baby comes, time will speed by and before you know it June will be around and we'll be together. For me, time is going by quite fast. These four months have really gone fast and days are going even faster now that the weather is good. We fly a lot now and don't have much time to waste. But we enjoy our evenings all the time. We cook out two to three times a week whenever we can get hold of some steaks or beef. The Cav is a real close group. I guess when you fly together with a group of guys, you develop a bond between you that is stronger than any friendships you had previously. I have no doubt that the pilots of the Cav are the finest in Vietnam and the most professional. We have such a variety of missions and do jobs that no one else can do. When anyone ever wants help, they call the Cav first because they know if it's at all possible to be done, the Cav can do it. These guys are all real professionals and I'm honored to fly with them. They're the best in Vietnam and the best of all of them that went into Laos. I've got a lot of stories I can tell you in June—should take two weeks to tell them all.

The 2/17 Cav is the most decorated unit presently in Vietnam. In many ways we're the best of the air aces. We can't even keep track of ribbons here. The Cav as a unit was awarded the Vietnamese Cross of Gallantry and Air Medal of Honor for exploits in Laos. No other Cav unit received both awards. So far, I've been put in for an air medal with bronze V for valor for the Medivac mission we conducted last month. It was really no big deal; a Ranger was seriously injured in the valley and we happened to be in the area and monitored the call for aid so we went in and took him to a hospital. Reports are that, if he had had to wait for a Medivac to get there from Eagle, he wouldn't have made it, so that makes it worth every risk we took. When you personally save a man's life, it helps you feel you're doing something worthwhile over here.

John was awarded an Air medal with V device. In part, his citation reads:

Captain Speidel distinguished himself on March 30, 1971 while serving as the pilot of UH-1H helicopter during the emergency extraction of a wounded soldier. Upon being informed that an extraction was needed, Captain Speidel immediately piloted his aircraft toward the landing zone. While in the landing zone, he directed the fire of his crew to counter enemy small arms fire directed at his helicopter. Once the casualty was aboard, Captain Speidel directed the door gunner in first aid for the wounded man.

Eight days later, Louis John Speidel III was shot down on the edge of the A Shau Valley on his twenty-fifth birthday. While all death in war is tragic, John's is especially poignant. After he was downed it took forty-eight hours for him to be pulled out of the wreckage due to heavy enemy action. Numerous soldiers were killed and wounded during these two days in their attempts to get to John, and a couple more birds were lost. But the 101st was true to that age old Army philosophy, *leave no man behind.*

An entry on the Vietnam Helicopter Pilots Association website provides an account of the action in more detail, and includes memories of classmate Dave Ohle:

A Ranger relay team was inserted near the east side of the Ashau Valley on April 23, 1971 and made contact with the NVA seconds after insertion while moving off the LZ. The team leader [Duren] was immediately wounded and a B company troop ship returned an hour later with a new team leader. The bird was shot down while leaving the LZ and crashed over the east side of the ridge line and turned upside down, trapping the pilot [John Speidel], and co-pilot in the wreckage. Because of all of the enemy action, it was impossible to get to the site to check on survivors.

A medivac came in and successfully extracted the wounded original team leader and a wounded door gunner from the B troop ship. It returned a short time later to extract more wounded and was itself immediately shot down with the loss of two crewmen; a third was killed later. The survivors had no radio contact through the night, and the next morning D troop was inserted into a hot LZ, just north of the team's position. About this time a member of the Ranger team was shot while trying to retrieve a radio from the LZ and died shortly thereafter. The survivors on the ground finally had commo and started working gunships around their location. D troop made an attempt to reach the team, but was ambushed while attempting to do so, and had five killed and fourteen wounded. At some later time, B company, 2/502 was inserted, and later reinforced with the remainder of the 502 and A Company 1/327. Finally on the twenty-fifth a rescue team led by the Ranger company commander, classmate Dave Ohle, with some volunteers from his company, fought their way to the bird, and extracted John from the wreckage. Unfortunately, his co-pilot had died in the crash. Dave demonstrated exceptional dedication and heroism in mounting the operation to rescue his classmate. According to Dave, the NVA had used the troop compartment of the overturned bird as a command post during those two days, which causes one to wonder just what John Speidel went through, being grievously wounded and I'm sure in a lot of pain yet determined to not let the enemy behind him know that he was still alive. If they had known, there's not much doubt that John would have been executed.

John had hung upside down for two days, trapped by his legs being crushed by the instrument panel of his bird, and was evac'd first to an Army evacuation hospital, and then to the larger facility in Japan on Okinawa. A major effort by all involved, the final cost to rescue John was eleven killed and more than fifteen wounded, and the loss of two more birds.

This story is significant in that it's a clear demonstration of one of the true meanings of Duty, Honor, Country. In those days, and in that Army, I'm sure there was no doubt that all efforts would be made to rescue John and his co-pilot. I doubt that there was a soldier or commander who had second thoughts about the effort. It was a comfort to all of us in the field to understand that if something happened to us that everything possible would be done to bring us home.

Many of us who served then had a terrible time now coming to grips with the way we left Afghanistan in 2021. To slink out of Bagram Air Base in the middle of the night and not tell the local commander, and then to abandon the airport in Kabul leaving many Americans behind, is just not anything that we would have ever considered or tolerated. We had a duty to all of our soldiers, and the honor of the unit, the Army, and the country dictated that we would do whatever was necessary to take care of our own and fulfill that duty.

John received the Distinguished Flying Cross for his actions that day. From the DFC citation:

Captain Speidel distinguished himself on April 23, 1971while serving as pilot of a UH-1H helicopter during a troop insertion in the A Shau Valley. Upon arriving at the landing zone, Captain Speidel successfully inserted a Ranger team despite intense enemy ani-aircraft fire. Captain Speidel maneuvered his aircraft to avoid increasing enemy fire but was unable to depart the landing zone. Captain Speidel's aircraft received numerous direct hits and was downed, trapping him in the aircraft.

Ellen needed to remain in Ohio to have their child, but the Army arranged for John's mother to fly to Okinawa to be with him for many weeks. The family received almost daily reports from the Army documenting John's condition with details like "drank a malt today" or "sat up in a wheelchair for a while." After several weeks of reports like this and a cautious "progress guarded," a report came to tell his wife that he was completely out of danger. While they believed this when the report was written, unfortunately John could not survive his wounds. On June 25, Ellen and her father-in-law were in the San Francisco Airport ready to board a flight to Okinawa when she was paged to meet two Army officers, who informed her that he had passed.

Randy White, whose direct relationship with John is unknown, posted the following tribute on Westpoint.org:

> John Speidel was wounded with B Troop, 2/17 Cavalry while performing the duties of a pilot. John died of his wounds a month after being recovered from his helicopter that was shot down in the A Shau Valley on April 23, 1971. I recently met with family members of his then wife Ellen, and others involved in the battle. If it's true that you're not really gone if you're not forgotten, then John lives on in the hearts of those who knew him. Many former members of L Company Ranger, 101st Airborne owe their lives to john and men like him. Thank you.

This was a fitting tribute from a soldier who probably fought with John. There is not a finer tribute for a combat soldier that to say that his service and heroism saved the lives of others. A family member of John's copilot on that fateful day added a memorial comment on the Wall of Faces:

> **Remembering Louis and my Big Brother Capt. William Collum. I never had the pleasure of meeting Lou, but his name will forever be attached in my mind & heart. Lou & my**

big brother Capt William "Billy" Edward Collum were in the same helicopter when they were shot down. They crashed on Louis BD & my brother; Billy died in the helicopter on 25 Apr 71 ~ my 14th BD. I think of Lou's family often & would love to connect with you.

John Speidel's memorial article for the Association of Graduates of West Point, written by his roommates Dale Hansen and Dan Robinson, opens with a very appropriate quote from T. S. Elliot:

> We die with the dying:
> See, they depart, and we go with them.
> We are born with the dead:
> See, they return, and bring us with them.

The memorial also includes other tributes that demonstrate John's personality and the love that his classmates had for him.

"When we think of John as a cadet, we remember his consistent willingness to help his classmates. He was a good student and was always able to explain a difficult idea or concept to his less academically gifted friends. We also remember his love of music."

His commanding officer wrote of John as a fine leader, an outstanding officer, and an exceptionally brave man. His mother, who was with him for his last seven weeks in Okinawa, remembered his bravery in those final, painful days. As was his character, through his last ordeals, he never complained, never was bitter, and his only concern was for his friends left behind in Vietnam.

Again, from John's memorial article: "We stand by the black granite memorial walls, an attendant takes a rubbing of your name, the emotions of loss flood our eyes and we walk slowly away, the memories locked for almost twenty years, rushing back. We, the survivors, have aged and gray is coming to our hair; you, who died on those fields half a world away, are never forgotten. Though years may separate us from the time, they can never separate us from your memory."

In an emotional tribute to her husband, Ellen described the wonderful time that they had together, even though it was for a relatively short time:

John and I had more in a short time than many have in years of marriage, and I have been blessed with a daughter, Gretchen, who is incredibly wonderful. She is bright, talented, and has accomplished much in her own lifetime, but more importantly, she is a sensitive and compassionate young woman. John would be so very proud of his daughter. Grief does not have an end point, beyond which anything can be said or done. I know that the circumstances surrounding John's death were painful for his parents to their dying days, and still grieve my daughter, my sisters-in-law, John's West Point classmates, and other close family and friends.

Louis John Speidel is interred in the Greenlawn cemetery in Milford, Ohio.

The final six months of 1971 saw no more casualties for the class. The war was winding down in terms of US participation as more and more units rotated home, and fewer classmates deployed to the combat zone. Since the first of the class had arrived in Vietnam in the early days of '69, nineteen had lost their lives.

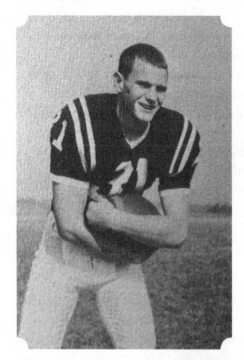

David Alexander—high school football at Harrisburg, PA Central Dauphin East HS

David and future bride Louise Waltman

Hank Spengler and Bill Reichert—both KIA

Russ Baker,
Andy Anderson,
Bill Reichert and
John Strand

Lou Schlipper, Dan Robinson,
Lou Speidel—Cow (junior)
year roommates

Pete Bonasso,
Ace Reichert,
John Strand, Andy
Anderson at John's
bachelor party

Lou on Vietnam
Departure day.

Lou and bride Ellen
at flight school
graduation dance.

David and Louise at flight school graduation ball.

High School sports complex named for David

VIETNAM: 1972

Henry Mershon Spengler III

U nfortunately, the war was not done with us yet. On the fifth of April, 1972, some nine months after John Speidel, we lost Henry Mershon Spengler III, the last in the class to die in Vietnam, and the last classmate to come home.

On August 28, 1989, family, friends, and classmates gathered around the grave of Henry's father, Brigadier General Henry M. Spengler II, as Henry's remains were interred next to his dad, seventeen years after his death. Henry was brought to his resting place with full military honors, which included the Army Band, a company of soldiers from the 1st Battalion, 3rd US Infantry (The Old Guard), and a color guard, all escorting him as his flag-covered casket was borne on an old artillery caisson pulled by six beautiful horses and flanked by eight soldiers who moved Henry's casket to the burial site. Already in place was a squad of seven soldiers to fire three volleys, and a bugler from the Army Band to play Taps, that haunting final tribute to a fallen warrior.

Waiting on the curb was an Army chaplain and the officer in charge of the funeral detail who would escort Henry to the funeral bier as he was caried by the eight-soldier casket team.

While I was not at Henry's funeral, I can see every detail very clearly in my mind's eye, as I commanded a company in The Old guard for almost two years after my return from Vietnam. One week a month my company had primary responsibility for all Army funerals in Arlington National Cemetery, with another week as the back-up company. During these weeks I was the OIC for all officer funeral details, and figure that I participated in maybe as many as sixty or seventy.

We all—officers, non-commissioned officers, and enlisted soldiers alike—felt that this was the most sacred of our duties. There was no greater honor for us than providing full honors to a fallen soldier, and no greater responsibility than to make sure that it was done formally and precisely to honor that soldier's family. Our casket teams practiced their movements for hours, moving a heavy, rock-filled casket up and down stairs, over uneven ground, and any other scenario that could be envisioned. The firing parties also devoted many hours to ensuring that all of their movements were in sync, and that a volley from seven rifles sounded like the shot of one. Additional endless hours were devoted to drill and ceremonies to ensure that we presented the best possible image to the family and other mourners. The entire funeral detail was subjected to a detailed inspection, including me, to make sure that we looked as sharp as possible, for we might be the last representatives of the Army that the family would see, and we wanted to make certain that memory was the best it could be.

The most difficult part of the ceremony for me was to receive the folded flag from the casket detail to present to the family, normally a mother or wife. I would kneel on one knee, look the person in the eye if at all possible, and present the flag with words that started "On behalf of the president of the United States, and a grateful nation..." One can just imagine the grief and sorrow of the family member at this time, normally with tears flowing, and even though it certainly affected me, I was not allowed to express or show any emotion. Sometimes, on a really bad day, I might do this two or three times.

If you're human, it's impossible to not be emotionally affected by the day's events. Often, when I got home at night after a day of funerals, I would go for a run in the cemetery to cleanse my heart.

Jim Locher, a close friend of Henry's from high school and West Point, spoke at the graveside: "We still remember Henry's kind and generous spirit, his quick, warm smile, his gentle goodhearted nature. He was the best of friends and the best of companions. He always enjoyed life to the fullest, whether loving his family, singing in the Cadet Glee Club, or playing handball. Henry especially loved to laugh, to hear a good story or tell one."

Turning to Henry's military career, Locher continued: "With great pride, Henry followed in his father's footsteps: first to West Point and then into the Army. He remained true to his high ideals and exacting standards throughout his military career, and made us proud of him, his accomplishments, and what he stood for. His father would have been proud too."

Tears flowed down the cheeks of Mrs. Spengler and her two teenage grandchildren, Shawn and Lissa, as each was presented with a folded American flag. The ceremony ended with Henry's wife, children, and mother each placing an American Beauty rose on the coffin.

For his mother, Henry's death was the third aviation fatality for a family member. Her first husband was killed in a plane crash while working for Boeing. Her second husband, and Henry's father, was killed in the crash of an Army helicopter in Germany just days before Henry's fifteenth birthday. Still, she had no objection to Henry's desire to become an Army aviator.

Henry was an Army brat and spent his life moving between Army bases. His father graduated from West Point in 1937 and went to Corregidor in the Philippines to command a coast artillery battery of Philippine Scouts. While there he met Henry's mom, Betty Mae Murrell, and they were married in Berkeley, California in 1941. During World War II he served in the China-Burma-India Theater. After the war, he served in a progression of assignments in Japan, California, New York, Washington, DC, and Paris. His dad's final assignment was to command the 32nd Artillery Brigade in Germany after being promoted to brigadier general. Four months later he died in the helicopter crash while on an inspection tour of his command.

Following the general's death, the family moved back to Alexandria, Virginia, where Henry enrolled in Francis C. Hammond high School as a sophomore. As it was close to the Pentagon, it was filled with military brats, and five other graduates of Hammond High joined the Long Gray Line and the class of 1968 with Henry. Henry made friends easily and quickly became a star member of the class. He excelled in academics and participated in three varsity sports, crew, cross country, and track. In the summer of '62 he and Jim Locher rowed competitively for Old Dominion Boat Club in Alexandria. Jim Locher remembered:

> The highlight of that summer experience was having President John Kennedy watch us row on the Potomac River. He was on board the Presidential Yacht, *Sequoia*, which slowed to keep pace with our crew. Henry and I could see the president leaning against the railing and watching us with pleasure. After ten or fifteen minutes, he waved and continued his cruise.

During the summer of 1963, the family traveled to West Point for a special ceremony commemorating his father. The officers and men of the 32nd Artillery Brigade presented a restored Revolutionary War cannon to West Point in honor of their former commander. It was a sixteen-pounder built by the French in 1761 and was used during the War for Independence. It was accepted by the Academy superintendent, General William C. Westmoreland, and placed on Trophy Point.

As a high school senior, Henry helped coach the freshman football team, which finished with a 6-1 season. During crew season he and Jim Locher were members of the varsity four-boat team. At the Old Dominion Boat Club, he learned to play handball on a one wall court and it became a lifelong passion. He and Jim played nearly every day during crew season.

Henry represented his homeroom on the student forum and served as a Big Brother to incoming freshmen. He was a member of the Varsity Club, the International Club and the Junior Engineering Technical Society, and even dated the Homecoming Queen senior year. He also participated in Boy Scouts and attended Westminster Presbyterian

Church, where he sang in the choir. During his senior year, Henry won a competitive appointment to West Point from Senator Henry Byrd (D-VA). Henry had eighteen days after graduation before reporting, but he and Jim, along with other classmates, rented a house in Virginia Beach for a week to relax one last time.

When they entered West Point, they were told that they'd not see each other again, as the Academy took pains to separate friends. However, when roll was called for the first time in Fourth New Cadet Company, a platoon leader called out the names not only of Henry and Jim, but also three other Hammond classmates as well! So much for separating friends.

After five weeks of Beast Barracks, the new cadets had an opportunity to see family for the first time. It was just the luck of Henry and Jim that Henry's mom knew the dean of the academic board, Brigadier General William Bessell Jr., who had invited Mrs. Spengler to use their back yard for the get together—just the place two nervous new cadets wanted to go! At the end of the picnic, Mrs. Spengler gave Henry and Jim snacks to hide in their room, twenty-four Three Musketeers Bars. Henry asked, "Could we not have had some variety?" Back at the company, the company commander warned at the dinner formation that there would be an inspection of new cadets' rooms looking for *boodle* and warned that punishment would be severe if any was found. After being forced to eat multiple ham steaks, many new cadets had a tough time after dinner. Henry, believing the threats, ran back to his room and ate all twenty-four bars. Jim said that he looked green the next morning.

During the regular academic year, both Henry and Jim were assigned to Company H-2, later to become B-4. After struggling with academics, Henry's life brightened when Jim's girlfriend, and later wife, introduced Henry to Bette Scott during spring break. The ladies were sorority sisters at the college of William and Mary in Williamsburg, Virginia and both were destined to become class wives. Their first date was the Army-Navy game yearling year, they became engaged during Army-Navy firstie year, and were married three weeks after graduation.

Pete Bonasso developed a relationship with Henry during our firstie year:

Hank Spengler and I were in the same company (early H2 then B4), but we'd never struck up any kind of relationship until senior year, when we had military art papers due. In class, the P said we could collaborate, and since he was in my class and lived just down the hall, I asked him if he'd like to be my partner. I was a little surprised when he said yes since we'd hardly said two words to each other. We worked together for the next several weeks on the paper, and during that time, we forged a friendship. So, he invited me to his bachelor party and his wedding right after graduation. He was very smart and had a wicked sense of humor that had me rolling on the floor at the party. I never saw him again after that. I was at the advanced course at Fort Knox when his wife emailed me of his passing. Side note: we got 17.0/18.0 on the paper.

Possessed of a superb singing voice, Henry sang in the Protestant Chapel Choir for all four years, and as soon as he was able during yearling year, tried out for and was accepted into the West Point Glee Club. Participating in these two outstanding organizations afforded Henry many weekends away from West Point, normally about one a month. The glee club was featured on the Ed Sullivan Show, with Henry in several closeups (found on YouTube and the class of '68 legacy site), a taped performance with the Rockettes of Radio City Music Hall, and a taped Christmas Mass for the Cadet Chapel with the Goucher College Women's Choir. Skeeter Kympton remembered: "Throughout the three years, he lent his unique, ever-present sense of humor, joy of life, friendship, and mature perspective to all of us in the club."

Henry's high class standing allowed him to pick the Corps of Engineers on Branch Night. At graduation he was presented a silver box with the inscription, "Presented to Henry M. Spengler III, class of 1968 USMA, From the class of Your Father, 1937 USMA." Henry and Bette were married on June twenty-ninth in the Old Post Chapel at Ft. Myer and honeymooned in the Bahamas. Upon arrival there, they discovered that Henry's brother Jim had pulled a good one; he had emptied all of the clothes out of Henry's suitcase and replaced them with barbells. They went shopping right away!

A few weeks later, Henry reported to Ranger School, where classmate Bill McCrone was his Ranger buddy. Bill recounted an incident where he passed out from heat stroke on a run; Henry picked him up in a fireman's carry, grabbed his weapon, and carried him to an aid station, where he woke up after dawn. Bill was about two inches taller that Henry and weighed about twenty pounds more. During the last, or Florida phase, one night's patrol involved moving through a mangrove swamp. Bill was point man that night, but Henry was right behind him. The swamp was waist deep and filled with Mangrove tree roots that could block your movement. Bill felt that about every twenty-five yards or so he would step into a deep hole up to his neck, and sometimes over his head, but Henry was always there to pull him out and then lead the rest of the patrol around the obstacle. The worst thing Bill recalled were all of the alligators. Even though the Ranger instructors assured them that alligators don't attack at night the students were scared to death.

Following Ranger School was Airborne School and the Engineer Basic Course, followed by his first assignment to the 23rd Engineer Battalion in Hanau, West Germany, where he was a platoon leader and then company commander. Bette loved living in Germany and spent time traveling when Henry was in the field, which was a great deal of the time. Henry commanded C Company, 23rd Engineers.

Early in his tour, Henry had the opportunity to award a military performance trophy named for his dad. Henry and Bette traveled to Kaiserslautern on November 4, 1969 to the 32nd Army Air Defense Command, the renamed unit that his dad had commanded. He presented the Henry F. Spengler Trophy to the commander of the best Nike Hercules Missile Battery in the command, which just happened to be commanded by a classmate Albert "Jim" Madora. Another classmate and B-4 company mate, Ed Thal, was the aide-de-camp to the commanding general.

On May 24, 1696, Henry and Bette's child, Henry Mershon "Shawn" Spengler IV was born in Frankfurt. Henry had volunteered for flight school, but Bette had asked him to wait until after their child was born. So, in August, they returned to the US for the series of schools that Henry needed to attend, the last being at Hunter Army Airfield in Savannah, Georgia for training on the AH-1G Cobra attack helicopter. Bette reported that, "Henry loved all aspects of flight school. I got to ride in a helicopter at Fort Rucker—my one-and-only time." One of Henry's friends in flight school said, "Henry was very humble about being a West Pointer. Always with a big smile. A great family man, friend, and flight-school classmate. He had a beautiful wife and infant child."

Flight training ended, and Henry left his family to report to Vietnam. On August 16, 1971, he reported to A Battery, 4th Battalion, 77th Aerial Rocket Artillery (ARA), 101st Airborne Division (Airmobile) in the Republic of Vietnam. These special birds carried two rocket pods on each pylon and had a minigun and a 40mm grenade launcher in a chin turret, as opposed to one rocket pod and a minigun on two pylons with a 40mm grenade launcher in a chin turret for the Huey model gunships. The Cobra could carry seventy-six 2.75-inch unguided rockets while the Huey carried forty-eight. Each of the airmobile divisions in Vietnam, the 101st and 1st Cavalry, had an ARA battalion assigned. In a change from the normal chain of command, ARA assets were controlled by the senior artillery officer, not the aviation boss.

Although the 4th Infantry Division where I was assigned did not have ARA assets, I had cause to be supported by two ARA Cobras in a particularly fierce firefight, but I'm not sure where they were from. The amount of ordinance they carried was astounding, and they could put a heck of a lot of high explosive (HE) on target in a very short period of time. I thought that in this particular case, they were more effective than tube artillery.

In January 1972, Henry was reassigned to the 1st Cavalry Division when the 101st went home to Ft. Campbell. This was the only ARA unit left in Vietnam and Henry wrote to Bette that one reason he wanted to be transferred "was to go where the action was." Of this transfer his new roommate said, "Hank had been in-country for less than six months when he requested to be moved south so he could get a *full tour* on his record (he could have taken a *drop* and gone home early)." Henry was assigned to F Battery, 79th ARA, known as *Blue Max*. Of Blue Max, the Vietnam history of the First Cav reports, "Greatly appreciated by troopers of the 1st Cavalry, its heavily armed Cobras flew a variety of fire missions in support of the 3rd Brigade. The pilots of Blue Max were among the most experienced combat fliers in the Vietnam War.

Many had volunteered for the extra duty to cover the extended stay of the 1st Cavalry Division." The 3rd Brigade stayed in Vietnam when the rest of the division redeployed to Ft. Hood, Texas."

The unit's name, Blue Max, came from an informal title given to the *Pour le Mérite*, a Prussian order of merit award established by King Frederick in 1740. The first recipient during World War I, and first aviator ever to win the award was Max Immelmann. In his honor, the award unofficially became known as the Blue Max. Presentation of this award ceased with the end of the Prussian monarchy in 1918. The pilots assigned to Blue Max were expected to perform above and beyond the call of duty at all times, which they did. They were often viewed with awe by those whom they supported. They would respond immediately to any call for help from a ground unit. As one pilot explained, "They parked us within five minutes' flight time of our guys in the field. We sat with a radio operator who would have contact with guys on the ground. If the radio operator yelled, 'Fire Mission,' we'd run to the aircraft and have to be off the ground in less than two minutes. As soon as we took off, the guy would give us the heading to follow and then he'd read the mission." One of the ground guys reported that when they needed their support they just radioed back "Bounce Max!"

According to Warrant Officer (WO) Jim "Jet" Jackson, "Blue Max was a close-knit unit with quite a reputation for excellence." He continued, "Anyone selected to serve in the unit was honored to do so. We spent a great deal of time together in our own little O club we had on our home base, called *The Plantation*, near Ben Hoa." Jackson added, "Because of the prestigious reputation of Blue Max, we had quite a few captains, some fairly senior, serving as pilots in our Cobra unit. There was also a fair number of West Point graduates among them." One of those West Pointers, Captain Alan Russo ('64), Blue Max's Executive Officer, came to know Henry fairly well. He said, "Hank was well-respected in our unit; he was a good leader and listener."

In March of 1972, Henry returned home for two weeks of R&R. Everyone believed that the war was winding down and so all had an enjoyable time. Henry joked and seemed to enjoy himself a lot. When he returned to Vietnam, he had only a few months remaining on his assignment.

Only three weeks after Henry returned, North Vietnam launched its spring, or Easter Offensive. On the fifth of April, three NVA divisions attacked the town of Loc Ninh in Vinh Long Province. The town was defended by about 1,000 South Vietnamese troops with a small number of American advisors. The NVA attack was fierce, and that afternoon Blue Max was given the mission of attacking the NVA positions and delaying their advance to prevent the town from being overrun. A Blue Max heavy fire team of two Cobra ARA ships responded to the alert to support friendly troops dug in around the little air strip. The lead aircraft was commanded by Chief Warrant Officer Charles E. "Windy" Windler with Henry in the front seat as co-pilot and gunner. The second Cobra was commanded by Captain Mike Brown. The team made the first of two gun runs.

Jim Locher described what happened that day:

> A second heavy fire team was preparing to relieve the first team. The lead aircraft was commanded by Bill "Lurch" Leach with Warrant Officer Jet Jackson as the co-pilot. The second Cobra was commanded by Chief Warrant Officer Barry "Magilla" McIntyre. Jackson reported, "As we approached at [an altitude of] about 4,500 feet, we could see Windy and Mike making their attacks using a traditional race-track pattern, with each Cobra being 180 degrees opposite the other. They were starting at our altitude and terminating their rocket runs at about 1,500 feet. We had made radio contact and informed them that we were approaching to relieve them. They were in their last attack run on the enemy when we were still two miles away.

Jackson recalled, "When Windy was just finishing his last run on the target, we heard him mention on the radio matter-of-factly, 'I think that I took a .51 caliber hit that time.'" Windy's wingman, Mike Brown, continued his dive on the target until he heard Magilla "yell into his radio, 'Windy, You're on fire! Get it down! Get it down!'" Brown looked up and "could see that the entire exhaust stack of Windy's bird was in flames."

Jackson related:

Those three words "you're on fire" are the most dreaded words that any aviator can hear. Windy immediately put his Cobra into a dive and began a rapid descent toward the ground. Unfortunately, placing the aircraft into a dive only increased the fire, and as it grew, the entire tail boom of the craft was being consumed by the flames. Windy and Hank had selected a clearing southeast of Loc Ninh as the place for their intended emergency landing. The other three Cobras were now in hot pursuit of the burning aircraft and ready to defend our friends' lives to the last man once they made it down.

At about 100 feet with the flames still completely covering the tail boom, Windy and Hank began their deceleration maneuver by flaring the aircraft's nose upward. . . Captain Spengler's radio was tuned to UHF instead of intercom and he could be heard hollering at Windeler to get the aircraft down. As they did, the tail-boom of the aircraft suddenly buckled and separated from the aircraft. The remaining piece of the helicopter with the crew inside yawed violently to the right and impacted the ground, exploding into flames.

At that moment, we were all in shock of what we had just witnessed. We circled the burning crash site several times, hoping in vain that someone had survived. While all this was happening, the North Vietnamese Army had continued firing at us with their heavy anti-aircraft weapons, but we were totally oblivious to it. Once we were convinced that there was nothing we could do, we were forced to retreat as the hail of fire increased. The aircraft was totally consumed by the fire, and there was no chance anyone could have survived.

Because of heavy enemy action in the area, and that the cockpit was seen to crash, explode and burn, no effort was made at that time to recover the remains of the crew; they were initially listed as Missing in Action (MIA). Ten days later their status was changed to Killed in Action (KIA). Captain Henry Spengler was the last Engineer and the last member of the West Point Class of 1968 to die in Vietnam. Alan

Russo, Blue Max's executive officer, praised Henry: "Hank Spengler was a hero and he died as he piloted a Cobra helicopter against the vanguard of the North Vietnamese invasion in April 1972 at Loc Ninh. This vanguard was the lead of three NVA divisions that would overrun Loc Ninh and Quan Loi and attempt but fail to overrun An Loc in a classic, epic three-month battle." Russo continued, "Hank's heroism, along with CW2 Charlie Windeler (the aircraft commander) allowed US advisors in Loc Ninh to escape successfully from their encampment. I was proud to have served with Hank in the small battery of Cobra helicopters that had such a big part in the defense of An Loc."

On May 19, forty-four days after Henry was lost, there was a memorial service held in the chapel at Ft. Myer. Those who had come to remember and honor Henry were still in shock and disbelief. The three readings from the Holy Scripture were comforting, especially from John 14: "In my Father's house are many mansions: If it were not so, I would have told you. I go to prepare a place for you."

I was still commanding in The Old Guard at this time, but I heard nothing of this service, which I could have attended with classmates and family. What a terrible circumstance. I could even have arranged for my company to have Henry's memorial detail. I'm deeply saddened and troubled by that fact.

Henry was awarded a posthumous Silver Star for his actions on his last day. It reads, in part:

Captain Spengler was flying in the lead aircraft of a heavy fire team in support of ARVN ground troops and US Army advisors, who were surrounded by an NVA Division in the city of Loc Ninh. Captain Spengler was at Lai Khe rearming his aircraft when he received information of a large enemy force forming west of the city of Loc Ninh. Captain Spengler's aircraft proceeded to the target area. Upon arriving he observed an enemy force of battalion size forming for an attack on the city. Unhesitatingly he maneuvered his aircraft for an attack on the enemy force. On his first attack Captain Spengler received a heavy concentration of anti-aircraft fire. Throughout the ensuing battle the ground to air fire increased in volume. Realizing the hazard the enemy fire presented,

Captain Spengler, with disregard for his personal safety, took the anti-aircraft position under attack, which resulted in breaking up the attack on the city. Captain Spengler continued engaging the enemy position until his helicopter was brought down by enemy fire.

The beginning of Jim Locher's eulogy captured the somber moment: ". . . my heart is heavy with sadness." He continued, "I am grateful for the opportunity to pay tribute to a man whose friendship enriched the lives of many and to honor a dedicated soldier. Henry Spengler was a sincere and generous friend. He was an uplifting spirit in our lives, a source of strength and comfort, a comrade with whom we could share our joys and sorrows, an unselfish companion who stood by his friends in times of need, regardless of the hardship."

Reflecting the feeling of grief, Locher lamented, "Those of us who loved Henry and those of us who cherished his friendship have suffered a great loss. We cannot replace the warmth of his attention, the sound of his laughter, nor the joy of his presence. He has touched our lives; we are thankful for the time that he spent with us." Of his military virtues, Locher remarked, "Henry had the courage to overcome adversity, the confidence in his judgment and sense of values to be a decisive leader, and the perseverance to achieve difficult objectives. His honesty, loyalty, and devotion to duty, together with his abilities, distinguished his military leadership." After Jim finished the eulogy, he sat down and cried.

When the Vietnam Veterans Memorial (better known as *The Wall*) was dedicated on November 13, 1982, Jim Locher recalled, "Henry's death ten years earlier was still a raw memory. The wounds of his loss had not yet healed. Many classmates came then and repeatedly to honor those lost during the Vietnam War." Locher continued, "Tracing Henry's name, chiseled into the black granite, with my fingers was a moving experience as was making rubbings of his name. It was a time of remembering but also a time of grieving."

On Friday, August 18, 1989, Henry's son, Shawn, received a call as next of kin that his father's remains had been found and identified. Betty had married Mike Meuleners, from the West Point class of 1970, a few years after Henry's death and they were living at that time at Fort Ord, California, where Mike was stationed. Bette, Shawn, and daughter Lisa traveled to Northern Virginia, where they and Henry's mother met with an Army representative who showed them the evidence of the recovery of Henry's remains. Vietnam had repatriated the remains of twenty-one US servicemen on April 29. In mid-August, Henry's became one of only five to be positively identified by the Military Central Identification Laboratory in Honolulu. The other member of the helicopter crew, Chief Warrant Officer (CWO) Windeler, was also identified. On August 23, the flag-draped coffins of Captain Spengler and CWO Windeler arrived under military escort at Travis Air Force Base in California. The caskets were carried past an honor guard in a small ceremony. Bette's husband, then Lieutenant Colonel Mike Meuleners, escorted Henry's body from Travis to Washington, DC.

Of these events, Henry's mother said, "It will be a final chapter in a long, long wait . . . We feel like after all these years he's coming home." Of the planned burial service on August 29, she remarked that it would be "a tribute to a fallen soldier who made the ultimate sacrifice to a country he loved." She also noted, "It does raise a lot of grief, but it does take away the waiting time to get the remains and have the final internment." Mrs. Spengler was right, the burial service on August 29, 1989, was a sacred tribute to a fallen warrior.

> Jim Locher provided a fitting final testimonial on Captain Henry Mershon Spengler III: You could not know Henry Spengler without being changed for the better. We learned from what he did and how he did it. Henry always excelled, but with ease and grace. He embraced life with wit and charm. He was dedicated with courage and conviction. He loved his family and friends with gentleness and passion. He lived and died by West Point's motto: Duty, Honor, Country. We felt Henry's tragic loss so deeply, but we have held onto him in his glory in our hearts.

Henry Mershon Spengler III is interred in Arlington National Cemetery.

Henry and Bette at West Point

Henry and Bette
wedding at Ft. Myer
chapel, June 29, 1968

Bette, Shawn and Henry just before departure for Vietnam

Henry Spengler and Capt. Henry—77th Aerial Rocket Artillery

"WE FELL"

By Dutch Hostler, '68

We fell.
We fell... in and swore an oath...
to protect and defend.
We fell... in for training...
'til war was no more pretend.
We fell...in growing numbers...
where the bombs and bullets flew.
We fell... for one another...
and we fell... as well... for you.
We fell... until the last report
and ricochet carom.
We fell... and bled on foreign shores...
and then... we fell... at home.
We fell.
We fell... as victims vilified
for answering the call...
berated... yes... and hated...
after we had risked it all.
We fell.
A fallen delegation... touched
by fire meant to kill...
in service to our Nation...
yes... and we are falling still...
to all the ills of body
Agent Orange can beget...

to terrors of the mind and soul...
that haunt and daunt us yet.
We're falling like our brothers fell...
at Dak To...
... Hue...
... Ben Het...
... Phu Non...
... Na Trang...
... Khe Sanh...
... Ia Drang...
so please... do not forget...
that there are wounds
you cannot see...
and we cannot conceal...
but their invisibility
renders them no less... real.
Our very lives a story
that with earnest angst we tell...
of who we are...
and how we served...
and why... and how...
we fell.

NOT THE LAST STORY . . .

In this book I've tried to relate the all-too-short stories of twenty American heroes, our classmates, for that's what they were in every sense of that now overused word; they were real heroes. Not only because they fell in combat, but because after facing sometimes almost insurmountable odds, and knowing with almost certainty that they would go to war shortly after graduation, they didn't falter. They accepted their responsibilities for the lives of others, and willingly went off to do just that. Many of our guys paid the price while trying to safeguard the lives of their soldiers, or while galloping off like the John Wayne cavalry of the past to help those in need. We should all be proud to call them classmates and need to keep them all in our hearts until we enter Valhalla and are reunited.

As I was putting this book together, I heard some incredible stories of how some of our fallen classmates made themselves known after their deaths. Most of these incidents are very emotional, and in some cases, I'll leave the recounting of the story in the words of those who experienced the event.

First, a story of Ken Cummings from classmate Ross Irvin. He had an experience, an epiphany, that is so meaningful, so emotional, that it needs to be quoted in its entirety:

> All of us have memories that lie like a patient, faithful dog in a compartment of our minds, unattended and neglected for years, yet always remaining in the background. Sometimes in our otherwise humdrum daily existence an event occurs that

releases a memory and the enormity and consequences of it springs into the present. The released dog raises his head, wags its tail, and tugs at our heart. This is such a story.

It is a tradition in our class during our reunion year to hold a memorial service in Washington at the Vietnam Memorial for our classmates who had fallen in Vietnam. It is always a somber and well-organized event put on by our classmates who live in the greater Washington area. I always go because I owe them. Dave Sackett and Jeff Riek, my best friend in the world, were my roommates at school at one time or another. In the fall of 1968 at the Infantry Officer Basic Course at Ft. Benning, Georgia, I roomed with Rick Hawley, famous as graduating last in our class; then later during Airborne school, I shared an apartment with Ken Cummings, our swim team captain.

Before the memorial service in 2008, Joe and Maureen Guignon hosted a party for company E-3 and swim team classmates. I was introduced to Franki Cummings Bennett, an attractive middle-aged woman who was Ken Cummings's widow. I had known, of course, that Ken had been killed and vaguely remembered that he had been married, but that was all.

"I would like you to meet our daughter Kim," she said softly. I turned to my right and staggered back in shock, for Kim was the literal image of Ken. She had the same red hair, the same freckles, even the same warm smile. My mouth desperately tried to respond, but it was overwhelmed by released memories of times long ago. I just stared and gaped.

"And this man knew your grandfather," came the gentle voice from behind. I turned quickly away from Kim, more to avoid my embarrassment than anything else.

I found myself looking down at three handsome children of ages ranging from eight to ten years old. Their earnest faces turned up to mine. I believe I said, "He was a brave man, you should be proud of him," or something like that, but my words choked in my throat as I held back the tears.

I grasped the enormity of this event. I had been privileged to share something that Ken, the rightful heir of this moment, had never experienced. Ken had a lovely daughter with a devoted son-in-law and three beautiful grandchildren, yet he had never seen or held any of them. He had died too soon, unfulfilled, performing his duty in a far-off land.

When one loses a loved one, especially in combat, I think it natural that those left behind want to know all of the details of their loved one's death. How did it happen? Did anyone try to take care of him? Did he die immediately? Was he a hero? Was he in pain? These are all understandable and legitimate concerns. And many times, these questions can't be answered for any number of reasons. In one case, however, those questions were answered because of research for this book, some fifty years after the incident, and if this book accomplishes nothing more, then I consider my effort a success.

Jim Gaiser's sister, Carol St. George, had lived all this time with questions surrounding her brother's death. These were common issues with her mom and other family members, all of whom passed before they had the questions answered. But here in Carol's words, are the answers. Because of her effort to research information for this book, she finally found closure:

> My parents wrote multiple letters to servicemen who should have been there that night, but no one replied. Then, in an effort to find Jim's best friend, Bob Hoyle, who would have been best man at his wedding, I discovered the entries from Dan Goedken. Had I not been looking for information for your book I might never have seen the entry. I contacted Dan and he readily agreed to a phone call . . .three hours long—my fault. He answered all my questions and patiently explained the living conditions as they were and the facts of Jim's injuries. I was so happy to know that he thought perhaps Jim had lived. His willingness to speak to me has brought closure and peace, most certainly a rare gift for a

relative in wartime. I told him that he was as much of a hero as my brother was, for he had gone without thought for his own safety to help a fallen comrade.

Dan Goedken is a medic who treated Jim that night and had been on a quest for fifty years to find out more information about the young officer he had treated, an action for which he had received a valor award. Here is his story in his words:

I have vivid memories of that early morning attack in Vietnam. I was a combat medic with a battery of the 1/92 Artillery. On this firebase we might have had forty-five to fifty guys. I had never met James, as he was on temporary assignment to my 155 Howitzer artillery battery. In the dawn hours, when our firebase received heavy incoming enemy missiles and small arms fire, James went from the safety of his command hooch to the most exposed lookout above the firebase, attempting to detect the direction of enemy fire. His only protection there was a three-foot-high sandbag turret-type enclosure. When that enclosure took a direct hit, either via a missile or mortar, he was severely wounded. I, as the only medic in our firebase, made my way to his location, perhaps 175–200 feet away. I mostly crawled to the base of his hooch, as a firefight was still underway. I scaled the hooch and found James responsive but severely wounded. Detecting his level of injury, in the semi-dark circumstances, while also trying to stay below the significantly destroyed sandbag turret, amidst the loud and smoky firefight, was the work of a medic. I had been in-country for ten months and was sufficiently experienced with combat injuries. We never spoke, and his wounds were knowingly grave. I bandaged all I could. Come daylight, I summoned a medivac. I stayed with him and helped load him aboard the helicopter. I then went to the side of five others, also wounded but all less seriously.
        Because James was a temporary assignment to the 1/92, I never knew his name. Nor did I know if he lived or died. One

has to understand the fragility of combat to comprehend this unawareness. A year later, in 1970, I was awarded a Bronze Star with V for valor device for my actions assisting a yet unknown officer, whose survival was unknown. For years thereafter, I felt conflicted. To be awarded the medal, for a distinguished officer's efforts, yet he remained nameless, and his fate remained unknown.

I have been to the Vietnam Wall many times and had many conversations with folks trying to reverse engineer and discover the name and fate of that officer in which we shared a fateful time in a faraway war-torn land. I was just never able to connect the dots. After retiring in 2017, I chose for the first time to attend a reunion of the 1/92 in Colorado. My mission, besides the communal desires to be with my fellow veterans who served fifty years ago, was to try and discern who that officer was, and his fate, and full story. I spoke with everyone there, everyone, all twenty-eight attendees. A few key admin folks had a hunch or two. By happenstance, my wife and I were with two other couples on a jeep tour of some canyons, and I brought up my search. One fellow 1/92 veteran, Mike, somewhat casually, or hypothetically, mentioned that a distant relative, an officer, had been assigned temporarily to the 1/92. And that he had been killed in action. Mike asked me the date of the firefight, and I said November 7. It seemed too unlikely that it would all come together, after fifty years. He gave me the name, Lt. James Alfred Gaiser. But when I searched his obituary info, it did not list the firebase. And this was most critical. The date alone was probably, but not the certainty I needed. Then, again with almost random happenstance, a few weeks later a friend at my church in Minnesota said she was raised at West Point, and said they have a vast database that I might be able to have access to, not to just validate a name but his story. It all, after fifty years, came personally together last fall, 2019. Thank you on this portal for allowing me to bring witness to James, on that firebase, and to add to his story. So it is with great sympathy that I offer these words. I now know the officer's name, and more of his vast story. And the people who loved him. As with so many that we lost, I firsthand saw his courage under fire, his steadfast and selfless leadership. And to know he was also awarded the Bronze Star with Valor device is personal and profoundly moving.

So, as stated, I only knew James but for thirty minutes or less on that ill-fated morning. But his life was big and impactful. Personally, my search story is now complete, and I thank all of you for recording his abbreviated life and story herein. It helps me to heal, also. For in life, we never know how critical paths may cross with someone. A vulnerable bond fixed in a moment long ago. A bond yet broken. And if troubling answers will ever, ever come to the many unknowns from that distant moment. God speed to James's family and friends.

From this story of comfort and closure we have a story of an abiding presence, the spirit of a lost comrade that lives on. This is a story of Jeff Riek's nieces from his sister Muffie:

Both of the girls turned out to be runners like their uncle. Daughter Natalie started in high school and encountered some trouble. She asked Jeff to run with her and consequently became so good that she received a full ROTC scholarship, became a captain in the Army, and deployed during Iraqi Freedom. She was one of twenty-three women that were Airborne, Air Assault, and Pathfinder qualified. The other daughter, who was all *girlie* as a cheerleader and singer, started running just recently. She, too, asked Jeff to run with her and is now doing half marathons. Jeff has never not been in our family. He continues to run with his nieces, just a foot behind and on their right shoulder. They know that Uncle Jeff will always be with them.

And to continue with Jeff's story, classmate Ralph Tildon recounts a Founder's Day event in 2001:

It was USMA Founders' Day, 2001, at the officers' club in Fort Bliss, Texas. Each West Point class present had a table with the class year prominent in the middle of the table. When eating time began, class members and spouses left the table and got into the buffet line. I remained behind— the sole person left at the class of '68 table. A guy in dress blues entered the room, looked around, saw the '68 table, and came to me.

> **Him (I don't remember his name):** "Hi. You're class of 1968?"
> **Me:** "Yes, I am."
> **Him:** "Do you know your classmate, Jeff Riek?"
> **Me:** "I sure do. I last saw him at Travis Air Force Base an hour before he flew to Vietnam August 1969."
> **Him:** "He and I were platoon leaders in the same company [in the 9th Division]. He was the best officer I've *ever* known. When we were in combat, he could call in and direct artillery and tactical air fire as though he were conducting an orchestra. He was just *outstanding*. The day he and his RTO were killed, I was on another ridge. We couldn't get to them in time."

At this point the man was fighting back tears as he continued.

> **Him:** "I named my son after Jeff. My son became an Army officer, too. He was killed in training at Fort Riley, Kansas, when the track [mechanized infantry vehicle] that he was in went over a sharp road edge, fell on its side, and crushed him. My son Jeff is buried at Fort Riley."

The guy again was fighting back tears. I believe that the guy said that he contacted or tried to contact Jeff Riek's mother when he returned from Vietnam.

◆ ◆ ◆

There is another story, this one about Rick Hawley and Tom McConnell, that is truly incredible—perhaps supernatural—while at the same time a testament to life after death. To read the story about this experience after Rick's death, will certainly get one's attention. Given the fact that Tom was a deacon in the Catholic Church adds even more credibility to his words:

After graduation and all of the schools, we were stationed at Ft. Bragg when Brenda became pregnant with our first child. I knew that Rick was getting ready to go to Vietnam, but I called him and asked if he could stop by to see us because I wanted to ask him to be our daughter's godfather when she was born. He said of course and spent a couple of days with us. Rick went on to Vietnam and Brenda and I went to an assignment in Germany. We had a great set of temporary quarters, it had eight bedrooms. The bedrooms were off a long hall, and ours was at one end and our newborn daughter's was down the hall from us. We named her Mary Catherine.

It was in Germany that I learned from my folks that Rick had been killed. That hit me emotionally in a way that is almost beyond description. I couldn't believe it and couldn't mentally process the information. Rick was dead. I called my boss and asked for a couple of days of leave, a strange request as I had just taken command of a company.

When I got the okay, I told Brenda that I needed to go out and then left the house. I know that I didn't take the car as we only had one. I don't remember anything about where I went or what I did, that is all just blank space in my mind. I remember leaving and the next thing I remember was climbing the stairs to our quarters. When I went in the door Brenda was standing there anxiously looking at me. She had been extremely worried and naturally asked where I'd been. I told her that I didn't know, that I had no idea. I had just needed to get off by myself to process that nightmarish information. I asked her how long I'd been gone and when she told me two days I was dumbfounded. I couldn't believe it.

One night shortly thereafter, I woke up in the middle of the night for some reason and couldn't get back to sleep. I got up and walked into the hall just to check to make sure that everything was okay and saw that the door to Mary Catherine's room was closed, something that shouldn't be. I quickly walked down the hall and opened the door and just stood there. There by Mary Catherine's bed stood Rick Hawley, dressed in the uniform in which he'd died, as it was burned and in tatters. He bent over the bed and kissed Mary Catherine on the forehead. How do you deal with something like this? I asked, "Rick, is that really you," and he replied, "Yes, I'm here." I asked him, "What are you doing here?" He told me, "I couldn't leave and not say goodbye to my goddaughter." I walked over toward him as if to put my arms around him and he said, "No, no. Don't touch me. I haven't left yet." He bent over the bed and gave her another kiss, and then started towards the door. I walked over to check on my daughter and then went out into the hall. Rick was gone.

How does one explain this kind of experience? Is this something spooky and supernatural, or can one come back after death to visit someone he loves? Obviously, the latter because it was Rick who was there that night—I have no doubt of that—and he obviously was proud of being a godfather and loved his goddaughter, whom he'd never seen, and had to say goodbye.

There was a story in the *Cincinnati Enquirer* on May 27, 2002, that was reposted on the Vietnam Helicopter Pilots Association website concerning the legacy of John Speidel.

In a three-fourths acre greenhouse, a stocky fifty-one-year-old walks with a slight limp past hundreds of plants. Mr. Duren, owner of Marvin's Organic Gardens in Lebanon, was seriously wounded in an ambush thirty-one years ago. On the hot afternoon of April 23, 1971, a Huey helicopter from the Army's 101st Airborne Division landed on a ridge in the A Shau Valley of South Vietnam. Six Rangers from L Company, 75th Infantry jumped out, including the twenty-year-old team leader, Spc. Marvin Duren, to establish a radio relay link for a Ranger platoon on the valley floor. As Spc. Duren led the Rangers out of the landing zone, they met a flurry of rifle fire and hand grenades from North Vietnamese Army troops, hidden in bunkers. Two bullets from an AK-47 ripped into Spc. Duren's right hip; shrapnel and gunshots also penetrated his stomach, left chest, left arm, back, spleen, appendix, left lung and small intestine. He radioed for help as the team medic tended to him. The first step in the rescue: get a Huey pilot to fly a replacement team leader into the battle zone to replace Spc. Duren. The pilot chosen was Capt. Louis J. "John" Speidel, Milford High School class of '64 and a 1968 West Point graduate. It was his twenty-fifth birthday. He knew the pilot was highly regarded by Ranger team leaders because he, too, was a Ranger. Capt. Speidel succeeded in delivering Spc. Duren's replacement, but heavy enemy fire hammered his Huey. It crashed near the landing zone with Capt. Speidel trapped upside down, his legs pinned in the wreckage. Meanwhile, as North Vietnamese continued pounding the Rangers' positions, a medevac helicopter rescued Spc. Duren. For the others, hope of a quick rescue soon faded. The enemy thwarted attempts to reach the Rangers and helicopter crews for two days. On the third day, a Ranger team rescued Capt. Speidel and other survivors. By then, eleven Americans were dead. One had been captured. Another was never found. Mr. Duren received a Bronze Star and Purple Heart for his actions that April day. In the late 1970s Mr. Duren opened a Waffle House at I-275 and Ohio 28 in Milford. About that time, he recognized that his restaurant landscapes lacked curb appeal. He needed advice from a gardening expert. He found one, at a place called Speidel's Garden Center. The easygoing proprietor, a man named Louis Speidel, loved to grow things. Says Mr. Duren: "He was so patient with me." Mr. Duren never thought to ask Mr. Speidel if he was related to a helicopter pilot who served in Vietnam. Mr. Duren, after all, had no idea that Capt. Speidel's full name was Louis John Speidel, or that he was from Milford. Capt. Louis John Speidel died of cardiac arrest on June 24, 1971. About a year ago, another Army Ranger mailed Mr. Duren a packet with a list of those killed in the April 1971 mission at A Shau. The list included Capt. Louis John Speidel, of course. But it was his hometown that stunned Mr. Duren: Milford, Ohio. And Mr. Duren was astounded to learn that Louis Speidel, the friendly man who for years had sold him plants and mentored him, was Capt. Speidel's father. In a perfect world, Mr. Duren would have visited Louis Speidel once more. They would have discussed their mutual love of plants. They would have talked about Capt. Speidel's final mission, and Mr. Duren would have praised the Army pilot. "Had he not come in to deliver that team leader," Mr. Duren says, "I wasn't going to be (rescued)." But Mr. Duren and Louis Speidel never met again. Mr. Speidel, suffering from a form of dementia, spent the last years of his life with a daughter in California. Mr. Duren wants Capt. Speidel's family and friends to know: He will always remember.

As a combat infantryman I have a special place in my heart for Army helicopter pilots; they took us into sometimes hellish places, but they invariably returned to haul out our dead and wounded, or to drop off more water and ammo, or best of all, to take us out of that place. They were some of the bravest soldiers I've ever known, making those ungainly looking flying machines do things their designers never imagined. I've seen them fly through incredible enemy fire to accomplish their mission, putting their lives, and those of their crew, in jeopardy to help and support us on the ground. The *wop, wop, wop* sound of Huey helicopter blades still makes my heart pound, and my eyes moisten. As Joe Galloway of *We Were Soldiers Once and Young* and Ia Drang fame once said, helicopter pilots are "God's own lunatics." While I honor several in this book, there are many more pilot classmates who deserve our thanks and respect.

Greg Camp, when he was involved with the building and content of the National Infantry Museum, had an experience with the memory of Pete Connor that played an instrumental role in the completion of the museum:

In 2008 we got an appointment with Harry Gray to seek a donation for the National Infantry Museum. Harry was the retired Chairman and CEO of United Technologies. We knew that Harry had received a Silver Star as an infantry company commander in WWII, hence the connection. I sent Harry a package and MG White (our chairman at the time) and I called on Harry at his home in North Palm Beach. When we met, we briefed him on the project and he basically chewed us out, as what we told him was covered in the read ahead. He asked some specific questions about how we were going to cover the Battle of the Bulge, as that is where he received his Silver Star. Neither MG White nor I had the details of that exhibit as we were still in the big picture phase of development.

Harry had pity on us after chewing us out and invited us to lunch before we headed back to Columbus. During lunch he mentioned his WWII hero, Lt. Col. Connor, his battalion commander, which went unnoticed until later in the conversation when he told us he was the godfather of Connor's oldest son and that he'd tried to talk his godson out of going Infantry when he graduated from West Point but the "kid did it anyway and got killed in action." Slow though I am, I began to put the pieces together and asked if Pete Connor was his godson and he said yes. I told him that Pete and I were classmates and Pete was in 1/12 Cav when I was in 2/12 Cav and Pete was killed one ridgeline over from where we were. Harry then said for us to "do our homework" on our Battle of the Bulge exhibit and come see him a couple months later at his Connecticut summer home.

As it turned out, the day we were to see him was the day after our 2008 remembrance at the Vietnam Memorial Wall and all of Pete's brothers and sisters were there. I told them what I was going to do, and they told me to make sure to give "Uncle Harry" their best. We had created an architectural mockup of the Battle of the Bulge exhibit that we briefed him on. Hoping to get $250,000 he sent us off to change into comfortable clothes and return for lunch. I had briefed him on the exhibit, but MG White was always the *asker* for the gift. Before MG White could ask for consideration, Harry said he'd give us a million dollars. Stunned, I mentioned that a gift of that amount would make him a four-star donor to the museum. He immediately asked what it would take to become a five-star donor and we told him $2.5 million. He then asked what we could do to honor a gift at that level and come back to see him again in three months.

We created an animated video of a dedication of one of the prime spaces in the museum that would become the 2nd Infantry Regiment Mezzanine/Gallery (named after his unit in WWII under then Lt. Col. Connor). In the animated video he was next to the Connor children as they cut the ribbon. Once he saw the video, he immediately upped his gift to $2.5 million. In March of 2009 he came to the museum to dedicate the 2nd Infantry Regiment Mezzanine/Gallery and all the Connor kids where there for the event. Harry died three months later but his widow honored his gift. This was a gift from Pete from beyond the grave.

And one last story from Jeff Riek's sister Muffie:

One of the last letters I received from Jeff, a birthday letter, was longer than most and completely prophetic. The tenure of the letter was that you can "never ask why, as there is no answer." I denied his death for several months until I had a dream. One night I dreamed I saw him in his whites at a big inside party. I ran to him, held him and said, "I knew you weren't dead." I could feel him and smell him and knew I was holding him. Glass mirrors surrounded the room and when I opened my eyes while holding him, he had disappeared. Then I knew he was really gone, and I began my grieving for this great guy who came to me to let me hug him one last time.

These stories surely prove that the influence of our fallen Twenty did not end with their deaths. From the stories in this chapter, and the memories of many more of us, I'm convinced that the spirits of those we lost have never left us. They have lived on in our hearts and minds, sometimes making themselves obvious, but always present when we think of them. I'm convinced that I've communicated with Don Colglazier on some of my stops to say hi to him at the North Carolina Vietnam Veterans Memorial. Sometimes there's a specific incident, and sometimes it's just a feeling, but they're surely Gripping Hands with us as we so often do with them.

LEGACY

This book is the story of the class of 1968's time at West Point, the background of the war in Vietnam, and a brief description of what that war was like, and a recounting of the lives and experiences of some outstanding young men who lost their lives in that far off land. For some Twenty of us, the war was the fatal culmination of five or more years of hard work and training, all in preparation for serving our country in a very hostile environment. As stated in a previous chapter, I firmly believe that we in the class of '68 shared an unbreachable love of country and all that America stood for. We willingly signed on for the four years at West Point and for all of the training and five years of service after graduation. We all knew at an early time that chances were pretty good that we'd be sent to the war zone; most of us served a total of 591 combat tours. A large number of the Twenty we lost died due to enemy action, although one was murdered and two were lost in flight accidents. I believe that every member of the class of 1968 can see himself in the lives of our Twenty. I believe that we will each reflect, from the vantage point of more than fifty years, that there but for the grace of God go each of us, for we each rode, walked, or flew through the valley of death multiple times.

We look back on these roommates, teammates, good friends, and some of those whom we may not have known and have a new appreciation for their sacrifice. We have lived full lives, most of us are secure in our families, our wives, kids, and grandkids, have enjoyed a successful career, or careers, and are now enjoying a well-deserved retirement. The Twenty that I've tried to honor with this book are names on a black granite wall. They stare back at us as we knew them then, names that represent a life that ended all too early and are forever young. Yet I hope that this book makes them more than just names, that with this book they become individuals with living personalities, with differing backgrounds, and different experiences in life, at West Point, in the Army, and in Vietnam. I hope that this book portrays them as young men, alive and full of hope for the future, filled with love of country, dedication, and valor, willing to put themselves in harm's way for a cause greater than themselves. A theme that appears in many of the stories is the remark about how gentle and kind our lost classmates were; yet when the need arose, they became superlative warriors, putting their lives on the line for others.

Many of those of us who did return carry visible and invisible combat wounds of an entirely different type. There is one aspect of the war in Vietnam that has become a lasting legacy for those who served there. It is known as Agent Orange and was a chemical defoliant, sprayed from the air, to destroy vegetation on the ground. It was claimed to be of no threat to humans or animals when the reality was much different. Most who served in Vietnam, and the sailors who served on the surrounding waters, were exposed to this agent and as time has gone on it's been discovered that Agent Orange has, in fact, long term lethal effects on many who served in-country. Before the dangerous effects were known, most of us on the ground welcomed the use of the agent because it deprived the bad guys of a place to hide, or uncovered access routes for supply or to attack our bases.

As time has passed, more and more of our number have been afflicted with many different lethal ailments—usually some form of cancer. Since we started reunions of my Vietnam recon platoon in the year 2000, we've buried ten of our brothers, an enormous percentage of a unit that normally only included maybe twenty-five guys. The Veterans' Administration now recognizes several of these ailments as associated with Agent Orange and provides some type of compensation. The hard fact is that the use of Agent Orange by the US military has resulted in many more casualties than the number lost to combat. The effects can sometimes be recognized over a couple of generations. Commonly accepted statistics say that over the course of the war about 2.5 million servicemen actually set foot on the soil of Vietnam. According to the American War Library, as of February 28, 2019, it is estimated that approximately 610,000 Americans who served in the land forces during the Vietnam War, or in air missions over Vietnam, between 1954 and 1975 are still alive to this day, or about one fourth of the total who served. That's a staggering statistic fifty years later.

The other major long-lasting effect of service during the war is PTS or Post Traumatic Stress. I refuse to call it a *disorder* because that does a disservice to those who experienced that war. No man who served in-country, particularly in the combat arms, came back the same as the boy who went to war. In addition to Vietnam having been a brutal small unit war, as stated earlier in this book, we had no time to decompress since our return trip was so rapid. We had dreamed about returning to *The World,* where we'd find our wife or girlfriend, could get some of mom's great home cooking, and could buy a fast car, but our actual return turned out to be a reception unlike any we had ever imagined. It was not an unusual experience to get off of our *Freedom Bird* at a US airport and be subjected to yelling and cursing, having unidentified materials thrown at us, and being called some of the vilest names imaginable—rapists, baby killers, druggies, etc. This was the reception we received at a time when we were feeling proud of our service and thankful for being alive and being able to return home, and left many returning vets feeling confused, angered, and embittered. Because of this reaction, many Vietnam Veterans held their experiences and fears internally, causing them to fester over time. I think that's why so many of us have wrestled with demons and dragons for so long, and why many have succumbed to their nightmares and memories. That, plus the early societal stigma of needing help with mental health issues led many guys to not even seek help. Veterans of the Vietnam War went to and returned from war alone, and in many cases, they've had to deal with their memories alone, and have taken their own lives while alone. There were even cases of veteran organizations such as the VFW (Veterans of Foreign Wars) refusing membership, and maybe even entrance to Vietnam vets as we hadn't fought a "real" war, or, if they gave us that credit, they prohibited our entry because we'd *lost.* This has been part of the problem that led to so many PTS and suicide cases; not that we were weaker in some sense, but rather because of the unique aspects of our service and the policies that governed it. Vietnam Veterans fought as heroically and nobly as any generation of Americans in any war in which we have been involved.

As the class of 1968 takes our last ride to Valhalla, most of us will leave behind a long legacy of achievement in a variety of fields and endeavors. Some of us served at least twenty years in the military and then went on to other successful careers. Others left the Army long before that time to pursue other goals. We have been fortunate, blessed with the camaraderie of classmates, and in many cases their families, some of whom we've known since day one, and others who have come into our lives at a later time. We've been able to meet every five years, during a memorial at The Wall on the anniversary of our graduation to honor and pay our respects to the Twenty whose names grace several of the panels, or at a formal reunion at West Point in the fall. Many of our cadet companies have held mini reunions during the intervening years because waiting five years is just too damned long. During these times, we've reveled in the company of our classmates, sharing bonds that are surpassed by few others. As the years have passed, we've realized more and more just how special are the bonds which tie us all together. These are the guys we shared Beast Barracks with, were our roommates, were the guys who provided support in many forms during plebe year, those with whom we walked the area, played sports, shared classes, and sometimes shared summer leaves with. We got involved with them and their One and Only, who many times became a wife and in an impressive number, still are. In some cases, we were Ranger buddies, in other cases we fought together, and in easier times we travelled and vacationed together. It's been a heck of a life.

And yet, during these times we remember that valuable friends, brothers in the truest sense, are missing; they will never be able to share the experiences we've had. While they were our brothers, close friends, roommates, or teammates, we can't call or talk with them or share experiences or stories with them. But they remain with many of us, always in our minds or hearts. I've learned through putting this book together that some of us treasure one of our Twenty as though they truly were lost family members. Some of us think of individuals we've lost on an almost daily basis. Some of us have named children after one of our fallen. Some of us maintain a life-long dedication to keeping the memories of one or more of our lost classmates alive. Some of us have dedicated ourselves to maintaining contact with the families. Certain occurrences will trigger memories and maybe make our eyeballs sweat just a little (combat soldiers don't cry). As a class, we've done a great job of keeping in touch with their families or widows with our get togethers at The Wall, letting them know that we've not forgotten their soldier or them. For this we owe a debt of gratitude to a few of our classmates who have put this remembrance together every five years. And in the truest sense, we have gripped hands with those who we lost in combat, as well as all others who have left our ranks, during a memorial service at our reunions.

I think it fitting and necessary that we remember our Twenty, that we continue to reach out to their families and loved ones, for they can't do that. We need to stand for them as we celebrate our milestones as a class, for they're still a very important part of us. We can't forget them or their achievements and successes in their short lives. I've learned that every one of our guys was special and unique in his own way, every one of them left an indelible mark on those who loved and respected them. They answered those questions of earlier in this book about the doubts we all held as we flew off to combat. And they answered in the affirmative with their lives, they did not shirk their duties.

Many of us who served in Vietnam want to move on from that war, on the surface many already have. But in our hearts and memories total divorce from our experiences and memories is impossible. While trying to forget is sometimes a necessary thing for us as individuals, we can never move on from our memories of those who we lost. To do so would be a sin against them and our class, for they epitomize what we have served to uphold: Duty! Honor! Country!

I've done my best to tell each individual story of each of our fallen. After more than fifty years it has been difficult in some cases to gather memories of their childhood and stories of their high school years. Many direct family members have passed on, as have classmates and other friends. With the incredible help of many classmates and surviving family members who have provided input or sources, the narratives give as complete a story of each of the Twenty as has been possible to assemble. These are our classmates who gave their all in service to our country. These are their stories and their all-too-short legacies. These are our guys who sacrificed for Duty, Honor, Country. These are our buddies whom we can never forget. I sincerely hope that I've done them proud. If you've not yet done so, I encourage all of you to visit the Vietnam Memorial, The Wall, to pay homage to these young warriors of our cohort. It's one of the few places you can go and pay your respects to all Twenty in one place.

And while I've tried to honor our classmates, there are still more than 58,000 other names on that Wall. I wish that something like this book could be done for each of them. As Joe Galloway once observed, "The guys who went to Vietnam may not have been part of the *Greatest Generation*, but they were certainly the greatest of their generation."

DUTY! HONOR!!
COUNTRY!

And when our work is done,
Our course on Earth is run,
May it be said "Well done:
Be thou at peace."

—From the West Point Alma Mater

"TOAST TO A DEPARTED CLASSMATE"

By Dutch Hostler '68

Our ranks are thinned. Death's icy wind has sadly swept away
A comrade of our callow youth when we were hearts in gray.
It falls to us to close our ranks and contemplate the day
We'll once again assemble . . . far beyond life's fickle fray.
The warmth of camaraderie transcends death's icy chill.
Our friend still lifts our spirits . . . and so shall we . . . until
we join that ghostly muster . . . as we must . . . for 'tis God's will.
So now lift your spirits fellows . . . and be careful not to spill.

EPILOGUE

Photo thanks to Dave Dostie of Dave Dostie Photography.

As a moving final tribute to our Fallen Twenty, I offer the incredible dedication of classmate Stott Carlton, who has demonstrated an abiding devotion to our classmate Don Workman and all of the others lost in the war. Since May 2020 he, accompanied by his dog Skip, has carried the nation's colors in their honor across the Donald Davey Bridge over the Sheepscot River in Maine several days a week. The bridge connects the towns of Wiscasset and Edgecomb. He performs this tribute between St Patrick's Day and Veterans Day, and so far, Stott and Skip have logged 241 miles as of January 2022.

THE WALL

History of the Vietnam
Veterans Memorial

[*Contributed by Jim Knots, president and
CEO of the Vietnam Veterans Memorial Fund*]

B orn and raised in rural Bowie, Maryland, Jan Scruggs was just
eighteen years old when he volunteered to enlist in the Army in
1968. Debate surrounding Vietnam was escalating. The war's length
and the growing number of casualties were fueling tensions. Within
months after he recovered from his own wounds and returned to the
199th Light Infantry Brigade, the American public was learning the
details of the events at My Lai. By the time he returned home, the
country was even further divided.

Over the next few years, as the war ended and more and more
troops returned home, the media began to paint a picture of the
stereotypical Vietnam veteran: drug addicted, bitter, discontented,
and unable to adjust to life back home. Like most stereotypes, this
one was somewhat unfair.

The truth was, veterans were no more likely to be addicted to
drugs than those who did not serve. And if they were bitter, who could
blame them? When they returned home from serving their country,
there was no national show of gratitude. They were either ignored
or shouted at and called vicious names. Veterans frequently found
themselves denying their time in Vietnam, never mentioning their

service to new friends and acquaintances for fear of the reactions it might elicit.

By June 1977, Scruggs was attending graduate school at American University in Washington, DC, and had joined a research group exploring the social and psychological consequences of Vietnam military duties. The group found that returning veterans were finding it hard to trust people. They were feeling alienated from the nation's leaders, and they had low self-esteem. He also found that those veterans whose units experienced high casualty rates were experiencing higher divorce rates and a greater frequency of combat-related dreams. Using these findings, Scruggs testified at the Senate hearing on the Veteran's Health Care Amendments Act of 1977, with the hope that he could help veterans gain access to the services and support they needed.

He also wanted to find a way to help them heal and suggested that the country build a national memorial as a symbol that the country cared about them.

By 1979, the country was beginning to have more positive feelings toward Vietnam veterans. One film that came out early that year, *The Deer Hunter*, explored the effects of war on three friends, their families, and a tight-knit community. When Scruggs went to see the movie in early 1979, it wasn't the graphic war scenes that haunted him. It was the reminder that the men who died in Vietnam all had faces and names, as well as friends and families who loved them dearly. He could still picture the faces of his 12 buddies who were killed, but the passing years were making it harder and harder to remember their names.

That bothered him. It seemed unconscionable that he—or anyone else—should be allowed to forget. Filtered through his own post-traumatic stress, for weeks he obsessed about the idea of building a memorial. "It just resonated," he explained. "If all of the names could be in one place, these names would have great power—a power to heal. It would have power for individual veterans, but collectively, they would have even greater power to show the enormity of the sacrifices that were made."

His research had proven that post-traumatic stress was real and had shone a light on the challenges faced by a significant number of military veterans. The idea for a memorial seemed like a natural extension of his academic work and his growing desire to find a way to help veterans. He had studied the work of psychiatrist Carl Jung, a student of Sigmund Freud, who wrote of shared societal values. As Scruggs analyzed the concept of collective psychological states, he realized that, just as veterans needed psychological healing, so too did the nation.

"The Memorial had several purposes," he explained. "It would help veterans heal. Its mere existence would be societal recognition that their sacrifices were honorable rather than dishonorable. Veterans needed this, and so did the nation. Our country needed something symbolic to help heal our wounds."

Once Scruggs decided to build the memorial, the next step was to get some people behind him. An ad hoc group of veterans had scheduled a meeting to try to use Vietnam Veterans Week to generate publicity for veterans' needs, and Scruggs thought that would be a good time to announce his plans.

But instead of enthusiasm, he received skepticism. Most at the meeting told him they didn't want a memorial; they wanted more benefits and government support. But the meeting gave Scruggs his first ally: former Air Force intelligence officer and attorney Robert Doubek, who thought a memorial was a good idea. "When I was attending law school, Vietnam veterans were an anomaly among the young single professional set of Washington, so it was something you didn't mention." remembered Doubek. "It seemed unfair and inappropriate that there should be no recognition."

Doubek approached Scruggs after the meeting and suggested that he form a nonprofit corporation as a vehicle to build a memorial. On April 27, 1979, Doubek incorporated the fledgling entity, the Vietnam Veterans Memorial Fund, and Scruggs asked him to be an officer and director. To make his dream a reality, he planned to get support from people as diverse as former anti-war presidential candidate George McGovern and Gen. William Westmoreland, who commanded US forces in Vietnam. Scruggs took two weeks off from his job at the Department of Labor to develop the idea further.

Wheeler recruited others to help, starting with a group of professional men, all Vietnam or Vietnam-era veterans: George

"Sandy" Mayo, Arthur Mosley, John Morrison, Paul Haaga, Bill Marr, John Woods and certified public accountant Bob Frank, who agreed to become VVMF's treasurer. Paul Haaga's spouse, Heather, soon came forward to lend her experience in fundraising. William Jayne, who had been wounded in Vietnam, volunteered to head up public relations activities.

The greatest challenge VVMF faced, said Doubek, was "to put together a functioning organization with people who didn't know one another, people who were very young and didn't have a lot of experience. We had to constantly find the most effective next step to take and be sure not to get waylaid by tangents." The group started to hold regular planning meetings

Their initial timeline was aggressive, with a goal of dedicating the Memorial on Veterans Day 1982—just a little more than 36 months away. The list of tasks to achieve such a goal seemed endless. They needed to secure a plot of land, raise funds and public awareness, design the Memorial, coordinate construction, and organize the dedication ceremonies. Most importantly, they needed to navigate the channels of government authorizations and approvals.

Never in the history of the United States had a national memorial been conceived, approved, built and dedicated in that short an amount of time. But if the challenges seemed insurmountable, no one expressed any fears. And none of them discussed their own personal feelings or political views regarding the war. All of them realized how critical it was that a memorial be apolitical. They set their sights in support of the clear, simple vision Scruggs outlined: to honor the warrior and not the war.

The VVMF organizers soon learned that it required an Act of Congress to build a memorial on Federal land, and Scruggs first called one of the senators for his home state of Maryland. Charles "Mac" Mathias, a Navy veteran of World War II, had been opposed to the war in Vietnam, but he had always respected those who served in it. Mathias had grown increasingly concerned about how veterans had been treated on their return. Because he possessed great knowledge of history, he understood the extensive healing process required after war. A memorial made perfect sense to him. It would be a way to honor the veterans and to help them—and the country—heal.

Scruggs and Doubek met with Mathias to outline their plans. They stressed that all funds for the Memorial would be raised from private donations. No government funds would be given. What they did need, however, was an acceptable location for the Memorial and enough support to push the idea through various governmental committees and agencies.

One of Mathias' early key suggestions was that the memorial should be on the National Mall, especially because the anti-war demonstrations had taken place there. Wheeler had the idea to bypass the traditional site selection route and have Congress pass legislation to award a specific area for a memorial site. Scruggs, Wheeler, and Doubek then scouted the Mall— sometimes by bicycle—to identify the ideal spot: a stretch of parkland known as Constitution Gardens, located adjacent to the Lincoln Memorial.

As they forged a partnership with Mathias and his staff, VVMF also set out to establish other key relationships. Scruggs took a bold step in contacting Virginia Senator John Warner. Warner, who had served as Secretary of the Navy during the war, was himself a veteran of World War II and the Korean War. After meeting with the VVMF officers and advisors, Warner volunteered to help the organization raise the seed money needed to launch the fundraising campaign.

On November 8, 1979, VVMF held a press conference in which Mathias, Warner, and several others announced the introduction of legislation to grant two acres of land near the Lincoln Memorial for the Vietnam Veterans Memorial. With the introduction of legislation, the VVMF leaders realized that it was time to transition from a volunteer committee and to open a staffed office. In December Doubek became the Executive Director, working on a half-time basis for the first few months, and opened the VVMF office on January 2, 1980. He organized the advisors and volunteers into task groups: public relations, financial management, fundraising, legislation, site selection, and design/construction. The priorities were to launch fundraising and achieve passage of the authorizing legislation.

Early in his efforts Scruggs had called on Emogene Cupp, then the national president of the American Gold Star Mothers. "Jan came to our headquarters to see if we had any room to help them get started," Cupp remembered. "We didn't have any space, but I liked their idea and told them I would volunteer to help with all that I could." The Gold Star Mothers is a group of mothers whose sons or daughters have died serving their country. Their motto is: "Honor the dead by serving the living." Volunteering to assist VVMF was an ideal opportunity for Cupp to do just that.

Cupp had experienced firsthand the pains caused by the war. Her only son Robert, an Army draftee, was killed by a land mine on his 21st birthday, June 6, 1968. Compounding the pain was that society's ill treatment of the veterans extended to their families. "It was very hurtful," Cupp recalled. "They treated the moms the same as they treated the vets. They weren't nice. At that time, they just ignored you and wished you would go away. Or, people would tell me, 'Well why did you let him go?' Of course, what choice do you have?"

Just before Christmas 1979, Warner hosted a fundraising breakfast in his Georgetown home. He made an impassioned plea for funding to his guests, members of the defense industry. Before he spoke, however, all eyes had turned toward the kitchen door, from which had emerged his then-wife, actress Elizabeth Taylor. She greeted each visitor in a regal fashion, wearing a dressing gown, perfect makeup, and beautiful shoes that curled up at the toes. "I'm sure I looked like a deer in the headlights, I was so nervous," Scruggs recalled. "I think I even spilled my coffee." But, her presence made a difference. "I heard that those present agreed to double their contributions after Taylor completed her remarks," Scruggs said.

With the seed money from several defense industry donors, especially Grumman Aerospace, VVMF launched its first large-scale direct mail campaign to reach out to the public. To create credibility for the fledgling effort, they formed the National Sponsoring Committee, which included then-first lady Rosalynn Carter, former President Gerald Ford, Bob Hope, future first lady Nancy Reagan, Gen. William C. Westmoreland, USA, Vietnam veteran author James Webb, and Adm. James J. Stockdale, USN.

By early 1980, contributions started to arrive. Millionaire H. Ross Perot made a sizeable donation. Direct mail was proving to be a highly effective fundraising tool. Letters came from moms, dads, grandparents, sons and daughters with heartfelt notes accompanied by checks and dollar bills. They came from veterans and from the neighbors, teachers, coaches and friends of veterans. The public wanted to have a hand in helping to build the Memorial and in honoring the warrior, not the war.

On April 30, 1980, the Senate approved legislation authorizing the Memorial, followed by approval in the House on May 20, 1980. Although differences in the two bills required a Conference Committee to meet, on July 1, at a White House Rose Garden ceremony, President Jimmy Carter signed legislation providing two acres for the Vietnam Veterans Memorial on the National Mall.

With the site approved, VVMF scrambled to address the issues of what the Memorial would look like and who would design it. A few preliminary concepts were embraced. As Scruggs had always envisioned, the Memorial would feature all the names of those who had died. Wheeler suggested that it should be a landscaped solution: a peaceful, park-like setting that could exist harmoniously with the Washington Monument and the Lincoln Memorial.

They were also keenly aware that the legislation made the Memorial's design subject to the approval of the Commission of Fine Arts (CFA), the National Capital Planning Commission (NCPC), and the Secretary of the Interior. It was decided that VVMF would hold a design competition, open to any American citizen over 18 years of age. Just as the American people could be a part of building the Memorial through their contributions and support, they could also have an opportunity to participate in its design.

Arthur Mosley headed the site selection task group and was assisted by John Woods, a structural engineer, who had been permanently disabled in a helicopter crash in Vietnam. (Woods continues to serve on VVMF's Board of Directors to this day.) There were four phases to the design competition spanning almost one year: planning and preparation; the launch; the design phase; the design evaluation and selection; the press conference and public presentation. The selected design then had to go through Federal agency approval and development into finished plans.

"The first phase encompassed the detail planning and preparations for holding the competition," said Spreiregen. "Holding a competition is like launching a rocket. Everything has to be thought out and in place before the launch button is pressed." The purpose of the Vietnam Veterans Memorial was to honor all who had served, with a special tribute—their names engraved—for those who did not return. The chief design criteria were that the memorial be 1) reflective and contemplative in character; 2) be harmonious with its site and environment, 3) make no political statement about the war itself, and 4) contain the names of all who died or remain missing. "The hope is that the creation of the Memorial will begin a healing process," Doubek wrote.

Healing meant many things to many people. Could a memorial accomplish such an enormous and daunting task? Could it heal the chasm within society, promote closure, show gratitude to those who served, comfort those in grief, and remind future generations of the toll wrought by war? Moreover, could it accomplish all of that while listing the approximately 58,000 names in an artistic, meaningful way?

Selecting a design that would meet the criteria demanded a jury that could grasp the significance of the Memorial's purpose and understand the unique needs of Vietnam veterans, their families, and a country divided. For weeks, heated discussions took place around the topic of who should be part of the design jury. Many felt it should be composed primarily of veterans; others felt it should be made up only of professionals; some thought a mix of the two would be best.

Ultimately, the VVMF Board agreed on a jury of the most experienced and prestigious artists and designers that could be found, since it took a mature eye to envision from two-dimensional renderings how a design would look when built. The reputation of the jurors was important to attract the best designers and to minimize second guessing by the Federal approval bodies

Spreiregen recommended having a multi-disciplinary panel: two architects, two landscape architects, two sculptors, and one generalist with extensive knowledge about art, architecture, and design. VVMF met the prospective jurors and scrutinized their credentials. The VVMF group liked them all and approved of them with trust and enthusiasm," even selecting three sculptors, making a total of eight jurors. The jury included: architects Pietro Belluschi and Harry Weese; landscape architects Hideo Sasaki and Garrett Eckbo; sculptors Costantino Nivola, Richard Hunt, and James Rosati; and Grady Clay, a journalist and editor of *Landscape Architecture* magazine. Four of the eight were themselves veterans of previous wars.

Each juror was required to read *Fields of Fire*, *A Rumor of War*, and other current literature about the Vietnam War. "Many had worked together, some in Washington. They were also the most collegial people, who would deliberate intensely but never argue or posture," Spreiregen remembered.

With the jury selected, the next task was to announce and promote the competition. In the fall of 1980, VVMF announced the national design competition open to any US citizen, who was over 18 years old. By year's end, 2,573 individuals and teams had registered—almost 3,800 people in total. From the registration forms, it was apparent that architects, artists, designers, as well as veterans and students—of all ages and all levels of experience—were planning to participate. They came from all parts of the country and represented every state. By the March 31, 1981, deadline, 1,421 design entries were submitted for judging. Each submittal had to be hung at eye level for review by the jury. But how and where could all the submissions be displayed?

Vietnam veteran Joseph Zengerle, then an Assistant Secretary of the Air Force, volunteered the use of an aircraft hangar at Andrews Air Force Base. The added component of military security made the location even more attractive, since it would ensure no interference with the designs or the judging.

In accordance with the strict competition guidelines, anonymity of all designs was carefully observed. Each contestant sealed his or her name in an envelope and taped it to the back of the submission. The designs were received and processed in a large warehouse east of Washington. They were unwrapped, number coded, photographed for the record, and prepared for display. The jury evaluation took place over five days, from April 27 through May 1, 1981. The jurors began by touring the site and then returned to Hangar #3 at Andrews to view each of the 1,421 designs individually.

"On the second day, the jury examined the designs together, walking the many aisles and stopping at each of the 232 designs that had been flagged by one or more of the jurors, pausing to discuss each design that had been noted. The first cut was further reduced to 90 by midday Wednesday. By Thursday morning, it was down to 39.

That afternoon, the winning design was selected," said Spreiregen. It was the most thoughtful and thorough discussion of design that I have ever heard, and I have heard many," he recalled.

With the winning design in hand, Spreiregen had less than 24 hours to craft an explanation of the decision—and the design—that would be suitable for presentation to VVMF. Throughout the judging process, one of the judges, Grady Clay, had taken meticulous notes of the jury's discussions. Together with Spreiregen, he composed a report based on these thoughtful comments. "They are a treasure of design insight and included many prescient thoughts as to how the Memorial would likely be experienced," Spreiregen wrote of Clay's notes.

The winning design was the work of Maya Ying Lin of Athens, Ohio, a senior at Yale University. At 21 and still an undergraduate, Lin conceived her design as creating a park within a park — a quiet protected place unto itself, yet harmonious with the overall plan of Constitution Gardens. To achieve this effect, she chose polished black granite for the walls. Its mirror-like surface reflects the images of the surrounding trees, lawns and monuments. The Memorial's walls point to the Washington Monument and Lincoln Memorial, thus bringing the Memorial into the historical context of our country. The names are inscribed in the chronological order of their dates of casualty, showing the war as a series of individual human sacrifices and giving each name a special place in history.

In August of 1981, VVMF selected a building company and architecture firm to develop the plans and build Lin's design. Lin became a design consultant to the architect of record. Early in the effort to get the Memorial built, there were traces of controversy. Some felt that the money to build a memorial could be better spent delivering the many services veterans needed. Others questioned the intent of the Memorial. When VVMF announced the selection of Lin's design, the initial public reaction was generally positive.

But several weeks after the announcement, a handful of people began to protest the design. A few of the most vocal opponents, including James Webb and H. Ross Perot, had previously been strong supporters of a memorial. They complained about the walls being black. They did not like the idea that it was below ground level. They did not like its minimalist design. They felt it was a slap in the face to those who had served because it did not contain traditional symbols honoring service, courage, and sacrifice. Some opponents simply did not like the fact that Lin was a young student, a woman, and of Asian descent; how in the world could she possibly know how to honor the service of the Vietnam veteran?

Then, in October 1980, veteran and lawyer Tom Carhart, also a former supporter, testified before the Commission of Fine Arts (CFA) against the design, saying that "One needs no artistic education to see this design for what it is, a black trench that scars the Mall. Black walls, the universal color of shame and sorrow and degradation." Lin moved to Washington and immediately became part of an internal struggle for control of the design. To bring the design into reality would require an architect of record. Lin and VVMF eventually selected the Cooper-Lecky Partnership as the architect-of-record, with Lin as the projects design consultant.

By early 1982, VVMF asked Warner to bring together both sides for a closed-door session to hammer out the issues. An article by Hugh Sidey in the February 22, 1982, issue of TIME magazine described the session: "A few days ago, 40 supporters and critics of the memorial gathered to try to break the impasse that threatened the memorial because of such features as the black color of the stone and its position below ground level. After listening for a while, Brigadier General George Price, a retired veteran of Korea and Vietnam, stood in quiet rage and said, 'I am sick and tired of calling black a color of shame.' General Price, one of America's highest-ranking Black officers lived with and advised the 1st Vietnamese Infantry Division.

"I have heard your arguments," said General Price. "I remind all of you of Martin Luther King Jr., who fought for justice for all Americans. Black is not a color of shame. I am tired of hearing it called such by you. Color meant nothing on the battlefields of Korea and Vietnam. We are all equal in combat. Color should mean nothing now." Sidey's piece continued: "At the end of five hours and much shouting, General Mike Davison, retired, who led the Cambodian incursion in 1970, proposed a compromise: add the figure of a soldier in front of the long granite walls that will bear the 57,709 names of those who died or are missing and the tribute to all who served. The battle was suddenly over."

VVMF agreed to the statue compromise, as well as to adding a flag and to reviewing the inscription on the Memorial, but they did not want to wait until a statue was designed before breaking ground. Waiting meant they would never reach their dedication deadline of November 11, 1982. Over several tense weeks, more debate followed, until CFA and NCPC gave their approval for a statue and flag in concept, pending suitable placement of those elements. Watt followed on March 11, 1982, by granting permission for the construction permits.

With permit in hand, Doubek instructed to commence construction immediately. His reasoning was that a complete mess would make it tough to stop construction. Scruggs added: "Make this place look like an airstrike was called in," he instructed. "Rip it apart." An official groundbreaking ceremony was held on March 26, 1982. General Price, along with Senators Warner and Mathias and future Secretary of Defense Chuck Hagel, gave moving addresses before the command was given, and 150 shovels entered the ground with enthusiastic veterans enjoying the moment.

As soon as the design was chosen, the next step was to consider the all-important details of getting it built. Maya Lin worked closely with Cooper-Lecky on all aesthetic aspects of the design. Lin knew it was critical to maintain the simplicity of the design throughout the design development and construction process. As the selection of the granite was narrowed down, Lin was keen on preserving the notion that the granite walls be reflective and thin—to help express a critical aspect of the design—that the memorial was a cut in the earth that had been polished. Working with the construction manager, Gilbane Building Company, the design team had to locate the appropriate type of granite: a flawless, reflective, deep ebony stone. In the end, the quarry in India was selected.

The choice of the lettering style—Optima, designed by Hermann Zapf—was a font Lin selected after considering a multitude of options. The font Optima seemed to fit that desire to match an almost printed quality with a hand-cut feel. The entire text size and layout Lin saw as an open book. The text size is less than half an inch, which is unusual for monument design, but was selected to make the memorial read more like a book. This lends a sense of personal intimacy in a public space which helps create a sense of connection to the memorial. Ultimately, one of the greatest challenges was how to get that many names on the wall panels in such a short period of time.

The design Lin envisioned listed the names chronologically by date of casualty. However, that posed a problem of how to locate an individual name. When Lin asked how many Smiths would be on The Wall, the team realized how important the chronological listing was to the design. A chronological listing would also allow a returning veteran to find his or her time of service on The Wall and those who died together to remain together forever on The Wall. The solution on how to locate a name evolved into a directory of names with an alphabetical listing and the panel and line number of each name. The families of service members who were missing in action originally wanted their names listed separately. Ms. Lin arrived at a design solution to note those that were MIA with a symbol (+) that could be altered if the service member was found.

The original design proposal called for all the names to be individually hand-chiseled in the stone, but it was soon realized the time and money it would take to do that were impractical. Instead, Lin found John Benson, a master stonecutter, to hand cut the text at the apex—the years of the earliest and latest casualties from the Department of Defense list and the brief prologue and epilogue adjacent to the dates. The design team and VVMF searched for a way for the names to be sandblasted rather than hand carved. Larry Century, a young inventor from Cleveland, Ohio, was selected to serve as a consultant to Binswanger Glass Company in Memphis, Tennessee, which was awarded the contract for inscribing the names.

As soon as ground was broken for The Wall in March 1982, planning for its dedication ceremonies began. They would include a big National Salute to Vietnam Veterans on Veterans Day. The American Legion, VFW, Disabled American Veterans (DAV), AMVETS, and Paralyzed Veterans of America (PVA) made sure their members knew that veterans were going to be honored and welcomed that week on the National Mall. More than 150,000 veterans, families, loved ones and friends made plans to attend.

The series of events began on Wednesday, November 10, 1982, and culminated with a service at the National Cathedral on Sunday,

November14. The Salute opened with a vigil Wednesday morning at the National Cathedral, where all the nearly 58,000 names on The Wall were read by volunteers around the clock, day and night, through midnight Friday. Every 15 minutes, there was a pause for prayer.

On Saturday, a grand parade took place where veterans marched joyously out of sync, some hand-in-hand or with their arms draped around one another, holding banners, flags, and signs. Many pushed friends in wheelchairs. The following week, Kurt Anderson recapped the festivities for TIME magazine: "Saturday's three-hour parade down Constitution Avenue, led by [Gen. William] Westmoreland, was the vets' own show. The 15,000 in uniforms and civvies walked among floats, bands and baton twirlers. The flag-waving crowds even cheered."

Over the four days there were also workshops, parties, events, and reunions. "It was like a Woodstock atmosphere in Washington for those who had served in Vietnam," recalled Scruggs. "After three-and-a-half years of nonstop effort and work, with all that you have to do to accomplish what we did, it was beautiful. It was surreal."

"The whole week was extremely emotional," Becky Scruggs remembered. "It was a whirlwind of events, and the press coverage was unbelievable. I remember The Washington Post had pages and pages of stories in the 'A' section." Vietnam veterans were, at long last, receiving the recognition they deserved.

ACKNOWLEDGMENTS

This book is really a product of the class of 1968—all I've done is stitch together memories and stories to try to present a more compelling picture of the twenty young classmates who we lost. I'm grateful to all who contributed a story or remembrance. The poems, some of the pictures, and the chapter about The Wall, included in this book, are copyrighted and are included with the express permission of the authors or photographers who own the copyrights to their respective works. If this book establishes a living legacy for those of our class killed in Vietnam, then it has been successful. As the West Point class of 1968 passes on to the Great Landing Zone in the sky, our warrior's Valhalla, I didn't want our classmates to be forgotten or to just fade into the other 58,000 plus names on The Wall. While that is certainly an honorable place to fade away to, I wanted to do something so that our guys from '68 could stand out. Hopefully this effort has accomplished that mission.

There are a few classmates who deserve special thanks and recognition for the assistance they've provided: Dutch Hostler the proofreader, Dale Hansen the consummate researcher, and Megan Hostler the communications expert. Of special significance are the following classmates who took on the task of writing and compiling major contributions: Jim Swinney, Jess Gatlin, Ralph Tuccillo, Gordie Tillery, Bob Brace, John Strand, Jim Locher and Rick Rhoades, along with Randy Pais from the class of '67. I owe all of them a heartfelt thanks for their dedication to our fallen and their willingness, even demands, to be responsible for a classmate to whom they were exceptionally close. A very special acknowledgment goes to classmate A. Patrick Jonas, who provided the inspiration for this entire effort. And of course, thanks to everyone else who contributed stories and memories that have enabled me to put these chapters together.

I would also like to thank Jim Knots, president and CEO of the Vietnam Veterans Memorial Fund, who kindly supported me with access to The Wall of Faces and a complete chapter on The Wall and its history.

I owe a special debt of gratitude to John Koehler, president and publisher of Koehler Books, who was willing to take a chance on me, and to Becky Hilliker, initially my editor, and then my partner, who guided me through the entire process of reorienting this book.

A very heartfelt and loving thanks to my One and Only, my soul mate, Margie, who put up with my eccentric schedule, my sometimes-overflowing emotions, and my sometimes hard-to-put-up-with persona as I made my way through this sometimes-heart-rending mission. Several times I needed her opinion and judgment or assistance on a particular part of this book, sometimes I needed her comforting. She never failed me. I could not have accomplished this without her love, help, and support. I'm truly blessed.

MILITARY DECORATIONS
OF OUR FALLEN COMRADES

THE DISTINGUISHED SERVICE CROSS

Second highist Army combat decoration awarded for
extraordinary heroism in combat while engaged in action
against an enemy of the United States.

First Lieutenant
William F. Little III

From the award citation:

The President of the United States . . . takes pride in presenting the
Distinguished Service Cross (Posthumously) to First Lieutenant
(Infantry) William F. Little III, United States Army, for extraordinary
heroism in connection with military operations involving an
armed hostile force in the Republic of Vietnam, while serving with
Company E, 2d Battalion, 3d Infantry, 199th Infantry Brigade. First
Lieutenant Little distinguished himself by exceptionally valorous

action on 11 November 1969 while serving as platoon leader during a reconnaissance operation southwest of Xuan Loc. After his point element discovered signs of recent enemy activity and three well-concealed enemy bunkers, Lieutenant Little started moving the rest of his platoon forward to the point element. Suddenly a concealed enemy force opened fire with small arms and automatic weapons, Lieutenant Little moved forward through the intense enemy fire to pinpoint the hostile positions. He then called in artillery and gunship support and remained in an exposed position to adjust the supporting fire. During a lull in enemy fire, Lieutenant Little and one of his men began to flank the enemy positions. When he suddenly saw an enemy soldier aiming at this companion Lieutenant Little pushed the unwary soldier to the ground and, in doing so, was seriously wounded. As Lieutenant Little fell to the ground, he fired his weapon and killed the enemy soldier. Almost immediately, Lieutenant Little was subjected to a burst of hostile fire and was mortally wounded.

THE SILVER STAR

Third highest military combat decoration awarded for gallantry in action while engaged in action against an enemy of the United States.

First Lieutenant William F. Ericson II
First Lieutenant Denny L. Johnson
First Lieutenant Kenneth T. Cummings
First Lieutenant David L. Sackett
First Lieutenant Peter M. Connor
First Lieutenant David T. Maddux
First Lieutenant Jeffery R. Riek
First Lieutenant John E. Darling
Captain Donald R. Workman
Captain Henry M. Spengler III

THE DISTINGUISHED FLYING CROSS

Awarded for distinguished heroism or extraordinary achievement
while participating in aerial flight.

Captain Louis John Speidel

THE BRONZE STAR WITH V DEVICE

Fourth highest military combat decoration
awarded for valor in combat.

First Lieutenant David L. Sackett (2)
First Lieutenant Harry E. Hayes (2)
First Lieutenant John E. Darling
First Lieutenant James Gaiser
First Lieutenant Jeffery R. Riek

THE ARMY COMMENDATIONMEDAL
WITH V DEVICE

Awarded for acts of heroism of a lesser degree
than that required for a Bronze Star V.

First Lieutenant David L. Sackett
First Lieutenant Jeffry R. Riek (2)

COMBAT INFANTRYMAN BADGE

Awarded to infantrymen who were engaged in active ground combat.

First Lieutenant William F. Ericson II
First Lieutenant Kenneth T. Cummings
First Lieutenant David L. Sackett
First Lieutenant Peter M. Connor
First Lieutenant Jeffry R. Riek
First Lieutenant Harry E. Hayes
First Lieutenant Richard A. Hawley Jr.
First Lieutenant William F. Little III
Captain Donald R. Workman
Captain Douglas Wheless

WEST POINT '68 KIA VN

Date of Death and Wall Location

1. Donald VanCook – 6/4/69 – 23W/68
2. William Ericson – 7/15/69 – 21W/124
3. Dennis Johnson – 9/2/69 – 18W/24/114
4. Kenneth Cummings – 9/4/69 – 18W/31
5. David Sackett – 10/24/69 – 17W/114
6. Peter Conner – 11/4/69 – 16W/28
7. James Gaiser – 11/7/69 – 16W42
8. William Little – 11/11/69 – 16W/58
9. Donald Colglazier – 1/18/70 – 14W/43
10. Jeff Riek – 2/25/70 – 13W/54
11. Harry Hayes – 3/31/70 – 12W/62
12. Richard Hawley – 5/6/70 – 11W/112
13. John Darling – 5/18/70 – 10W/61
14. Donald Workman – 7/21/70 – 8W/39
15. David Maddux – 8/9/70 – 8W/98
16. Douglass Wheless – 11/22/70 – 6W/78
17. William Reichert – 1/25/71 – 5W/66
18. David Alexander – 2/6/71 – 5W80
19. Louis Speidel - 6/25/71 – 3W/89
20. Henry Spengler – 4/5/72 – 2W/129

CONTRIBUTORS

This book would not have been possible without the incredible cooperation of classmates, family members, friends, and soldiers in units commanded by our Twenty. When I started this journey, I put out an email blast to the class asking for contributions of stories, pictures, anecdotes, and memories that any classmate might have of one of the Fallen. After more than a year of several solicitations, I amassed a great deal of information. I had initially committed to including everything I received in this book but, unfortunately, that proved to be impossible. I have so much additional information on several of the Twenty, I could almost produce a second volume. Some of the contributions didn't survive the several cuts required to get this final product to a reasonable size. However, I want to recognize everyone who made the effort to help. I'm indebted to each and every one. Below you will find the names of each of our Twenty followed by everyone who provided input for that individual.

DAVE ALEXANDER

Jim Swinney
Richard Rhodes
Steve Caldwell
Myles Crow
Robert Shimp
Anthony Ambrose
Sheila Lapean
Dale Hansen
John Oneal
John Kruger
Mark Hansen
George Fravel

DAVE MADDUX

Sheila Lapean   David Clappier
Jim Lancaster(USAFA '68)   Dale Hansen
Clare Barkovic   Gus Lee
Thomas Margrave   Renata Price

DAVID SACKETT

Jim Swinney   Jesse Gatlin   Randy Pais

(From Jim) We wish to acknowledge the enthusiastic support of the coauthors for our chapter, Randy Pais and Jess Gatlin, who embraced the project for their dear friend and poured their memories of him into this work. Dave's widow, Pam Stokes Sackett Rosenberg, contributed her cherished photograph. We send our appreciation to Sue Eldridge and the other members of the Welch High School class of 1964. We also wish to acknowledge the EM, NCOs, and officers of A Company, 2-12th Infantry who contributed so much to Dave's story. Sarge Bruce Holzhauer's battle logs filled in many gaps in the story of Dave's time in Vietnam and can be found at: http://www.212warriors.com/1969_3.html. Our thanks go out to Jeff Hinman, BN Correspondent for 2-12th Infantry, and James Wright, Ph.D., president emeritus of Dartmouth College, who reviewed drafts and made suggestions. For all involved in the chapter, this has been a labor of love.

DENNY JOHNSON

Ralph Tuccillo put this narrative together, with additional contribution from:

Dennis Burrell   Don Davis
Jon Dodson   Jimmy Earles
Steve Frushour   Jude Glorioso

Carl Hudson

John Johnston

Nick Kurilko

Tom Niebling

Lyle Pirnie

Glenn Sadler

Ralph Tuccillo (writer)

Danny Johnson

Glynn Kohler

George Mays

Dave Ohle

Jack Reid

John Throckmorton

Robert Turrell

DON COLGLAZIER

Joan Colglazier

Scott Vickers

Shirley Rollins

Dale Hansen

John Johnston

Tom Barnes

Carolyn Colglazier

Craig Carson

Steve Shaw

John Keane Jr.

DON VAN COOK

Larry Van Horn

Ross Nagy

Art Coogler

DONALD WORKMAN

Greg Unangst

Bob Stroud

Brian Utermahlen

Karin Loke

Michael McGill

Daniel Nettesheim

Stott Carleton

Charlie Lieb

Jeff Parsonage

John Dodson

Rick Fetterman

Dutch Hostler

DOUGLAS WHELESS

Bruce Korda

Gary Willis

Robin Willis

Jeff Rogers

Dale Hansen

Stephen Wheless

HARRY HAYES

Bob Brace put together and wrote most of the material for this section, with additional contribution from:

Jim Carman	Jim Hayes
Mike Shaeffer	Rick Fetterman
Jim Hayes	George Laswell

HENRY SPENGLER

James Locher put together and wrote most of the material for this section, with additional contribution from:

Dale Hansen	Bette Meuleners
Ralph D'Alessandro	Pete Bonasso

JAMES GAISER

Carol St. George	Renata Price
David Clappier	Dale Hansen
George Ziots	Joe Javorski
Sharon Miller	

JEFFRY RIEK

Ralph Tildon	Ross Irvin
Bobbi Munson	Lou Pierce
Natalie Manor	Jack Munson
Gordon Tillery	Bill Robinson
Dale Hansen	Tom Volrath

JOHN DARLING

Jeanne Sager
Patrick Okeefe
Julie Heck
Charles Canella
Joe Dooley
William Brown

Paul Joseph
John Cruden
Paul Joseph
Thomas Margrave
Les Krohnfeldt

KENNETH CUMMINGS

Franki Bennett
Renata Price
Brick Sweet
Alan Akers
Joe Guignon

Ross Irvin
Jim Tanski
Raymond Puffer
Stephen Harper
Dale Hansen

LOUIS SPEIDEL

Dale Hansen and Don Robinson helped put this narrative together, with additional contribution from:

Dale Hansen
Sam Wyman
Ellen Johnson
Mike Shaeffer
Greg Camp

David Ohle
Gretchen Hall
Don Robinson
Louis Schlipper
Al Vitters

PETER CONNOR

David Schulte
Franki Bennet
Greg Camp
Robert Keller

Liz Dabney
Robert Keller
Robert Connor
John Miller

Dick McClelland
John Hathaway

Dave Taylor
John Dodson

RICHARD HAWLEY

Meg Hawley
Mike Brennan
Ken Hauck
Dave Taylor
Ray Rhodes
Scott Vickers
Bob Hensler
Bruce Brown

Donald Hall
Tom McConnell
George German
Eric Thomas
Bruce Brown
Mike Patrow
Ted Trauner

WILLIAM ERICSON

Bill Barkovic
Alan Aker
Dale Hansen

Clare Barkovic
Gordon Tillery

WILLIAM LITTLE

Gordon Tillery was the primary researcher and writer for this section, with additional contribution from:

Patrick O'Regan
Greg Camp
Alison Saksena

Gordon Tillery
Bill Raines
Dave Prescot

WILLIAM REICHERT

John Strand was the primary researcher and writer for this section, with additional contribution from:

Gordon Tillery
Mike Havey
Pete Bonasso
Art Coogler
Pete Swan
Ralph Dalessandro

Jim Stefan Sr.
Rick Goodell
Gordon Sayre
David Ford
Dale Hansen

REFERENCES

New York Times, 1/3/2017
Vietnam Helicopter Pilots Association
Howitzer, Class of 1968, West Point, NY
Bugle Notes, West Point NY
Street Without Joy, Bernard B. Fall
Association of Graduates, West Point, NY
Vietnam Veterans Memorial Fund, Wall of Faces
The Coffelt Data Base of Vietnam Casualties, the Coffelt Group
American War Library
A Company Commanders Journal, Lt. Col. Michel Lanning
Ripcord, Screaming Eagles Under Siege, Vietnam 1970, Keith Nolan

CPSIA information can be obtained
at www.ICGtesting.com
Printed in the USA
BVHW041743040522
636156BV00001B/9